Wealth vs. Work

Wealth vs. Work

How 1% Victimize 99%

ALLAN C. ORNSTEIN

author HOUSE®

AuthorHouse™
1663 Liberty Drive
Bloomington, IN 47403
www.authorhouse.com
Phone: 1-800-839-8640

First published by AuthorHouse   01/03/2012

ISBN: 978-1-4670-3329-9 (sc)
ISBN: 978-1-4670-3330-5 (ebk)

Printed in the United States of America

CONTENTS

Introduction:
The Author, The Book

It is disheartening and disconcerting, at the very least, that here I am today—close to the end of my professional career, almost 45 years from the time I started teaching at the university—witnessing the decline of American power and prestige. The nation has become victimized by a shift in values—where greed, arrogance and corruption flourish among a small group of powerful people. The nation is in decline. Inequality is increasing. The middle class is struggling and shrinking, and education is no longer the great equalizer—not when the top 1 percent owns nearly 40 percent of the nation's wealth. Indeed, we have failed to learn the lessons of history, specifically the rise and fall of former great empires.

Just as there are stages and big ideas about history, I do believe that many authors go through stages or periods, whereby they have different interests and write on different topics. September 11 was a paradigm shift for the U.S., and it led to a major shift in my professional writing. Suddenly, in my 60s, I was radicalized, when most professors were thinking about retirement. I felt to some extent like I was a cast member of "Survivor." My former colleagues at my last university where I taught for 27 years had retired, and in my advancing age I had transferred to another university and another city and no longer felt part of a tribe or fraternity.

Now, sometimes I feel mixed up—slowly drifting form reality—what the Polish poet, Czelaw Milosz, one of my literary heroes, calls "moving away from the fairgrounds of the world." Ah, I guess, as you get older, time has a way of moving faster. It has a way of creeping up on you—sometimes clouding your thoughts and stealing your mind or sometimes making you aware of the thicket of history. Here I would like to think that Cicero, the ancient Roman orator, was right. "Old age, especially and honored old age, has such a great authority that it is of more value than all the pleasures of youth."

Personally, I would rather think of the sensual pleasures of youth and drink enough whiskey or wine to block out all the painful words that describe the human condition, all the con artists and crooks that cast their shadow over ordinary people (the masses of humanity). I'd rather not recall that Cicero was assassinated at 63 for speaking his mind against the rich and powerful, and I'm 70 and tilting to the Left. I rather not admit that my best days are over and sometimes I'm griped by physical vagaries, old worn-out memories and slow-moving dreams. Somehow I think that as we enter the "fuddy-duddie" years, these kind of witticisms from our Greek and Roman heritage seem to enter into our vocabulary—as a way to offset or slow down the "woe is I years."

Today, we live in a tragic world, as the Greeks knew and there can be no easy answers. We are surrounded by an unstable and chaotic world, by global poverty and misery, by inequality and injustice, by greed and materialism. The genre of tragedy points to centuries of human folly and suffering that defy rational thought and religious philosophy. By historical accident and geography, Americans have been spared much of the world's problems and poverty, its disease and hunger, and there are fanciful phrases describing our land as the "new Athens" and "new Rome." But these words mask our approaching decline, the growing dark hole in which we find ourselves, slipping downward as a nation and people. Like all great civilizations that have declined before us, we are a nation that needs to reexamine its values and social and economic institutions.

I am sure that most of you have a greater sense of hope and are more optimistic about our future. All you need to do is listen to the press conferences of President Obama. As for myself, I would like to think I still have some vim and vigor. In fact, since 9-11, I believe I have reinvented myself. After publishing more than 55 college textbooks, characterized by safe and sterile prose, and lack of controversy, I am now mixing vernacular and formal syntax, relying on bold language and strong opinions to describe (1) the plight of ordinary Americans, where elsewhere I refer to as the "bottom" 90 percent,[1] (2) how wealthy people exploit working and middle-class people and treat them as inferior or second class, (3) the financial and economic problems of the country, caused by U.S. overconsumption, China surpluses and the housing bubble, (4) the redistribution of wealth on a world-wide basis, from the West to developing countries, and (5) the nation's drift toward inequality and injustice, and the erosion of the American dream.

A related issue in the book is that the social and economic climate that we live in has made it nearly impossible for ordinary Americans to live a decent life—and is a microcosm of a deeper, more pervasive problem that has resulted in the average American to lose hundreds of thousands of dollars in retirement funds and home values and run up household debt to 119 percent and national debt ($14 trillion) amounting to $135,000 per household by 2010—all which places our nation in economic jeopardy for the future. Even worse, as businesses become more efficient, they generate fewer jobs. They use more machines and immigrant workers and outsource jobs to other parts of the world. The result is greater unemployment, especially for unskilled and semi-skilled workers. The problem is structural, not temporary nor cyclical.

Here I feel a twinge of sadness. When I started my professional career, the U.S. was on the top of the world, the only super power left intact from the ravages of war. It was the time when GM was the dominant force in the American economy, the symbol of our wealth and power, then representing the seventh largest gross national product in the world. To be sure, we have had our day in the sun, starting with the post-World War II era and ending with the election of Ronald Reagan. It had to come to an end, it had to happen—given his philosophy of free markets and small government and practice of undermining unions and providing tax reductions for the rich. All these conservative principles draw on the deeper springs of morality, test our democratic ideals and education purposes—and lead to outcomes where only a selected few manage to prosper. The issue is no longer between excellence and equality; it is between inherited privilege (1 percent) and the common people (99 percent). To be sure, my writings go in one direction. We are heading for a financial oligarchy—much worse than the aristocratic Old World that our Founding Fathers feared and tried to avoid.

The writing in this book consists of highly opinionated prose, and is sprinkled with gloom and doom. The world is seen around a simple organizing principle—a mix of Hobbes and Hegel, and a pinch of Michael Harrington and a dash of Paul Krugman (two philosophers and two economists on the left side of the political divide). The author's literary urges beckon to a different world and a different type of expression—one that deals with the "silent majority," the people who built this nation, protect its streets and defend its shores; about the increased power and wealth of the rich and the survival of the rest of us—whether the next generation will be fortunate enough to have the same quality of life as their parents. The book also deals with immigration, unemployment and underemployment, and a high-tech, computerized, and globalized world.

We live in a new world that benefits a few people who are highly innovative or willing to take risks and penalizes the masses who are unable to adjust or take advantage of the paradigm shift taking place. A few global firms and financial players dominate this world, and the vast majority try to hang on to their jobs and survive on a daily basis. To be sure, not too many people are clucking with joy or yelling hip hip hurrah—what a wonderful world we now live in.

As you read this pocket-sized book, you may criticize the author for being biased or too liberal, or that his ideological convictions are a distant mirror of the 1960s, an era of thriller and youthful plots to topple the socio-economic system. You may also question my assumptions and claim my facts don't fit your reality, or that I'm some kind of loon or balloon head. As a free person or someone with high-minded moral convictions, you have this right. And, it doesn't mean you are mean spirited or just plain stupid. The fact is, all authors bring their life experiences to their writing in some way. It is my working-class roots that partially explain my analysis of the rich and their ill-gotten wealth while the rest of us grapple for a meager piece of the pie.

The book is meant to be distinctive but not wild or outlandish, comprehensive in scope but not overly detailed or burdened by too many facts. The writing borrows from various genres and sources of knowledge, mixing classical and contemporary writings of business, philosophy, history, economics, and education. The long view in this book is that no single historical event matters more than another in describing the attitudes and behaviors of men and women of wealth. Throughout history, the economic elite have plundered the countryside, from the beginning of civilization to the present, as if they were gods. They have kept the common people, working people, ordinary people, masses, etc. in check under the guise that superior people reign over lesser individuals.

Why? Why should this be? are existentialist questions that have no particular right answer. Depending on your social, economic and moral lens, the answer can be found by reading Homer or Milton's "Paradise

Lost" which justify the ways of God or by reading Karl Marx or Milton Friedman who provide a framework for those interested in inequality, economic opportunity, and social justice. There are no be-end, end-all answers to describe the human condition, or the history of human affairs, unless you are a true believer—only antidotes to human folly and fanaticism, aggression and plunder, deprivation and misery.

Perhaps "the answer is blow'n in the wind," to repeat Bob Dylan, nothing more complicated than a few words in a song. Most likely, however, we all have a good idea what is right and just, but remain silent because it means questioning the heart and soul of America—the titans of industry, the super rich and the flaws of capitalism. It means being criticized for having progressive or socialist views, possibly unpatriotic thoughts. Not enough folks with political or economic clout are willing to speak out publically, make some tough choices and reform the system so it works for the less fortunate people who play by the rules and have just enough money to pay their bills (the so-called lucky ones) so long as they don't lose their job(s). (Many of us need more than one job to stay afloat.)

Anyone who believes in God or Kant—anyone who is pious or moral wants more equality, opportunity, and justice for all Americans (and for the world in general). We all want to hit the jackpot, but few of us want to buy the ticket to ensure we are better off today and tomorrow than yesterday. Sadly thousands of years have passed, and many working people in the U.S. and around the world are still trying to survive on a daily basis.

I guess it's much easier to say nothing, to go along with the system (because that's the way it's always been from time memorial)—and just fade away and count clouds or cars. Ah, everything is mighty fine so long as we don't have to think about or deal with poverty and human misery around us, why U.S. workers cannot compete on a global basis, or why the world is increasingly anti-American. It's a wonderful world in a rich man's world. Everything is "A-Okay" so long as dad can get you into Harvard or Yale, that is if you are a member of the privileged and powerful club. It does not hit home that the working people around the world, including here in America, are exploited by the rich and super rich or that the middle class is struggling and shrinking, not if you drive around in a Mercedes-Benz CL 600 coupe (cost $125,000) or carry around a Fendi handbag (cost $5,000).

It's "peachy keen" if your mom or dad manipulate markets and prices in business posts and live the life in F. Scott Fitzgerald's *The Great Gatsby*. Everything is "sunny" and "rosey" in the wonderful world of *Ozzie and Harriet* and *Mr. Roger's Neighborhood*. It's great to think of the old tiny town of Arverne (population 3,000) where I grew up, a pimple of a place that almost no one ever heard of, a time in America when burgers cost 25¢ and youthful friends from humble backgrounds were eager, optimistic and hopeful about the future. It was midcentury—an era with no plastic money and when people from across the oceans still thought the streets in America were paved with gold.

It's wonderful, today, to live in Kansas and recall that July 26 is "Turnip Day" or travel to the "Land of Oz" on the yellow-brick road, searching for brains, hearts, and courage. It's "cool" to call yourself Shrek, live in a swamp outside "Duloc" and search for the love of your life. It's great to feel hope and inspiration in a Frank Graham or Joel Osteen Sunday sermon—talking about the mind, body, and spirit. (And, as the good people might say: "Lord have mercy on us.") On a secular basis, however, it's a little like *Ragtime*, people coming to America with hopes and dreams and clawing their way from the bottom to the top. Perhaps the best antidote is escape: being old and overweight and cruising the Mediterranean Sea on a luxury liner, eating and drinking to your heart's content—or being rich and spoiled and sunning on South Hampton Beach, N.Y. or the French Riviera—ignoring the world that we are leaving for our children and their children. No wonder why so many people feel indifferent to the plight of so many other people within our borders and across the sea.

It's time to dispense with the philosophy and observations of life, to move from the readers' outsides to their insides, most important, to grapple with the ideas of the book. As for its potential success, the book lacks an upbeat message or advice on how to become a millionaire. The successful outcome is a long shot or "Hail Mary." But, hopefully, the book's story will flutter down to you in tantalizing bits and provide you with food for thought. Arm yourself with some apples and bananas or a legal sized pad to take notes. Here is a chance to catch up on thousands of years of world affairs, as well as the hard scrabble of the human condition and the high noons of history—all in a short read.

Overview:
Wall Street and the World

So here you are about to make a decision whether his book is worth reading. There is little wrong with this book if you read it from a liberal or Jeffersonian perspective. But there is a lot wrong with it, if you read the book from a conservative or free-market view. As for free or unfettered capitalism, I live with a puzzle that something so crazy and damaging to so many people can be so captivating to millions who are the victims of its outcomes.

Too many people believe that markets are self-correcting and people in the financial sector do a better job protecting the system than regulators. Not only do U.S. government agencies such as the Security Exchange Commission and Federal Reserve reflect this philosophy, so do the majority of American people. It's mythical—and ignores the human condition—incompetence, greed and arrogance—even worse, that Wall Street and corporate America can become reckless, mislead their employees and customers and defraud the public. Then, if and when they become too big, they can wreck the overall economy of nations.

Today, we have Wall Street and Main Street, the world of finance and the world of workers. As a result of government deregulation, the people who move money around with a mouse have changed a "static" part of the economy to a powerful engine that can sink whole nations and the fortunes of hundreds of millions of people. We are a long way from ancient Greece and Rome, but little has changed in terms of the human condition. The sword and whip, and later, the barrel of a gun, once separated those with power over the powerless. Now, it's people who wear pin stripe suits, crimson suspenders, and power ties who determine the fate of others and who believe they are doing "God's work" (at least according to Goldman Sachs' CEO Lloyd Blankfein). Alas, today, we are more civilized and rely less on brute force to check mate our opponents, but the political and economic structures are still ingeniously designed to keep the vast majority at the bottom—barely existing day-to-day, pay check to pay check. As workers, we are nothing more than economic units keeping the system intact, as did our ancestors for the last 5,000 years of recorded history. Of course, no American wants to hear this kind of news.

The news is more painful and perennial than we realize. Since the dawn of civilization, 1 percent of society have always controlled the lives and fortunes of 99 percent of society. Today, the people who run the financial industry consider themselves the "masters of the universe." The ordinary person still wants to believe in Wall Street and *laissez-fare* economics because they hope to live the American dream. The sheer complexity of the American dream is a welcome reminder that capitalism can be beneficial for society. The result is, there will always be "titans" of corporate America and "masters" on Wall Street ordering $500 bottles of wine to help see their way for masterminding their next easy-money contracts and get-rich financial schemes. Few people understand these transactions and they flip under the regulatory radar until the bottom falls out.

It's a zero-sum game, with winners and losers. Statistically, the odds overwhelmingly favor insiders. Periodically, those on the inside get caught with their "hands in the cookie jar," fattening their wallet while fleecing the public and defrauding ordinary people on Main Street. They produce half-hearted apologies, pay a small fine in comparison to the money illegally made, and life goes on until the next shoe drops on the little guy—and what John Q. Public has learned to expect.

"Money, money, money. It's a rich man's world," so go the lyrics by Abba, the Swedish rock group. Ordinary people cannot compete with the money class. Schooling cannot equalize the vast gulf between Wall Street and Main Street, the rich and super rich and the rest of us.

If we want to avoid a stacked deck, the existence of inequality must be addressed—and what constitutes a level playing field. The question eventually arises: To what extent and how much power and money should be concentrated in the hands of a few people. The potential effects are more than just economic; the outcomes have social, political and emotional consequences and affect the productivity and vitality of our nation. If you cannot find viable work and feel there is little opportunity, if your savings and pensions are at risk because of the quackery and corruption of the money class, if you feel the lawyers, accountants, and politicians who are supposed to protect your interests are "screwing" you, or if you feel that the rich and powerful do not pay their share of the taxes because of loopholes and tax havens, then the argument can be made: Why knock yourself out? Why go to school? Why knock yourself out on a job? The system is unfair. It is easier to dropout—and frolic on the beach or engage in criminal pursuits.

Now I certainly understand that we all have our own brand of history—forged and shaped by our cultural roots, personal experiences and socio-economic lens. That said, this book is written by someone who grew up knowing the mean streets of a small town called Arverne, a dot on the map that the readers are not expected to know. Although intensely grateful to this country for its opportunities, because of a mix of idealism, morality and small-town values, the author is saddened by growing inequality in America, the economic decline of the country, and the abuse and arrogance of a new class of robber barons from Wall Street, banking, and corporatocracy. He traces the rise of the money class in America backwards to the Gilded Age, then to European feudalism and the nobility class, then to the warlords who plundered the countryside, and eventually to Greece and Rome and the dawn of western civilization

The author claims that warlords still exist around the globe. They reside in New York, London, Zurich, Tokyo and Hong Kong. In Africa, Latin America and other parts of the third world, they live on mountain tops or in jungles and wear military fatigues and body armor. The economic system hasn't changed in the last 5,000 years. Working people are still pushing stones uphill and barely keeping their heads above water. In the ancient and medieval world, they were called slaves, serfs, and peasants. After the Industrial Revolution, they were called artisans, shopkeepers, miners and factory workers. The big fish have always eaten the small fish, and the economic elite have always tried to keep down the ordinary people—originally through brute force and more recently through laws and practices devised by a political system that favors the rich and super rich. This money class (who are defined as the richest top 1 percent) are still scooping up and redistributing wealth from the people at the bottom of the pyramid to the top.

The con artists and the crooks in the U.S. do not wears masks and tote hand guns; they sit behind mahogany desks in glass and steel buildings and use their power and wealth to perform favors and donate campaign funds to politicians; and, they hire lobbyists, as well as, lawyers, accountants and economists as experts—all to ensure the sympathy and cooperation of political brokers and pundits. Hence, they are able to amass fortunes—often by limiting the power and rights of labor—and rely on tax loopholes, tax credits, and other favorable tax treatment, sometimes even off-shore accounts, to expand their wealth.

Although the rise of Wall Street helped knit together a growing economy during the postwar years, the same financiers—driven by greed and risk—helped cast a bleak, dark shadow over Main Street. Today, the barons on Wall Street and in banking are viewed with loathing and disgust by the masses of Americans who have doled out trillions of dollars to save the fortunes of those high rollers (who were too big to fail). In the meantime, the employment outlook, pensions and small businesses of ordinary people have dramatically declined. Although the financial industry has recently fallen from favor, the handwriting has been on the wall for the last thirty years for ordinary people who work for a living. The problem affecting the masses of Americans is highlighted by flat wages for workers, despite the steady growth of the U.S. economy from 1980 to 2010. (The medium annual wage income in 1980 was $16,500 which translates to $47,000 in 2010 dollars). In other words, the profits for the last thirty years have been earmarked to a small percentage at the top income bracket. The economy is also characterized by increasing home prices and mortgages that outstripped wages and the ability for people to make payments for years; soaring consumer and national debt; the outsourcing of jobs; the decline of the U.S. manufacturing sector and the diminishing power of labor unions. All of these trends gravely impact on working and middle-class people.

A little like Tom Sawyer riding on a bike down a cozy country road, we remain oblivious to our own limited political and economic voice, and gloss over the poverty and misery infecting most of humanity. The vast majority of people around the world are chasing after dreams that cannot come true. They must learn, even here in America, to deal with failed aspirations and lament the daily struggles of life. They are forced to accept the realities of their subordinate status—satisfied there is food on the table and a roof over their heads. Think historically, think globally. This is the origins of the world, and much like it is today for several billions of people, while a tiny number of rich and super rich people who earn tens and/ or hundreds of millions a year, shuttle on private jets between multiple homes and have bottomless expense accounts, all-knowing attitudes, and run the affairs of the world—largely with their own interests in mind.

Warming Up, Getting Ready

Having read the introduction and overview, or at least skimmed them, you should have some thoughts on how I see the world. I hope I have given you something to think about because there is nothing worse than a boring beginning or one that is "loosie goosie" and says nothing. Those kind of introductions deaden brain cells, loosen nerve endings and cause readers to drift away, like a disappearing dream—or to count pages in order to get an idea of how long they have to endure the medicine.

Most important, I hope you haven't misinterpreted me or think I'm some kind of liberal crackpot. Although I have little patience with the central tenants of economics, for I think they are grand frameworks which often do not apply to the changing world, they are one-sided (in favor of the rich and super rich) and organized to keep ordinary people down. Despite all the gurus with big ideas who publish books or give speeches, and despite all the armies of politicians who claim to represent the people, the system has always worked for the favored few. Of course, if you believe in the gospel, or if you are some sought of Reaganite conservative, then you have a different explanation why there are so many poor and powerless people, so many working people who have to hold down two or three jobs to make ends meet, and why there are so many shameful social deficits within our society.

For prior centuries, the idea of massive deprivation and inequality was an accepted premise of how the world functioned. The masses were expected to live on the edge of starvation while the warlords and landlords were the natural beneficiaries of great fortunes. Membership in a family (or a clan, caste or class) determined the privileges, prestige and power among people in society. Nothing could be done to alter inequality or the norms and institutions of society, since the laws of nature governed. Ability was irrelevant, and it wasn't until the Industrial Revolution that new modes of economic organization surfaced.

The idea of competition, self-improvement, and individual achievement began to take shape with Adam Smith, and his publication of *An Inquiry into the Nature and Causes of the Wealth in the Nation* in 1776. Individuals were thrown into the market place and relied on their own resources and abilities to sink or swim. Then came the publication of Charles Darwin's *Origin of Species* published in 1859. It was explained that the system worked for those who possessed the elements of *adaptability* and were capable of modifying their behavior as society changed. The system also worked for those who were strong, smart and bold, and/or had special talents, that are required for advancement; that is, according to Herbert Spencer who added a social (as opposed to a biological) component to Darwinism and introduced the idea of *survival of the fittest*. For both Darwin and Spencer, the idea of social measures designed to protect or help individuals who could not complete were limited, and the idea of equality was completely rejected. Those who rise and those who fall were merely working out the laws of nature and God.

In the twentieth century, the link between competition and production was provided by Ayn Rand's *The Fountainhead* and *Atlas Shrugged*. Not only would anything in the name of social welfare or compassion interfere with the market forces, but also greed was considered good because it was the engine that drove the economy and enhanced productivity. Men (and women) who took risks and seized opportunities were praised and considered heroic. Free competition was thought to be the natural law of economics and any concession to "socialism" or social welfare was considered artificially induced and incompatible with high productivity. The idea that common people might share in the economic growth of the country was secondary; they should be satisfied with employment.

Arthur Laffer (Ronald Reagan's chief economic advisor), Alan Greenspan (a disciple of Ayn Rand and the former head of the Federal Reserve) and the financial and conservative base sanctioned these economic ideas. The market was considered a self-regulating mechanism and the best outcomes for productivity were free of union interference, government legislation, and social controls. In a world that for thousands of years has long been poor and plagued with deprivation and misery, as long as America prospered the new economic mood in America made sense. Similarly, the scope of social programs and safety nets designed to provide survival chances and protect the average person from privation and abuse from big business were minimized.

Whatever a person earned was his to keep unless fraud or larceny was proven. If people abused the system or the system failed to protect the average person from another person's greed or abuse, then it was the few bad apples at fault and the system would eventually self-correct. But in the race for enhanced efficiency and productivity, it was expected that ordinary people would lose the contest or merely work and pay their bills in this competitive arena called capitalism.

To be sure, America is still the place where the common people have a chance to succeed, and there are a sufficient number of examples to keep the idea alive in our folklore, literature, and church sermons. But regardless of how we slice the economic pie, those with inherited privilege and bloodlines to Ivy League colleges and corporate parents, and those with inherited parental talents, have more opportunity. Perhaps it can be argued that the cream rises to the top and that natural selection (Darwinism and Spencerism) functions to recognize the best and brightest in a competitive struggle. The rationale is, those who have become gazillionaires through hard work, even if they have sidestepped a few rules, deserve what they have earned. We know that competition is imperfect and luck is also a factor in the rise and fall of people. One might also argue that work is for less talented or inferior people, and their weakness subjects them to a master or boss, as well as to market conditions which they have little control over. Of course, all these underlying arguments do not help working people obtain the basic decencies of life—or obtain social controls over the economy, some sort of regulation to protect them.

So the million dollar question comes down to whether the so-called "superior" people, that is powerful and politically connected people, the people who play the system and know how to take advantage of it, and even the lucky few, are entitled to all they earn regardless of the fate of ordinary people. The next million dollar question is whether wealth should be concentrated into few hands and the gnawing implications it has for the foundations of the American way of life. I certainly realize that liberals and conservatives can make a case for one side or another, but who is supposed to protect the average person who works and plays by the rules.

In a democracy, a social contract must exist between government and the people. Only the government has the power to regulate big business and to protect the people from corporate abuse, fraud and corruption. But the people must also be convinced, regardless of the stories of conservative pundits, that it is in the best interest for government to restrain the so-called "superior people," the "titans of industry" and the "masters of the universe." America is the theater where the great struggle for the rights of common people is to be made; therefore, the government is required to protect the so-called common people, or the masses, from the hazards of economic life: Reducing *inequality* (the outcomes of competition) and enhancing *opportunity* (deserving beneficiaries for advancement).

I guess what it all comes down to is where you feel you fit or see yourself on the economic score card, what life experiences you have had—including the fortunes and misfortunes of living within the competitive model, and just how fair you feel are the institutions of society. Someone born and raised in the Bronx, NY or the Southside of Chicago will have a very different view from someone born on the upper-east side of New York or in Winnetka, Il. Someone who was educated at the City College of New York or Chicago State University will most likely have a very different perspective than someone who was educated at Columbia University or the University of Chicago—and so on. If you consider the title of the book, the majority of people (99 percent of the population) are being victimized by a tiny minority (1 percent of the population). Therefore, I do believe that my ideas will make sense to most people in the world, as well as in the U.S.

Now given all my excessive statements and uncomfortable arguments, and admitting to all my flaws of reasoning in advance that you may discover or think you have discovered, it is time to turn the page and read the next six chapters.

Chapter 1

QUESTIONS TO CONSIDER

1. Why is the middle class in America struggling and shrinking?

2. Is it fair and just (or unjust and unfair) to redistribute wealth? To what extent?

3. How do you reconcile the statement: Class differences and class warfare have existed since the beginning of civilization?

4. Why has the gap between the rich and the rest of us increased steadily in the last thirty years?

5. Who is the largest U.S. private employer? What is the average wage of their employees?

6. What is the average U.S. consumer debt? How much is the debt of the average college graduate with a bachelor's degree? A master's degree?

7. Does democratic society require a balance between performance and compensation? Should economic floors and ceilings be introduced in the wage structure of a democratic society?

8. Should John Q. Public or Joe Six-pack be expected to have a minimum decent standard of living in the U.S.? Or, should

"survival of the fittest" and the "law of the jungle" prevail in a capitalist society like ours?

9. To what extent should government play a role in establishing safety nets and social programs for ordinary people?

10. How should society balance the differences between excellence and equality?

11. Should government care more about people or property? Should government regulate or deregulate (stay out of the way of) big business? What is your preference: What is good for big business is good for the country or what is good for labor is good for the country?

12. Is the American dream alive and well? Or is it disappearing or being outsourced to Asia and Eastern Europe?

13. Do recent economic differences with Main Street and Wall Street reflect an aberration, a unique economic blimp, or does it coincide with hundreds of thousands of years of history?

14. How would you describe the difference between yesterday's serf, peasant or indentured servant and today's factory worker, migrant farmer, or immigrant laborer?

15. Given the wealth of the U.S. why is it concentrated in the hands of a tiny minority? How tiny of a number or percent?

16. Is America in economic decline? Why? Why not?

Chapter 1

A WAY OF LOOKING AT THE WORLD

And so it came to pass on a frosty winter day in the year 2009, I sat down to write a sequel to my last book, *Class Counts*. The book was full of *facts* and *inferences*, but never dry or boring, sprinkled with an ideology and alarmist view about the decline of the U.S. and the free fall in standard of living among Americans. The dust jacket of the book summed up the theme of the book and the preface or first three pages summed up the details (or facts) of the book. Allow me to replay these two quick snapshots in order to set the wheels in motion for this new book.

But wait. Let me add one happy thought to lift your spirits and give you a brief feeling of joy. In exchange for flashing these tidbits of information from my previous book, I promise to limit this new narrative so there will be little need to skim or skip. I also promise to keep it light (and sprinkle intriguing ideas into the narrative) so you can read the book on the beach, in the bathroom, or between sets on the weight machine in the gym or while you briskly walk on the treadmill. And, to add a little spice to your life, so long as you believe in the virtues of progressive or liberalism, you may find yourself high fiving and saying "Yes." Since the book is not neutral, sanitized nor plain, I do not expect this book to reach the shelves of Wal-Mart or Costco, but you should still find the book relevant.

So forget the history of Herodotus, Homer, and Thucydides that sit on your book shelves and collect dust. These books are too heavy for the X, Y generation and worse for Internet browsers. Allow me to vault through time, from the beginning of civilization to the present, and provide a lighter commentary: Not exactly like a fox to a "bunny wabbit," a John Grishom or a Stephen King thriller—more like a feature story for *Newsweek* and *Time* magazine readers and for urban dwellers living in Gotham, Chicago, Houston or Los Angeles, possibly London, Paris, or Mumbai (formerly Bombay) and Shanghai.

PREVIOUS COMMENTS ON CLASS

First, turning to the dust jacket of *Class Counts*—and into the specter of doom. "Class differences and class warfare have existed since the beginning of Western Civilization, but the gap in income and wealth between the rich (top 10 percent) and the rest has increased steadily in the past twenty-five years. The middle class is struggling and shrinking, the Medicare and Social Security trusts are drying up, and education is no longer the great equalizer. A moral society, one that is fair and just, sets limits on the accumulation of wealth and inherited privilege and also guarantees a safety net for the less fortunate. This book describes the need for a redistribution of wealth in order to make U.S. society more democratic, fair, and just, and outlines the ways in which we can begin to make these very necessary changes . . . and preserve the social fabric of American life."

For those who have a restless aversion to numbers, yawn at facts or have difficulty arriving at the truth through simple stats, please accept my apologies. The list of factoids below is meant only to provide a quick glimpse to my previous book in order to show the linkage of class and also that *class counts* in the new book. If you must, you have my permission to stop reading the list of facts at anytime. I promise not to provide you with this sort of detail in this new book, where the mind begins to fritter and lose access to the subject matter. Beyond the list, I promise to provide the reader with more old-timely talk that will linger deep in the recesses of your mind.

So here is a sixteen-point nest of facts from the preface of the previous book—and on the road to Leftville.

"1. Class counts. Class differences and class warfare have existed since the beginning of Western Civilization, with the Greeks and Romans, and since our nation was founded. It was reflected in the different philosophies of Thomas Jefferson and Alexander Hamilton and presently between liberals and conservatives. It is keenly expressed in who gets admitted to Harvard of Yale and who attends second—or third-tier colleges; only 3 percent of students at the nations top 146 colleges come from families in the bottom economic quartile (or the lowest 25 percent).

2. The gap in income and wealth between the rich (the top 10 percent) and the rest (the bottom 90 percent) has increased steadily in the last twenty-five years. In 2005 the average worker in the United States earned $43,506. Among Fortune 500 companies, the average executive pay was $11.3 million, not including stock options, which have the potential effect of doubling or tripling the earning of a CEO. The nation is heading for a financial oligarchy, much worse than the aristocratic Old World that our Founding Fathers feared and tried to avoid.

3. In 2005 the bottom 90 percent of the population earned $117,000 or less while the top 0.1 percent earned $16 million or more. From 1950 to 1970 for every additional dollar earned by the lower 90 percent—what I call the "new struggling class"—those on the top 0.1 percent earned $162. From 1990 to 2002, for every dollar earned by the lower 90 percent, these top taxpayers earned an additional $18,000. This kind of income gap is eventually going to shred the middle class and then the democratic process.

4. For the last twenty-five years, real wages of the working class have remained flat at about $15 to $16 per hour. Job loss and job insecurity are at an all-time high in the United States, as reflected in the loss of high-paying jobs and the outsourcing of white-collar jobs, as well as the reduction or elimination of company-funded pensions and health insurance. Replacement jobs result in a one-third reduction in wages, regardless of retraining and education.

5. Despite continuous growth in the economy since the 2000 stock market bubble, nearly two-thirds of new jobs—more than 5 million in total—pay less than $35,000 a year. The largest U.S. employer is Wal-Mart, where the average worker [in 2006] earned about $7.50 per hour and had minimal health insurance coverage.

6. As many as 85 percent of American families remain in the same class or move up or down one quintile three decades later. During a twenty-five-year period, ending in 2004, 61 percent of families in the

lowest income quintile were stuck at the same level. In reverse, 59 percent in the highest income quintile remained at the same level.

7. The middle class is struggling and shrinking. The average consumer debt was more than $9,300 in 2005; the savings rate was a negative .4 percent, the first time since the Depression in 1933 that Americans' spending exceeded disposable income. Educated young Americans are in worse shape. The average debt from student loans among college students graduating with a bachelor's degree was more than $18,000 and among graduate students was approximately $45,000 in 2005.

8. Tuition at private colleges has increased 110 percent in the last decade, compared to 60 percent for four-year state colleges; however, income for the bottom 50 percentile increased 35 percent and, after considering inflation, there was no gain. Measures designed to make colleges more affordable, such as tuition tax breaks and special tax-free savings accounts for college, disproportionally benefit families in the top 40 percentile.

9. Today 23 percent of all people sixty-five to seventy-four years old hold jobs, compared to 16 percent just two decades ago. The number of workers in the sixty-five to seventy-four groups grew three times the rate as the overall workforce in 2004 and ten million previously retired people were forced back to work in order to make ends meet. Although most seniors want to keep their homes, 44 percent of home-owners at age seventy will have sold their houses by age eighty-five to pay for living costs and basic needs.

10. The Medicare trust is expected to start running a deficit in 2013 and Social Security is expected to go bust by 2044. Looming deficits in both social programs are forcing the government to curtail benefits. Some 50 percent of the American populace are without pensions and are relying on Social Security for retirement. While hundreds of billions of dollars are passed on yearly to the offspring of the rich (the top 10 percent) and superrich (the top 1 percent), 86 percent of U.S. households will receive less than $1000 in cash value or no inheritance at all.

11. Education is no longer the great equalizer. Schools and colleges cannot overcome the difference between those born on third base and those who are struggling to get up at bat. The American dream is slowly evaporating and becoming more unattainable for the under-thirty generation.

12. So long as Americans have the view that the Michael Eisners, Michael Dells, and Michael Jordans of the world, and all their descendents,

are entitled to all their wealth because they worked hard, founded highly successful companies, or could shoot a ball through a hoop, then the millions they make will continue to create economic imbalance and doom the rest of us to a bleak future characterized by vast inequality.

13. A democratic society requires some kind of balance between achievement and equality. Endpoints or benchmarks are needed to establish economic ceilings and floors. A moral society, one that is fair and just, sets limits on the accumulation of wealth and inherited privilege and also guarantees a safety net for the less fortunate. Without such limits, social mobility and opportunity become abstract and unachievable ideals, representing nothing more than propaganda derived from a sham notion of a classless society driven by the American notion of equality and the Protestant work ethic.

14. Cultural and social differences and religious views, reflected in red and blue voting patterns, mask important economic and safety net issues such as jobs, pensions, Social Security, and health-care and college tuition costs. New laws and policies are required, including government regulation of Wall Street and the financial and banking industries, as well as increased safety nets for the American people.

15. There needs to be a redistribution of wealth in order to make U.S. society more democratic, fair, and just. Recommended are a host of taxes, including but not limited to luxury taxes, windfall profit taxes, estate taxes, and fuel taxes. Other recommendations include eliminating taxes on food, drugs, and low-cost clothing, free state college tuition for above-average students, and zero tax on the first $50,000 earned in annual wages for all Americans.

16. A strategy is outlined in order to restore the social contract that is supposed to exist between the government and the people. The U.S. standard of living and quality of life for the bottom 90 percent of the economic scale is at stake. The idea is for people to vote for their pocketbook, and not be derailed by secondary or side issues." [2]

Conversing With My Critics

For those who feel that I am distorting statistics, missing the whole picture, quoting out of context, or oversimplifying abstract economic notions, I would say either you have been living on Mars for too long or you are an ideological hard-liner clinging to out-moded ideas of free markets and smaller government. For the reader who feels distant from these facts, that I am blurring reality, or refuses to acknowledge what is happening to the core of the nation, the ordinary American or the bottom 90 to 95 percent who work for a living (and don't move around money nor have the proper DNA), then all I can think is your white, privileged and boring.

I realize truth cannot be grasped in a 16-point decaffeinated or artificial flash, and I don't think anything I say will have the slightest dent on public policy. Still, I speak from the heart, based on my childhood, hardscrabble experiences—and now speaking as a professor—I believe ideas do matter. You will be glad to know that I will not burden the reader in this new book with thickets of statistics so that you are forced to put down the book and look for hobbits of relief—or count the number of pages in the chapter.

We can talk ourselves to death about social and economic nuances. Professors do this as part of their living and in their desire to do good. But it boils down to taking a position. Should we assume that what is best for Wall Street is best for all of us, or what is best for Main Street is best for the nation? Should we believe that increased income tax rates for the rich are confiscatory and labor unions are a menace to the country? Or, should we redistribute wealth, so average working Americans—once called Joe Doakes and John Q. Public, now Joe-Six Pack and Joe the Plumber—can have a descent standard of life? The answer to these questions reflect to some extent whether you have grown up against a background of unstated but obvious labor or wealth, and what political and social lens you have in interpreting the unfolding episodes of life.

As the author sees it, the clash of opinions in this book is primarily one of class and culture—listening to Johnnie Cash or Sara Brightman, scoffing up a Budweiser or Miller Light or sipping Ketel One or XO Cognac, ordering the $9.99 Blue Ribbon special at the local diner or choosing the *prix fixe* menu (with wine, tax, and tip) $500 to $750 per couple at *Le Bernardin* or *Du Cas* in Manhattan, equivalent to the annual earnings of nearly one third of the world's inhabitants. This kind of discrepancy breeds not only resentment between classes within the nation, but also breeds malcontent and hatred toward America.

As in life, the meaning you find in the books you read depends on the author's viewpoint and whether he writes as an advocate (subjective) or scholar (supposedly objective). Here I profess to be more concerned about people than property, which makes me somewhere left of center on social and political issues. My writing is fairly charged and is not meant to be neutral, nor taste or look like vanilla ice cream. But readers must understand that no one lives with a calculator in his hand or a camera strapped to his head for research purposes. My writing is also abrasive and critical of people, pundits, and politicians who fabricate different statistics and sound bites, and who are governed by a different sense of truth than mine. Just how abrasive or critical the reader judges my writing will depend on his or her own experiences and social and political lens. What you think of this book also depends on what the author includes and excludes from the passages, as well as what statistics are selected and how they are interpreted to bolster a point.

The secret story revealed in this book is that government plays a key role in America's class structure and whether the American dream runs on or off track. The story involves more than just tax rates, minimum wages, and Medicare benefits, but which political party is in power—which philosophy or doctrine controls human services and safety nets for people, whether the party supports and protects labor or business, and what kind of policies and level of transparency and accountability govern finance, technology, and globalization. We would like to think that we are alive and well and we have it all under control, and the stuff we overlook or cannot control doesn't matter. But it does matter. It's just that we don't realize it or don't want to face up to it. We would like to think there is very little difference between Democrats and Republicans, between liberal and conservative thought, and between free markets and regulated markets, or what is good for big business is good for America. But there is a difference, and it is bigger than most of us think. What we need is a government that cares more about people than property, more about rising inequality and the shrinking middle class than denying it or arguing that what is good for the rich is good for the country, or what is good for labor or unions is nothing more than socialism.

Class war will not topple America, at least not in the form of overthrowing the system. But the struggle is fought on a daily basis and the desperate poor and disenfranchised working persons are left to care for themselves, even worse to compete and sometimes fight among themselves as they always have throughout history. The plot on Main Street is not against Wall Street, as it should, but about small rivalries and jealousies—not the ultimate show down between the rich and rest of us, or wealthy and working people. There are no sentimental victories for the masses other than keeping their heads above water.

In America, the underclass often deny their own condition, voiceless and unable to escape their hardworking and relentless grind. They still believe in the American dream. God bless them; they have not given up as they have been taught to believe in hope, ambition, and opportunity. It's a sentimental song to a part of America that doesn't have much of a chance—whose jobs first in steel and ironworks, then furniture, textile and garment industries, and now part of the auto industry have just about all disappeared, as are now thousands of white-collar and high-tech jobs being outsourced to Asia and Eastern Europe. The sad outcome is that more people now seek opportunities at Wal-Mart and McDonald's, two of the largest U.S. employers, than they do at U.S. Steel or General Motors. We live in a lost world, a lost dream, without many Americans wanting to recognize or admit it because it goes against the American spirit.

It is more than ordinary workers who suffer. Take heed of the next layer, the so-called middle class: teachers, social workers, fire fighters, nurses, and accountants. They live one or two steps above subsistence levels. If they loose their job or become bogged down with serious medical problems, then they experience a sharp break with the life they have known and become easy prey to the rising swath of castaways, down and out, and unlucky people trying to stay afloat—sometimes succeeding, often failing.

It occurs to me that some readers might ask how someone who is not an economist or banking guru has the audacity to write about wealth, work and inequality as if the author has a Peter Pannish faith in his own theories. How daunting it might be for my academic colleagues in business and finance if I got it right: facts and abstractions, syntax and slang, conventional wisdom and innovative ideas. My simple response is if Alan Greenspan, the "maestro" of Wall Street, that everyone in public office once seemed afraid to question, could get it wrong, then it is possible that one of his critics with a different flavor and form of capitalism could get it right.

And, here we are today, in the midst of an economic collapse rooted in Ronald Reagan's and George Bush's trickle down and privating economic theories. We are supposed to believe that recent developments portend a radically different environment for the American working and middle class; rather than grudgingly recognizing that such events coincide with hundreds of thousands of years of history. Working people have always been considered the target of the rich and ruling elite, a class to be preyed upon. In fact, for most of recorded time working people have been considered by the powerful and rich as "nonpeople," and now a cost unit or production unit to hire and fire at will.

Amid all this gloom and despair, you might just rationalize that the author is fond of the darkness—or that Thomas Hobbes, the ultimate seventeenth century pessimist, (who believed the peasant and labor class are subject to the wishes of the strong), has gobbled his mind and heart. Or, you might just say that Dickens and Dumas, and possibly Marx and Che, have imposed some benign control over the author. My only admission is that I wear sunglasses in the summer; possibly those secret glasses cause me to see the dark side of the world and to sympathize with the struggle of the "have nots."

A Trip Down Memory Lane

I have come to know two completely different worlds outside heaven and hell, an upper class bubble in Winnetka, Illinois and Manhasset, New York, as I once lived in a working-class world, a tiny town that is known for nothing, except possibly its beach. Winnetka and Manhasset introduced me to the Brahmins of Wall Street and the banking industry, where greed, selfishness, and the ethics of Enronism prevailed. Arverne made me aware of my blue-collar existence, where I learned at a very early age the scars of class welfare which started when I was about age six and made my first hour-long drive to K-Mart to shop with my mother for lower prices and start school.

My mother, rest her soul, knew the dreary side of life, mopping floors and bathrooms to supplement dad's income while slowly dying of cancer—ten years of pain and suffering—at the end 70 or so pounds of flesh. My mom's death represents the story of humankind across centuries—mountains of nameless and faceless people dying with only their kin besides them, fighting amnesia and holding on to fading memories—and eventually forgotten forever. Hopefully on the day she died, some 25 years ago, she began a new journey: Her soul merging with the universe (Hinduism), becoming part of a stream (Buddhism), or rising to heaven (Christianity).

The flashbacks of my mother's slow looming death are filtered alongside my father's years of unemployment and attempt to put food on the table. The struggles and loss of my mother, coupled with the loss of an unburdened youth, cannot be replayed or redone. There is no recourse in the face of severe hurt, perhaps only a concentrated stream of anger and gloominess that critics can argue filter through my words about the human condition.

I am sure the therapists, armed with a couch and pad, can explain how my childhood experiences filter through this book—and why there is passion and anger in my voice. Reflecting on hard times, knowing the dark side of the streets in which I lived, those little doses of childhood weave through the fabric of my adult dinner dances, summers in Martha's Vineyard and winters in Jackson Hole. My landscape and formative years are sought of the anti-thesis to the "sunny" and "rosey" world of *Ozzie and Harriet* and *Mr. Roger's Neighborhood.*

No wonder, then, Johnnie Cash remains my hero, since the age of fourteen, as he gains weight and significance over time, singing the common man's plight: Traveling dusty roads, dreaming about dead-end relationships and old loves, waking up on a Sunday morning hung over with unarticulated thoughts and unexpressed emotions about lost lives and lost memories, about getting older and not necessarily smarter.

Age has a way of making all of us think about the past—a world that could have been had we been dealt a different hand or made a few different choices. Although the past has become a place inhabited by those who feel the onset of blindness and deafness, and although some of all my senses are slipping away, I can still recall a lost world, when I was young and more optimistic, like so many others who grew up in the late 1940s and 1950s. It is now a dimming world I see, a past that grows increasingly distant, when the U.S. was more prosperous and egalitarian, when the nation had no economic rivals, and when the future seemed bright and the children of the common people had a real chance to achieve the American dream.

A BROKEN WORLD

So here are the major themes of the book. The history of civilization for the most part is a story of regression rather than progress, cruelty rather than civility, war and plunder rather than peace and prosperity. This is a Hobbesian view of the world which encompasses both the periods of civilization (5,000 years of recorded history) and barbarianism (another 5,000+ years of nonwritten history comprising story telling, folklore and pictures). In the barbaric or savage period, the passions and brute force of men led to invasion and destruction of one group over another group. Families, tribes, and clans of people pillared the countryside. Men lived by rape and plunder under the most primitive conditions and the only form of authority was based on the "natural force" of power.

A continuous struggle for survival and safety occurred as people waged war on each other for scarce goods, slaves or servants and land. Alongside the economy of plunder, a primitive code of honor developed which spared people and their animals and tools that were important for rudimentary existence. Nonetheless, it was still considered appropriate to rape women or extinguish an eye of an enemy soldier to weaken future opponents. The concern for human rights and world poverty, famine, disease, etc. was meaningless in this stage of history. Misery and despair were basic conditions of life; the masses were merely trying to survive and they could not take time to "dilly dally" with philosophy or preaching—or with debates about the human condition.

Civilization emerged from families and tribes which were enlarged by war, either for necessity to band together for security or when the victor increased his territory. This is how civilizations evolved, including Egypt and Persia, ancient China and India, the Greeks and Romans, the English and French, etc. Certainly Native Americans came to understand this policy as they experienced first the seizure of their land and then destruction of their civilization. Unless you believe in the second grade dittie that "George Washington never told a lie," it is safe to assume that America suffers from some of the same defects of all civilizations. Cruelty, war and plunder are part of the human condition. For most colored and formerly colonialized people of the world, this is how America is seen, despite how wonderful and magical we in the U.S. might see it.

And so, the great civilizations developed through war and territorial expansion, starting with Egypt around 3,100 BC, as primitive tribes and then small kingdoms were consolidated into monarchies, city-states, and later empires. Ancient Greece and Rome, however, emerged by human agreement—rather than by conquest. For Aristotle, in *Politics*, it is contended that civilization reduces the propensity for war, enhances the safety and security of the people, and leads to the good life; it is superior to all forms of pre-civil life. Hobbes has no problem with this interpretation, with the exception that he still feels civilization is governed by passions for profit, class conflict, economic competition and civil strife. He points this out in the *Leviathan* and *De Cive*.

Moving beyond Aristotle and Hobbes, the so-called superiority of civilization doesn't alleviate the precarious existence that plagues humankind. For 99 percent of the population there was little change in their standard of living for centuries, at least not until the Industrial Revolution. It mattered little if the person was a slave, serf, peasant, indentured servant, etc—an economy based primarily on agriculture and household production had limitations. Any surplus was subject to taxation by government officials or the church or to plunder from warring city-states, polities and kingdoms. The expectation was that people were destined to live a life of privation, misery and despair—to procreate and then die faceless and nameless. Their only hope was heaven—and under these conditions the influence of the church expanded in Western Europe.

Now back to Hobbes. He was fearsome of anarchy, civil war, and lack of security. The political, economic and religious institutions cannot be dissolved without a threat to society. He believed that rational people are willing to agree to a sovereign, noble assembly, even a dictator, to keep the peace and maintain order so long as it does not put their own lives at stake. In fact, he was willing to accept a monarchy or authoritarian leader, a nobility and priestly class, along with inherited privileged to maintain a civil society—a condition which allowed the elite to reap nearly all the fruits of labor of the working people.

Here the reader must understand that the nobility class can be traced back to the warlords who were given title and property for their allegiance to the small kingdoms and monarchs that developed over centuries in Europe. The rest of the people, the common people, were considered inferior to the nobility, with no political voice, nothing more than economic units to be utilized by the monarch, landowners and church. For nearly 3,000 years of so-called civilization, the masses were kept down by the system, living on a day-to-day existence, left on their own to work with no floor or safety net below which they could fall. If people, through their own perspiration or luck, were able to improve their condition the change was minimal, compared to the huge contrast between the top 1% and the bottom 99%.

That is how society evolved—rich and poor. If your name was John Locke, John Hume, or Jacque Rousseau, and you raised questions about life, liberty or property or about a social contract between government and the people, you were branded a nut. And, if you agree with this interpretation or accept part of this vision, then the world is pretty gloomy and civilization is not much better in some respects than savagery. You may not want to agree with this view, because your spiritual or moral values may get the best of you. But Hobbes also warns that language reflects "the nature, disposition, and interest of the speaker," and that is especially true in matters of "virtues and vices," and, if I may add, when it comes to power, privilege and money. These three driving forces result in desire. For Hobbes, "The object of man's desire, is not to enjoy once only, and for one instant of time; but to assure forever, the way of his future desire." This leads to a vast array of emotions and passions, including modern-day greed, abuse, and corruption—warlords yesterday and robber barons today in pursuit for power, privilege and/or wealth.

But desire is only one problem that characterizes civilization. Today, more than half the world is weighed down by the woes of poverty, hunger and sickness, by rape and plunder of warlords and militia groups, by autocratic and corrupt governments, and by sex—drug—and weapon-trafficking of criminals and rebels. America is supposed to be the exceptional place. As Thomas Paine once put it, "the cause of America is in a great measure the cause of all mankind"; or, as Lincoln said, we are the "last best hope of earth." Today some people might take exception. America is not so perfect, not so powerful, not so rich—and not so free from racial, religious, or economic strife. It is true that the American Revolution wiped out the monarchy and nobility class, the notion of inherited privilege, and weakened the influence of the Church. However, some of these threats seem to have reappeared in recent years with the rise of the conservative right.

I would also venture to guess that the spirit of American individualism, innovation and entrepreneurism forged a society very different from the Hobbesian world. But given American hubris and mythology of almost unlimited power and wealth, the same nation which militarily defeated Nazism and Communism in the twentieth century is now suffering on an economic scale never imagined by its people as we enter the twenty-first century. As a country, in the last thirty years, we have moved toward less manufacturing and productivity and to greater inequality and economic decline. We have also witnessed the decline of labor unions, the only large institution that represents working and middle class people against the lobbyists, lawyers and consultants of the money class.

The victims of this inescapable misfortune are the common people, the masses, who find it difficult to find good-paying jobs. Certainly centuries-old stagnation has disappeared and our economic model has engineered great wealth for Americans, but wealth not for the majority but a tiny minority. In good times, few people questioned the America model of free enterprise and free markets, despite the fact we were producing fewer things and our recent wealth was based on financial engineering and excessive consumerism which has driven us into massive debt. Today, liberal economists, G-20 members (especially the Chinese) and corporate leaders around the world are raising questions about the excesses of U.S. capitalism.

We are destined to an uncertain future, very different from projections of unlimited power and wealth that characterized speeches of our presidents and pundits from the Wilson era to the Reagan and Bush II era. President Obama inherited a misguided free-market system, with minimal transparency and restraint, and attempted to redefine American capitalism. He is not only trying to create a more intrusive government as a counter weight to market forces, but he is also attempting to represent the needs of working people and the middle class. His policy goals are an uphill battle, given the nonapolegetic and Darwinist history of American capitalism and a Hobbesian world that for centuries accepted the poverty and misery of the masses as part of the natural order.

THE DECLINE OF AMERICA

Today, as we enter the twenty-first century, I have come to the realization that the American dream is waning: The middle class is struggling and shrinking, inequality is growing, and social and economic mobility is grinding to a halt. All great civilizations whether they are nation-states or empires, grow and then decline—like plants, animals, and people. To be sure, Edward Gibbon's work, The *History of the Decline and Fall of the Roman Empire,* remains a classic for its monastic writing style, depth of information and insights, and its dead-end authenticity to the dialogue and the atmospherics of this twelve hundred-year period.

It is natural to make comparisons between Rome and that of modern history: The fall of the British Empire and the Soviet Union in the twentieth century, and all the other great empires of Europe since Charlemagne's Holy Roman Empire; Portugal, Spain, the Netherlands, and France during the sixteenth and seventeenth centuries; the Napoleonic Empire and Austrian-Hungarian Empire; and the other ancient empires including the Egyptians, Greeks, Persians, Mongolian, Turkish, Aztec, and Mayan empires in an earlier age. Following Gibbon's work, we now have Arnold Toynbee, the English historian, and Oswald Spengler, the German historian, claiming the rise and fall of all civilizations; they either wither away, crumble from within due to false values and virtues, or self-destruct because of military overreach.

At some point in their decline, if I may add a note, with almost all civilizations, their leaders think they speak to God (or are doing God's work), and believe they can reshape the world; humility and rational thought are replaced by fanciful or delusional visions of grandeur. As decline sets in, powerful civilizations curtail their imperialistic ambitions and lose much of their economic vitality. Henceforth, they are reduced to a smaller power and must learn to share power with rival nations or empires. Although this perspective may sound dialectic or oversimplified, this is the way of the world—at least it has been this way for the last 5,000 years or more.

Since 9/11, the U.S. has witnessed the emergence of new economic powers—China, India, the European Union, the oil rich nations, as well as emerging nations such as Brazil, South Korea, and Singapore—all challenging U.S. economic power. We have witnessed the effects of George

Bush's war in Iraq, one of the stupidest endeavors of the United States, or any great power, has ever undertaken—a keen example of our own hubris, unilaterism and delusional march to war—very much like the Greeks and Romans at the height of their power.

At what point does the rickety architecture of civilization begin to collapse? What are the limits of American power? Americans are an optimistic people. But make no bones about it—we are in decline, and our standard of living is bound to be reshaped, as other centers of economic growth reconfigure the world order. The 2008 financial meltdown, initially caused by Wall Street greed and irresponsible risk involving some $33 trillion in credit default swaps that few people involved fully understood not only dragged down the U.S. economy, but also the global economy. One interesting outcome was that the G-20 (not G-7), that accounts for 85 percent of the world's economy, met to come up with economic proposals. It was the emerging nations, not only criticizing the U.S. for dragging down global markets but also it was China, Japan, and Saudi Arabia surfacing as the nations with fat wallets and the likeliest candidates to assist distressed countries—all symbols of the shifting landscape of economic power and the future test of the American economy.

Here it is worthwhile to note that Merrill Lynch announced that the three countries with the most newly minted millionaires since 2007 were India, China and Brazil, in that order. Similarly, India and China now produce more billionaires than the U.S. These new millionaires and billionaires reveal that the sweet breezes of wealth are no longer confined to the American landscape and that gumption, knowledge and opportunity are no longer exclusive American characteristics. As more economic elites and entrepreneurs around the world, including those in emerging countries, challenge American economic superiority and jostle for position, power and wealth, there is bound to be a major distribution of wealth from the U.S. to the rest of the world. Morally, there is nothing wrong with this growing trend but economically the American people grudgingly are going to have to make some life-style adjustments and tighten their belts. There is an economic "reset" or "reordering" now shaping American society, a major shift in the American dream, and a world economic order that is slowly disappearing forever.

Under the guise of protecting or spreading democracy, we have become the most militaristic nation in history (a hard pill for some Americans to swallow). Might makes right in the world of realpolitik, but it inspires world opinion to resent and even despise Americans. Our 2010 military budget (not counting the war in Iraq and Afghanistan) was more than $500 billion and represented 50 percent of the world's weaponry spending. These costs are unsustainable and result in curtailed spending for real social and human needs.

Grand idealistic or imperialistic designs, call it what you want, will produce little benefit for America. It is one thing to forge a foreign policy based on protecting American lives, asserts Robert Merry in *Sands of Empire*, but it is dangerous to participate in illusions of American omnipotence. Merry, the president of the Congressional Quarterly, warns that American intervention around the world is based on hubris that considers U.S. hegemony to be beneficial and sustainable. History shows that such a policy is delusionary and disastrous for two basic reasons. First, there will always be multiple power centers, incompatible ideologies, and conflicts around the world. Second, such a foreign policy can only exhaust us and lead to decline, as every great civilization that continuously tried to impose its will on other parts of the world eventually learned.

As we barrel ahead with unaccounted military spending, we are being threatened by a host of economic issues: hypereconomic competion from Asian-rim countries and resource nationalism and energy intimidation from Russia, Middle Eastern and Latin American countries; U.S. corporate downsizing, layoffs, and outsourcing of jobs; consumer and government overspending; and huge budget and trade deficits. Adding to our problems, giant corporations dominate the American political and economic landscape and supersede the interests of the people. Society is being divided into separate estates, and catch phrases harshly sort people into "winners" and "losers," suggesting a struggling and shrinking middle class. A growing gap between the rich and the rest of Americans has been fostered by a newly imposed tax system—steming from the Reagan administration and bolstered by the Bush II administration—and designed so that the children's children of super millionaires (the top one-half to 1 percent of the population) have the chance to become billionaires while the masses shoulder the monetary burden. As we squeeze the average American household (earning approximately $50,000 in 2009), we are transforming American democracy into a financial oligarchy. [3]

We are at the crossroads of American society; and as we look at the facts, there is only one conclusion. All directions point to difficult and bumpy roads ahead. There is no rule, no formula, for predicting the level and rate of decline. An American trait is the yearning for a new president as the Moses to lead the people out of troubled waters and through turbulent times, to find the way toward the rising sun. But Presidents are human and America has had its day in the sun. It reached its *belle époque*, what the French called it, during the Cold War period (when Europe and Asia were in shambles).

Americans have been protected by the accidents of geography and history to fully understand the irrevocable, historical human battle with misery, squalor and cruelties that people hush up because of a mixture of naiveté, hope and faith. No doubt, we are the lucky ones. We have only to thank the old posh British disdain toward the thirteen colonies and that a sufficient number of Founding Fathers had an ideological disdain toward the injustices of the European aristocracy.

Now here is the rub. Americans are not that lucky anymore. We are no longer alone on top of the hill nor a unilateral power. The good days lasted less than 50 years, from post World War II when all the great industrial powers were shattered by the ravages of war to the rise of Reaganism. Much of his economic theories can be summed up as free markets (translated into unregulated business practices that unleashed unfettered greed), small government (meaning fewer social programs and safety nets), and tax cuts for the rich (resulting in greater inequality of income and wealth among Americans). The outcome is that we must now adjust to a new global village. The playing field is a little more even (or flattened) and a little more interconnected; wealth is being redistributed from the U.S. to China, India, and other emerging nations; and Americans feel squeezed and worried that their children will not have the same opportunities or standard of living they enjoyed.

If this is a fault with this account, it is its relentless gloomy view of the world order and my disdain toward the top 1 percent, the rich and powerful whose love of money and Machiavellian strategies form the basis for human desire and self-interest at the expense of many. Such one-sidedness reflects the author's mental map of the world and the foundations of this book.

CLASS STILL COUNTS

The story I weave is based around class, wealth and work. Class counts and it has always counted. For all the citizens of the world, class reaches back to antiquity and stretches across the globe. It is a defining element throughout history, shaping political, economic, and social attitudes and behavior. Class is the foundation for understanding human thought and the human condition. The choices are vividly portrayed in Victor Hugo's *Les Misérables*: Whether you are willing to steal a loaf of bread to eat or use the law to put someone in prison for trying to survive—whether you are a Jean Valjean, one of billions who are hungry, poor and desperate—or an Inspector Javert, just another ordinary person following the orders of the rich and powerful. For myself, class serves as the great divide: People like Jean Valjean (lower—and working-class people), Inspector Javert (middle-class bureaucrats), and those whom the Javerts work for (the rich and powerful).

"Class" is a metaphor for exploitation. Today's workers in some respect are indistinguishable from yesterday's sweatshop workers, the medieval serfs who tilled the soil, or the Greek and Roman slaves. They are the same people that fight all the wars from time immemorial. They are the world's workforce, the common people, the unknown names that built our railroads, bridges, and tunnels, that built the great churches and castles for Charlemagne, Peter the Great, and King Arthur, that built the Acropolis and Coliseum, and before them pushed the stones uphill to build the Pyramids. Sadly, we do not know one of them by name, though they number in the billions. They are the faceless people of the earth who for centuries survived through sweat and toil. Alexander Hamilton labeled them the *herd*. Marx called them the proletariat. Eugene Debs organized them as *union workers*. Ben Wattenburg, more recently, referred to them as the *silent majority*. I call them the "massline" and/or "multitude." Look in the mirror. It's a 99 percent chance that you are part of this group.

Class, today, can be used to divide people into social and economic categories, to show monetary gaps are growing between the rich (top 1 percent), and super rich (top .01 percent), and the rest of us (bottom 99 percent). The principles of democracy, the very foundation of America, are being threatened by increasing inequality and a diminishing middle class. We have reached the point—an economic divide—where education cannot easily compensate nor overcome economic inequality.

If you are some sort of a liberal that reads the *New York Times* and listens to CNN on a regular basis you have a different explanation than some conservative person who subscribes to *Fortune* magazine and listens to Fox news for why in America we have so many shameful social deficits such as decaying schools and neighborhoods, why tens of millions of citizens are without a decent job, and why so many working people have to hold down two or three jobs to make ends meet. It's a serious problem, masked by the notion of the American dream, which our children and youth don't recognize or fully understand because they have been seduced by it.

Riding the winds of liberalism, the common people (meaning the poor, working and middle-class populace, and most of the elderly) should be concerned that the network of public and private social and health protection is unraveling. There are fewer safeguards against downward mobility in a world pulsating with economic insecurity for the vast majority of Americans. Our society, today, is characterized by creeping unemployment, limited employment opportunities and low wages; loss of retirement investments and pensions; deflating home values and equity; soaring medical bills and health insurance costs; a strain in Medicare coverage to cover seniors' bills; and an uneasiness that Social Security is being depleted so that the retirement age will be bumped up or benefits will be reduced. Economic analysts warn that the flood of retiring baby boomers will cause federal spending on Social Security and Medicare to eventually consume as much of the nation's economy as the entire federal budget does now. Budget deficits that exist now, measured in the trillions, are forcing the government to borrow from (and some might say rape) Social Security and Medicare funds to finance current deficits.

It is not only the working and middle class that feel the strain and feel stretched thin. Upper-middle-class babies of the baby boomers, the under-thirty generation who have finished their MBAs, also feel that pinch—from corporate downsizing, global outsourcing, and vanishing pensions. Their moms and dads, with their two-earner households, feel the same pressure—often having borrowed on their home equity. (As many as 44 percent of American homeowners have refinanced and increased their mortgage or have taken a second mortgage, called a home equity loan.) The popularity of interest-only and low-rate adjustable loans rapidly increased from 2000 to 2007, suggesting more and more buyers were straining to qualify for housing loans. This made more people vulnerable to rising interest rates, especially those who had balloons or adjustable mortgages. New loans quickly ran into trouble, reflecting hard times among homeowners, what was later to be called the "housing bubble." Even worse, personal bankruptcies increased six-fold from 1980 to 2008, largely due to loss of jobs or high medical costs.

Corporations, attempting to keep competitive in a global market, have shifted health costs and pensions to employees. Even worse, conservative policymakers see the need to dismantle social and health programs to balance budgets, as part of the new economic realities and the desire to diminish and decentralize the roles of the federal government. They dismiss safety net proposals as a form of welfare, and as subsidizing people who don't want to work or prefer to play the system to their own benefit at the cost of the public good. Only with the entire economic system in disray, and their own lifestyle and measures of wealth threatened, is the money class and conservative pundits now willing to help out the people who live on Main Street. Reluctantly, after much discord, they were willing to assist the auto industry—that is blue-collar country. But the traditional lifetime employment arrangement, with health and pension benefits, often referred to as the old GM model, is out the window—replaced by less stable, less secure and lower-wage marketplace.

What we have, today, is a growing number of working-class and middle-class Americans spiraling downward, what I call "struggling Americans," trying to make it on a daily basis, often in hock, while conservative policymakers lobby hard to shift the tax burden from the rich to the non-rich, from wealth and assets to labor and earnings, from income to consumption (sales tax). The rich obviously do not need government help. They are rich because they know how to take care of themselves and know how to make money. The rich need to be impeded, brought down a notch or two—to try to level the playing field. Of course, conservative pundits would argue that the rich pay most of the taxes and their taxes need to be further reduced to stimulate the economy.

Bless these economic pundits, including Milton Friedman and Alan Greenspan, for hoodwinking the American public on small government and free markets. Now we are paying dearly for what experts on Wall Street and the banking industry call a "bubble," that is when sectors in the economy plummet. Sadly that's what happened in recent years. And it all happened out of the pockets of the U.S. Treasury and Congress. What started as a $700 billion bailout package on "loosey, goosey" terms with limited transparency and accountability that would make Forest Gump blush, expanded to trillions to combat a pending Depression—all in the name of the free markets, greed is good, and the rich should not be overly burdened with taxes.

EXCELLENCE VS. EQUALITY

The issues concerning *excellence* and *equality* are also examined in the book—issues which go back to Greek civilization, when Plato wrote the *Republic* and the *Laws* and tried to define universal concepts such as truth, goodness, justice and the spiritual world of ideas. These twin issues continue to impact on society and involve a delicate and shifting scale with regard to the kinds of performance society chooses to reward, resulting in the conditions of social and economic mobility and the degree of stratification within society.

Most liberal and conservative pundits have their own ideas about excellence and equality of opportunity in education, jobs, and society in general. Many of us are unable to agree on what is equitable or fair, and how much we can stretch the embodiment of reform or the fiber of society. When large numbers of people perceive the system as unfair or rigged so that no matter how hard they work few rewards are achieved, the people who feel discriminated will stop working hard and thus fulfill preconceived expectations about their lazy or inadequate performance. The subordinate group may even adopt the terminology of the dominate group, especially if the latter group controls the institutions of society and the media.

Too much emphasis on egalitarianism can lead to mediocrity, indifference, and economic decline. Extreme egalitarianism leads to policies that handicap or penalize bright and talented people, whereby the goal of equal opportunity for individuals is replaced by the goal of equal results among groups. Such a society devaluates the use of tests and other forms of objective data. On the other hand, excellence carried too far can create social and economic gaps, hostilities among groups, and a stratified society. Even worse, over emphasis on achievement and unbridled individual performance can lead to a discussion of the unequal capacities of individuals and groups, and an excuse for keeping people in a second-class status and for violating basic human rights.

Democratic societies tend to ignore differences in intelligence where possible; when it cannot be ignored, the blame is shifted to the institutions or agents of society. No group is supposed to be regarded as better or smarter than another group. Whenever differences in capacity are recognized, the politically correct view is that differences vary among individuals and not groups. In a heterogeneous society like ours, when we focus on differences in achievement or economic outcomes, the result can lead to a host of hotly contested issues.

Given how American society has evolved, the ideal is to search for the golden mean which goes back to Aristotle, and to achieve a balancing act which rewards merit and hard work and provides a floor or safety net for low-performing, slow running and weaker individuals. But despite this ideal standard for society, we are confronted with the harsh truth that this nation remains much more stratified than what its principles suggest. We shall see in the remaining parts of the book, there is very little movement from one class to another in American society. We would like to believe that through merit and hard work anyone can achieve the American dream. Our Founding Fathers, rejected aristocracy and inherited privilege. Yet we are heading toward the creation of a new aristocracy—rooted in Wall Street and the banking industry, the entertainment industry and the captains of industry. At the same time, we are witnessing the destruction of the middle class.

In a more egalitarian society, the people who work at unskilled jobs or low-status jobs are paid relatively higher wages than would otherwise be paid in a society that fosters inequality. In such a society, a full range of excellence would be rewarded, and provisions would be made for those who do not come out on top because of lesser abilities, motivation, drive and—or just bad luck. In this type of society, policies require decent wages and working conditions for those jobs that few people want to perform (i.e. landscaper, hotel chamber maid, janitor, etc.) but are necessary to society. No matter how excellent they perform in these jobs, their rewards will be limited. For example, how much extra should society pay for and excellent janitor? Compare that to an airplane pilot or surgeon.

In an egalitarian society, safety nets and social programs are needed to help the less skilled and less fortunate (who may be skilled but unlucky), including the poor and working people, sickly, disabled, and aged. Policies also require an education program for all children and youth not only to enhance mobility among the lower and working classes, but also for purpose of the nation's growth and productivity so that all its citizens can improve their standard of living. Finally, society requires some cap or limit on salaries for jobs that are considered highly skilled, high status, and high paying. Government regulation is appropriate, not only for purposes of protecting the slow and weak runner, but also to curb the "champions" of exploitation, greed and avarice.

Here we are going down a "slipping slope," where the "masters of the universe," the titans of industry, and conservative pundits argue that we need to reward high standards of performance to the fullest in order for society to achieve greatness. The realities of competition and the "sorting out process" operate best in a free market, we are told, with no government interference, no regulations, no quotas, and no limits on rewards. In a highly competitive society, one that fosters social conditions under which the benefits go to a small group of people because of performance, (or even worse, because of inherited privilege or advantage), class conflict can escalate to the point that the underclass threatens the rich.

Where the costs of protecting the more affluent against the masses outweigh the costs of redistribution of resources or wealth, at that point society collapses or is overthrown. Obviously, the U.S. has not reached this point. But we should pause and take heed that hundreds of societies over centuries have reached the point of breakdown or upheaval because of government authoritarianism and corruption, hereditary privilege (membership in a family, class or caste) is viewed as iron clad, and/or the inability of society to constrain human greed and avarice. Recent events in Africa and the Arab world reflect this type of flash point or revolt. Jealously of ill-gotten gains among political leaders is acute among the youth and educated cohorts across Africa and Middle East—and other parts of the underdeveloped world.

At home, the financial meltdown of 2008 and 2009 is an example of the near economic collapse of society because the free market was considered the driving engine of the economy, and it was believed by ideologs that the market, if left alone, would correct itself. The idea that competition leads to increased productivity and greed leads to increased efficiency is rooted in the minds of Darwinism and Spencerism, and to a kind of "survival of the fittest" and "law of the jungle." Similarly, the notion that shrewdness and strength will create the rise of obscure and uncultivated men to great wealth is at best a false free-market assumption and at worst a class-interest philosophy that ignores the human condition. Greed and corruption will always prevail when the money class is permitted to act without restraint or regulation. These kind of values will almost always trump excellence and equality—sought of a Hobbesian view of life described in *The Leviathan*.

In his *Life and Letters*, the words of Henry Lee Higginson, the Boston financer, ring loud today as they did some 90 years ago. In his plea to wealthy colleagues to endow Harvard liberally, he bluntly asserted that the wealthy class had fast hold of the world and that superior education was essential "to save ourselves and our families and our money from the mobs." In the twenty-first century, the "masters of the universe" and "financial wizards" continue to prevail, fortified against possible misfortunes through the acquisition of values and interests unconnected with Main Street or the common good. In picturesque words, they have become marred in the crude and conspicuous enjoyment of the feast—evidenced by their king-sized mansions, lavish parties and lifestyle—and displayed and celebrated by the media in popular magazines, cable television, and the Internet. Spokesman of big business and banking remind the American public, more precisely dupe the people, that that acquisition of wealth has always been the crucial index of civilization and without it no great achievement nor innovation, no long-term productivity nor jobs could be realized. Celebrated in song and story, they are allowed to squander hundreds of thousands of dollars on private jets and big yachts, on old wine and rare paintings that may be unpalatable and ugly—or worse, counterfeit—and boast on the air waves and in print how they made their first billion dollars and how you and I can still achieve the American dream. Although they provide us with stories about inspiration and perspiration, their view of excellence has little to do with merit or performance. Their achievement is based primarily on political clout and power, the right social clubs and network of friends, or being born in privileged status.

In the most recent bubble, all the profits went to Wall Street and all the losses were absorbed by Main Street. It was working people, ordinary Americans, with diminishing retirement pensions and investments for their children's college education, who saw their world shattered. They also paid the bill for the Wall Street and banking bail out—as will their children and grandchildren in terms of possible governments deficits, reduced Medicare and Social Security benefits, higher taxes and/ or inflation—or all four.

Under the rules of corporate America and Wall Street, this is the way of the world. The little person tries hard and often believes in the good of people but gets devoured by the sharks or drowns, while the wealthy, with their clout and inside information, know when to jump ship. We would like to think we are all in the same boat, one nation indivisible. But then my thoughts drift to the movie *Titanic*—a great metaphor to explain who drowns and who gets to live another day. Because of class differences Jack was denied space in a lifeboat—and drowned. The first class passengers were evacuated and given access to boats and lived.

THE SUPER RICH AND THE REST OF US

Let's define terms, so allow me to introduce the *rich*, *very rich*, and *superrich* (sometimes referred to by others as the *ultrarich* or *mega wealthy*.) The average household income of the top 1 percent of Americans, the so-called *rich*, was $940,000 in 2004. These numbers compare to the *very rich* or the top tenth of 1 percent, whose household income was $4.5 million or more and the *super rich*, or the top hundred of 1 percent who income was $20 million or more. [4] By 2010, the top 1 percent of Americans earned 22 percent of the nation's income and held nearly 40 percent of the nation's wealth; this gap in income and of wealth tops the inequality index among 32 industrialized country (except Singapore and Hong Kong). Similarly, nearly 40 percent of the wealthiest 1 percent of the global population are Americans, although this inequity is about to gradually shift to China and India. [5] (Why the richest 1 percent cannot afford a graduated income tax beyond 35%, and the top .1 percent still a higher rate, is beyond reason.)

When it comes to wealth or assets, a million dollars is not what is used to be—certainly not when I grew up during the Truman and Eisenhower years. About seven percent of U.S. households are millionaires and some may be your next door neighbor, according to Stanley and Danko's recent book, *The Millionaire Next Door*. But you should not assume that it will make you deliriously happy or give you sufficient security to quit your boring job. Ironically, the authors found that thrift, inheritances and social class had stronger correlations with money that did intelligence or education.[6]

When people of wealth, with al least $500,000 to invest, were surveyed by *Worth* magazine in 2008, as many as 48 percent defined the rich as having a net worth of at least $5 million, 25 percent said $25 million, and 8 percent said those with $100 million were truly wealthy. Now I think it is safe to say that someone is *truly rich* with $25 million in assets, and *superrich* with $100 million—that is "mega wealthy" or just "plain wealthy" if you like vanilla ice cream.

The difference between wealth and work is simple. Wealth is passed on from generation to generation, and includes assets that are taxed at a lower rate than work. In 2010, capital gains were taxed at 15 percent while earnings of $50,000 or more for a single person was taxed (including federal, state, and social security) at nearly 50 percent. It is nearly impossible to accumulate wealth by working for a salary; the tax system prevents it.

Given these conditions, it is nearly impossible to narrow the gap between the rich and the rest of us. In fact, the wealth gap is just as unequal in the U.S. as it is around the globe. No joke! About 99% of the U.S. population depend on work in order to put bread on the table. They have what is called a job. About 1%, the rich, do not work at a 9 to 5 job, rather move around money and invest—thus creating more wealth—based primarily on acquiring stocks and bonds or property. The vast majority of these people do not care about the plight or condition of ordinary Americans, and are more concerned that the masses don't "storm the Bastille" or break down their doors. They care more about which patrician spouses they marry, about their summer homes and gardens, and their charming wine cellars or rare paintings. F. Scott Fitzgerald, the early twentieth century American novelist, put it aptly: "The rich are different from you and I." It's more than money and wealth; it deals with attitude, lifestyle, and social and political connections, and the fact they are part of the system or know how to play the system for their own gain.

New money—athletes, actors and singers, and entrepreneurs—do not have the same DNA or breeding as *old money*. New money often lacks political clout, as opposed to old money who are part of the ruling class. It is not easy being born into old money. These people rarely speak publically about their finances, in good times or bad. There assets most likely have dropped recently, but it is doubtful if it will cut into their lifestyle. New money is more overt in displaying their big yachts, fast cars, Rolex watches and $500 hair highlights, and they are less mum about their losses. Certainly, there is no need to feel sorry for them if they now have to cut down on their trips to the Riviera or sell a 4-carat diamond with the hope no one will notice that it is gone.

The simple truth is, in the last thirty years, the new money class have had the opportunity to make huge sums of money, largely because of mass media, technology, and market globalization. Entrepreneurs make products or provide services, but entertainers—well, they entertain us like modern-day gladiators or courtier jesters. Their names become brands and faces become images which are copyrighted, merchandised and sold, then plastered on television and the Internet.

One way to illustrate the rise of this new money class is to compare two household baseball names. In the mid 1950s, Mickey Mantle of the New York Yankees was in his prime earning $100,000 a year. Compared to the average working man's salary (few women worked) of $4,000, his salary was 25 times greater. By 2010, Alex Rodriguez of the same Yankee organization was earning $28 million, not counting additional monies for endorsements, while the average working person' salary was $35,000—more than 770 times what the average American earned. For older readers who golf, Ben Hogan's top annual earnings was $90,000 in 1948, compared to Jack Nichlaus' $320,000 in 1972 and Tiger Woods' $122 million in 2007. To be sure, wealth vs. work has become increasingly skewed because of mass media and globalization, as well as a tax structure that has increasingly favored the rich since the Reagan administration.

The issue can also be stated in terms of pricing seats for sporting events. In the last twenty-five years, the average baseball ticket increased 300 percent, more than 5 times the inflation rate and during the same period when the average working wage (after considering inflation) remained flat at $16 per hour. Add in parking, burgers and cokes, and a family of four at the ball game spends a few hundred dollars to sit in the bleachers. What used to cost $1 to $2 per seat now costs $30 to $35 per seat. And, what used to cost $5 to $7 for a box seat now cost $100 to $250 per seat. The main reason is competition for scarce seats which corporate business people can right off as a tax deduction. The bidding process by the rich for good seats has not only driven up luxury skyboxes from $500 to $2,500 (in Yankee Stadium) per seat, but also the box seats behind home plate which are second-choice seats.

The same situation holds true for center-court seats at basketball games and fifty-yard line seats at football games. The endless-demand by the rich in the sports market, fueled by entertainment deductions for big business and the wealthy distorts the market and cheats the public out of tax revenue. Of course, in the grand scheme of things this coincides with American capitalist system. One solution would be to limit the amount of deductions for expensive tickets. Another solution would be to cap salaries of modern-day athletes who make nothing of worth for the common good and merely entertain the masses in the way gladiators did for Rome while it was declining.

It's nice to know the rich and super rich are human and vulnerable to rocky times. During the last financial meltdown, the nation's 400 top-money people lost a total of $300 billion in 2008, according to *Forbes*. This brought down their combined net worth to $1.27 trillion, about 19 percent. Of course, the super rich are more insulated and knowledgeable than average folks who work for a living. Their percent loss of assets was about half the percentage lost by America's pension funds and stock portfolios. Moreover, it can hardly hurt or change the life style of Warren Buffett, the "Wizard of Wall Street," who lost approximately $10 Billion or 20 percent of his wealth that year. Nor can it change the life of Kirk Kerkorian, the corporate raider who lost $8 Billion and had only $3 Billion left. Then there is Bill Gates, the number one "geek" and America's richest person for the sixteenth straight year. He lost 7 billion or about 12 percent of his wealth.[7]

To be sure, inequality of income and wealth is a byproduct of capitalism, pushing the well-connected, under the guise of the best and brightest, to the most profitable positions. But the system falls apart when the plutocrats run the world as if it was their play ground. They may encourage young college students to work hard and start their path to Wall Street or banking. However, the system is not sustainable if the vast majority are told they must excel for a $1 dollar more per hour or a $1,000 more a year, while the upper crust gobble up millions or even billions.

So in a nut shell, who is the ruling class? Who runs the world? Certainly not those families earning $250,000 a year, a magical number the Obama Administration wanted to use for increasing taxes. In fact, on the East and West coasts, where living expenses are higher than the rest of the U.S., $250,000 suggests nothing more than middle class or upper middle class. For some pundits, however, $250,000 suggests the top 2 percent. As for running the world, ordinary Americans (the bottom 99 percent) have no say. They now have trouble holding on to a job and paying their bills, in fact, most Americans live just above subsistence level but don't realize it—until they lose their job. But, then, that has been the human condition since the crack of civilization. And, we are the fortunate ones. As Otto Bismark, the Prussian chancellor, once muttered: "God has special providence for fools, drunks, and the United States of America."

The rise of the nation-state, coupled with the global economy, has given rise to what David Rothkopt in *Superclass* calls a "national ruling class" and a "global power elite"—business and financial titans who run large public companies and banks, supra organizations such as the World Bank and International Monetary Fund, and have huge influence on political leaders around the world.

These super elites have all the characteristics of the old Protestant elite, but with the essential difference that they operate from a global market and they have sway over more money and a larger share of the economic pie. They attend the same elitist universities such as Harvard, Yale, and University of Chicago, attend the same forums such as the Council on Foreign Relations and World Economic Forum, travel in private gulf stream jets, vacation in private ski havens like Yellowstone Club, where they can mingle discreetly without bodyguards (since the place is protected by the Secret Service), invest in the same hedge funds such as the Carlyle Group and Blackstone Group and often illegally bury money offshore and thus avoid or delay for years the need to pay taxes. They get together at meetings and resorts with former presidents, prime ministers and CEOs; invite or nominate each other to corporate boards and foundations; trade inside information; and make each other richer. The world may be flat, according to Thomas Friedman, but it is also tilted in favor of the rich and super rich—and it's always been like that.

For the greater part, the rulers of the world are the global elites—along with top business people and financial wizards of the world, as well as old money. It is not all that complicated. A small number of families dominate business and political interests in the United States and Europe. They are in the position to provide lucrative favors for each other and a mass wealth, more than the old "robber barons" dreamed during the Gilded Age. The key to their fortunes is not excellence nor individual genius, it has to do with family ties and social and political clout, who they know and who they do business with. It is what one insider, John Perkins in *Confessions of and Economic Hit Man*, calls "corporatocracy," the bond that ties together families, corporations, and government in the United States and other parts of the world. It is the same system of inherited privilege and political power that allows for the Bushs, Kennedys, Rockefellers, and DuPonts to live in splendor and influence, if not dominate, the world stage.

"SPLAININ"—WHERE THE U.S. IS HEADING

Alan Beattie, the conservative editor at the *Financial Times*, contends that every country is in control of its own economic destiny. As we try to recover from the 2008-09 financial meltdown, the reversal of our own fortunes depend on what political leaders decide to do. "We created this mess, and we can get ourselves out of it," he says. Beattie maintains that the choices we make as a nation will determine our future economic health. He fails to consider, however, that the ordinary working person has little to say and depends on its political leaders who are often in bed with and to some extent depend on Wall Street and the banking industry to keep the economy running, which in turn is fueled by greed, arrogance and self-interest. Obsession with money overtakes morality and any concern for the common good. The more money someone makes, more often the more greedy someone becomes.

While Beattie and other conservatives talk about choice and free markets, they also mention how the role of history plays in the economic success or failure of a nation. In *False Economy*, Beattie argues that neither the laws of nature or scripture, nor luck or even abundance of fertile land or natural resources, explain why some countries end up rich and prosperous and others poor and unstable. Economic outcomes of a country largely depend on choices of its political leaders and the spirit and creative passions of its populace. These are all intangible or hard-to-define items, but they often make the difference between how nations manage and build or mismanage and squander their wealth.

Obviously, history has been kind to America, not only in terms of geography (the oceans protected us until 9-11) but also natural resources (abundant in America) and climate (mild weather has allowed for abundant food production). But, given the historical context of America, Beattie and others fail to consider how the corruption of the Gilded Age of the nineteenth century served as a model for the Gilded Age II (the last thirty years). He fails to see or admit that the flaws in our financial system can break our economy, or that the growth in inequality and shrinking of the middle class for the last thirty years, unless check mated, can lead to a financial oligarchy and the collapse of American democracy.

The recent Gilded period has shown that people in finance are just as unethical, arrogant, and fraudulent as they were when they were called *robber barons* more than one hundred years ago or *warlords* more than 1,000 years ago. The difference is that more money is now at stake because the market has expanded on a global basis and there are more ways to fleece the public.

The warlords, and then the nobility class and monarchs, once taxed its citizens. Now Wall Street brokers and traders, as well as investment bankers, have privatized the same function by convincing ordinary citizens with 401Ks and workers with government pensions to purchase stocks, bonds and mortgage securities and charge profits and fees for their services. The financial industry around the world has gained access to capital with minimum regulations and transparency, and has convinced the victims on Main Street including local and state government bureaucrats in charge of billions in pension money, that bankers are the "pillars of society."

The Securities Exchange Commission and other regulatory agencies (like the Federal Reserve and rating agencies such as Moodys and Fitch) are supposed to protect the people, uncover huge risk, and lock up the thiefs. However, the reader needs to understand the SEC officials who are supposed to check and regulate Wall Street and banking often look to use their present position as a stepping stone or resume indicator to land a job as a Wall Street executive or banking investor where their potential earnings will be four or five times more. Hence, it doesn't take a rocket scientist or math whiz to figure out why the cheats in business and finance continue with almost complete immunity. When the Federal Reserve thought about more regulation, tried to scrutinize credit-default swaps or question bond ratings, which led to the subprime mortgage crisis in post 2008. It was often rebuffed as stifling free-market capitalism and competition. The Feds rescued big banking, we are told, because it was afraid the entire economic system would collapse. No one thought of small companies or the ordinary people; they were left to drown or swim on their own.

In the most likely scenario, the economic giants like Goldman Sachs, J.P. Morgan and Citigroup now report billions in profits and bask in reverent applause. Nonetheless, millions of jobs have been lost, tens of millions of jobs have been reduced to short schedules or completely outsourced to foreign workers, and billions of dollars in wages have been extinguished. China will eventually supersede America as the engine of growth and production within the next 20 to 25 years. Africa, and especially the vast resources of the Congo, will become the new battleground in diplomacy and trade between the Western world and China which is starved for resources and commodities such as oil, copper, tin, etc. Latin America, which the U.S. has taken for granted as its sphere of influence, will also become a new economic battleground between China and the U.S.

The extremes of wealth in the Western World and the "old boy club" of the rich nations of the world, notably the G-8, reached its apex at the turn of the twenty-first century. Gone are the days of Pax Britannical (Roosevelt-Churchill to Reagan-Thatcher era) and Pax Americana (Bush I to Bush II era), when Britain and the United States determined the rules of the world order. Economically, the new world we live in is highlighted by America drained by military overreach and China clutching a fist full of dollars, actually U.S. banknotes, but also the stark reality that the U.S. consumer can no longer prop up the global economy and continue to chalk up increased debt.

On a moral basis, the madness of the U.S. capitalist system is characterized by assorted ways of making piles of money among a tiny minority while millions of Americans are plagued by debt, struggling with and either unemployment or underemployment, and worried about how much money they have left for retirement. President Obama, speaking at the G-20 meeting in 2009, and again in 2010 and 2011, assured the leaders of the world that America is not in decline. He rejected the idea as an old theory which flys in the face of "a vibrancy to our economic model, a durability to our political model, and a set of ideas that has sustained us through difficult years." All well and good, a great piece of rhetoric, and an uplifting pinch of sugar and spice.

But go tell that to the average worker in Wisconsin, Ohio, Indiana or elsewhere in the Midwest and South who in 2011 were fighting to retain their rights to collectively organize. Conservative governors claim the unions are breaking the middle class. No, unions are the backbone of the middle class. The titans at the top, the rich and superrich, are pitting ordinary workers against each other, union workers against nonunion workers under the guise of "shared sacrifice" and balancing budgets.

Recent presidents have failed to consider that the U.S. has moved from a manufacturing society, whereby Americans made products for the world, to a financial-based economy, whereby services are provided for a fee which in the long run is unsustainable. Much of the financial industry hoodwinks and traps consumers and home owners with the small print that few people, even with a Ph.D., can understand. It produces windfalls for bankers, mortgage brokers, hedge fund managers, and insurance agents—and resentment for the rest of us. It drives up the cost for everything—from the cost of a hamburger to a house—until the cost becomes unreasonable which in turn leads to a correction or bubble.

Our economic system is partially based on a culture that thrives on independence and individualism, not on the collective good or about what happens to our neighbors. It is fueled by the spirit of hard work and inner-directed (not group-based) behavior. If I work hard, and with a little luck, I'll get what I need and I don't have to be concerned nor worry about the person who cannot or will not work as hard. It's a cynical view but pretty much sums up western values and the notion of individual freedom in the U.S. Not only does this point of view prune away the "weak links" in society, it also corresponds with the notion of Social Darwinism, popularized in the nineteenth century, and the Gorden Greco model (in the movie *Wall Street*) that greed (sometimes called self-interest) is good.

Our economic system has also been corrupted by a financial model that is based on quick profits and/or phoney profits—and riddled by the likes of Enron, World Com, AIG, and Madoff. Hence, profits and gains for the last thirty years or more have flown disportionately to the rich, defined as the top 1 percent, at the expense of the bottom 99 percent. In simple mathematical terms, as many as 25 percent of the *Forbes* 400 richest people owe their fortunes to the financial sector, compared to the 10 percent in 1982 (when the U.S. was still a manufacturing society).

Using more exotic, statistical jargon, the top .01 percent of Americans earned 20 times the income of the bottom 90 percent in 1979 and 77 times the amount in 2006; the bottom 90 percent of the population earned $117,000 or less while the top .01 percent earned $16 million or more. Education levels, technological change, and globalization may explain why uneducated workers and poor people have lost ground to college graduates and skilled workers. But it does not explain the growing inequality between the super rich and the rest of us—or why the middle class is being wiped out. You might say that hard work and luck help explain the differences, but that's old hat. Most ordinary people are beginning to think the system is rigged—where the powerful and rich play by one set of rules and the rest of us play by another set of rules, one group is born on third base with a batch of trusts and the majority are merely trying to get up at bat and get a decent education and job.

One group (about 1 percent of the American populace) is front and center with a long standing mix of huge salaries, bonuses and pensions while ordinary Americans are struggling and angered. They are barely getting by, sinking in debt, and worried about their jobs—and whether they will be able to continue to pay their home mortgages and save enough money to pay for their children's college education. A growing number, perhaps the bottom 50 percent, are worried about putting sufficient food on the table. We have slowly descended into a two-tier society, a country run by a financial oligarchy (the political and economic elite), and a social order (in terms of inequality) that is coming close to the one that existed before the French and Russian revolutions. The average American refuses to admit that the deck is stacked, the bubble has burst, and the so-called dream is now more folklore than reality. Kiss Horatio Alger goodbye, at least for the vast majority of the people. The loss of competitiveness and increase in global competition adds to our economic downward spiral, particularly at the bottom and middle ranges of the American workforce.

The economic system that has evolved rewards people who are in position to make *profits* for a large corporation or financial institution by moving money around with a flick of a mouse, by fleecing the public and/or by entertaining the masses (as actors, singers, ballplayers, etc.) through the media. It penalizes people who are considered a *cost* factor for an organization or business, and thus wages are capped. We have unwittingly created a distorted system of rewards—a rigged game and an upside-down economy. The system has allowed the financial sector to become so gargantuan that when mistakes are made, they receive government bailouts so they can survive at the expense of the people who are struggling on a daily basis. This is not only stirring up questions of fairness and equity, but also old vestiges of class resentment.

For conservatives to yell foul—and put down or stifle critics of the system by labeling them as unpatriotic, jealous or stirring class warfare—is to mask the hypocrisy of big business and big money, and the negative effects of multimillion dollar contracts and the continual windfall of the superrich. Conservatives argue there is danger in taxing the rich, restricting their bonuses, or regulating their behavior. They fail to consider that anger on Main Street is growing toward the money class. When it comes to people who have earned their money in the financial sector, there are an increasing number of people—average working Americans who feel it is wrong. A class divide is growing. There is the feeling that the wings of the investment bankers, hedge fund managers, and Wall Street executives need to be clipped and that windfall profits, bonuses and retirement packages (often called golden parachutes) should be taxed at higher rates.

The economic calamity of 2008 and 2009 should have shattered some of the cherished tenets of capitalism. But, John Cassidy, a financial journalist, sizes up the problem in *How Markets Fail.* He points out there are no hard-and-fast principles to destroy. Capitalism means different things to different people; liberals and conservatives have very different views on how to reform it. It so happens that the free market system has dominated American thinking since the election of President Reagan, whose goal was to down size government and reduce taxes for the rich. Alan Greenspan, the chairperson of the Federal Reserve from 1987 to 2006, added fuel to the fire. He sold Americans on the ideas that financial markets are rational and self-correcting mechanisms. The outcome was the worst financial crisis since the Great Depression, with no one held accountable for their role in the crisis (except in the case of overt fraud—such as with Madoff).

The conservative movement in the U.S. is anti-government, resents government regulation of corporate America, and views it as "Big Brother." So long as the American economy is marked by the closure or bankruptcy of plants making cars, clothes, and electronics—where the losers are working people—there is little concern for government regulation. When banks and Wall Street go under and stocks plummet, conservatives take note and rally and come forth with government assistance. The argument is these institutions are "too big to fail" and must be saved in order to ward off financial disaster and save jobs.

Conservatives fail to recognize that manufacturing in the 1960s represented 35 percent of the U.S. work force and now it is slightly less than 10 percent—and these pundits just watched labor groups suffer without lifting a finger. The class war has ended. The people lost. Throughout history, they have always lost. The global pie has expanded, making the rich richer. But for every super rich person, there are millions who are starving or barely making it day-to-day. Then there is the government-capitalist divide—or myth. The more government regulations are considered a violation of individual liberty, or that they are believed to limit the vitality and innovativeness of society, the worse off its workers. The conservative pundit relies on a "Trojan horse"—a backdoor attack for limiting the size of government in order to enhance free markets—whereby the winner is the corporate or banking titan (or capitalist) and the loser is the worker. Why ordinary people are seduced by the notion of free markets probably has something to do with partisan politics and cultural issues that divide the nation. Of course, there is always Alexander Hamilton's viewpoint. The masses are stupid; they adopt herd behavior, and they will always be second class to the banking and manufacturing class.

While conservative economists and the moneyed class try to play down the misadventures and malpractices of Wall Street and the banking and insurance industries, and then try to resurrect the reputation of the financial sector, the losers of the economy (the bottom 95 to 99 percent) should expect to feel the long slog of the economy: Unemployment, underemployment, foreclosures, and loss of pension funds. In the meantime, the financial sector has quickly returned to the festive days of huge profits and bonuses; the public now assumes the game is rigged and that the government merely protects the rich and powerful in corporate America and on Wall Street at the expense of the people. To be sure, the people on Main Street are simmering with rage—a period in time similar to the French monarch and nobility class viz-a-vie the peasants that stormed the Bastille.

Conservatives talk about economic blowback: Hindering competition, choice and free markets will wreck the economy and will have ripple effects on jobs and ordinary Americans. Nonsense. What we have now is a loss of community, runaway individualism and the accumulation of great wealth in the hands of a few. During the Eisenhower administration the tax rate was as high as 90 percent—and the country was growing at a faster rate than the last several years when the rate was 35 percent. Similarly, there is no such thing as "now is not the best time." The time is now. Reform is necessary—not only in terms of tighter regulations and early warning systems, but also higher taxes for the rich. It's hard to see how we emerge from this economic downturn. Indeed, the country's political leadership seems unable and unwilling to help the people, to provide a sense of common purpose that filters down to everyone.

CONCLUSION

It is hoped that some of the statements in this pocket size book may pop the seams of the reader's trousers. I do not believe myself to have any original genius, nor any economic wisdom that match the minds of a Paul Krugman or Robert Reich, two economists who I would enjoy drinks with before one of us fades into ambiguity.

I am basically conveying simple ideas that characterize history, starting with Chapter 1 that the gap between the rich and the rest of the people has been the rule of the social order—even before the Pharaoh's days when the working class were pushing stones uphill. Whereas the bottom 50 percent of the global population own 1 percent of the world's wealth, the wealthiest 1 percent have gobbled 40 percent of the global wealth.[8]

To be sure, our present is connected to all our pasts. There is no single timeline, no specific historical period, separate from another time period. History has a way of repeating itself. A tiny minority—rich, powerful and politically interconnected—has ruled over a vast majority. All our eras and epochs, all our social and economic times, are alive and with us now. As the present is merely the accumulation of the past, the author intends to highlight certain periods of time to share the building blocks of ideas, permitting the reader to think and rethink the idea that America is divided along the lines of wealth vs. work. Inequality is growing within our nation, and the achievement of more equality is nearly impossible unless those in power are willing to set floors and ceilings of poverty and wealth—and redistribute wealth.

In simple terms, the issue is how much present levels of inequality should be tolerated, and just how much equality is plausible within our political and economic system. The flip side is that if we fail to modify the skewed income and wealth curves, we may surrender the principles of democracy that require a strong and vibrant working and middle class. Shared communal and economic interests are a strong antidote to the dark dimensions of a financial oligarchy—a money class running the government and economy and ruling the people. As we shall see in Chapter 3, our Founding Fathers came close to implementing this type of governing structure, as so many of them adopted the manners and ideas of the European aristocracy. It was mainly the influence of Thomas Jefferson and few other liberal thinkers that thwarted the notions of hierarchy and hereditary privilege, and it was not until the election of Andrew Jackson, in 1828, that American politicians begin to boast of having been born in a log cabin. As for you literature buffs, it was not until the publication of *Moby Dick* by Henry Melville and *The Last of the Mohicans* by James Fennimore Cooper that did the dignity of ordinary men become ascribed by well-known American writers and poets.

And, now, I hope to take you on a breathless ride across time. For me it is an apocalyptic landscape, peopled by powerful and wealthy elites who have regularly sort more power and wealth at the expense of common people. The outcome is, today, we have entered a trapdoor, a new paradigm or shift in society. It is fostered by the most extreme disparities of income and wealth in the U.S., worse than the Gilded Age or era just prior to the Great Depression, because the economic pie has expanded. The new paradigm is also characterized by the loss of jobs to China and India and other emerging nations; the manufacturing prowess of America has vanished, and we import much more than we export—making us a debtor nation. The result is a struggling and shrinking middle class, fewer prospects for mobility than the previous generation, and a weaker nation.

Now working Americans, the common people, even the middle class are plunging toward a lifestyle reserved for the working poor—not so far from the destitute and subordinate classes that have suffered through the ages. The catalog of transgressions by the rich and powerful against the interests of this country, spearheaded by marauders of the financial/banking world, has wrecked the most powerful economy and ruined the lives of many of its people.

Fifteen trillion dollars was squandered by free markets and market manipulators, during the housing bubble and Wall Street plunge in 2008 and 2009. Then taxpayers bailed out many of the same companies and executives that abused, tricked and robbed them. Add up all the recent damage, deceit and mishaps—and consider how each reader has been affected by events impacting on the economy: Housing mortgages, college loans, savings and retirement, credit and debt, unemployment or underemployment, and future relations with China (our new banker)—and you should now understand the fiery in my writing. After reading this book, the "Real Pepsi Challenge" is to understand this is how the world has always worked—political and economic elites gobbling up enormous benefits for themselves at the expense of ordinary people. To be sure, money does not trickle downward. Money always flows upward, from poor and working people to the rich, from the bottom sectors to the top.

Keep in mind a financial system, centered in the U.S., lending ridiculous sums of money to unqualified businesses and homeowners, as if the laws of supply and demand had vanished. Based on fantasies and phony ratings of credit worthingness, easy money fueled economic growth and riches for the rich until the bubble "popped." Then consider the effect on the America people: hundreds of millions of workers have been hurt, tens of millions devastated. To be sure, it may take years, possibly even a decade, to fully recover. Actually, the meltdown may be systematic of a worse situation that experts prefer not to discuss: A structural change in the amount of good paying-jobs, the deterioration of the America standard of living and the redistribution of wealth from the U.S. to emerging nations and from the Western world in to Asia and Latin America. It may just reflect a new generational underclass (millions of Americans): Born of less income equality, fewer chances to succeed and few chances for mobility than we have been taught to expect. And, if you believe in the tooth fairy, or perhaps the Tea Party, then the new likes of Alan Greenspan and Gordon Greco will come to our rescue.

Chapter 2

QUESTIONS TO CONSIDER

1. Since the beginning of civilization, which groups have controlled the political and social order?

2. For most of recorded history, what percentage of people have lived at the margins of poverty, famine, or disease?

3. Why was there always the expectation, since the dawn of civilization, that humans must live on the brink of squalor and starvation?

4. Compared to other past civilizations, how did ancient Greece and Rome differ in their political and social order?

5. In the ancient civilized world, how were the warlords who commanded armies paid for their loyalty to monarchs? Why did the masses so willingly surrender their rights to the warlords?

6. Given centuries of change in civilizations, why did philosophy, art and science do little to change the conditions of ordinary people in the Old World?

7. How did the Industrial Revolution change economic conditions in the Old World? Why did a different type of social and economic order unfold in America?

8. Why (and how) did the "zero-sum game" between the power elite and common person unfold in a different way in the New World than the Old World?

9. From the ancient world to the birth of the New World, how was power, authority and wealth derived? And perpetuated?

10. How do issues in education, namely what type of education and for whom, compare between ancient Greece and Rome and the U.S. today?

11. How does Rome's gladiator world compare to the U.S. sports industry today?

12. How does the decline of Greece and Rome compare with U.S. military overreach, the Bush doctrine of war, and Obama's notion of U.S. political and economic global limitations?

13. In the ancient world, survival amidst plunder and chaos was common on a daily basis. How does this differ in most parts of the world today?

14. Prior to the Industrial Revolution and to mid—nineteenth century, life was depicted as a gigantic struggle for existence. How does this differ from today's theories of unfettered capitalism, *laissez faire* doctrines, the profit system, survival of the fittest, greed is good, or that the big fish eat the small fish?

15. What political and economic conditions exist that prevent working people from gaining power over the capital or property class?

16. Why is it that the interests of the few (who are powerful) seem always to prevail at the expense of the many (who work for a living)? What, then, has changed in economic terms during the last 5,000 years of recorded history?

Chapter 2

A GLIMPSE INTO THE PAST AND PRESENT

The unifying theme in this chapter, as well as in other parts of the book, is that the long view and big idea are crucial in understanding humankind. To this extent, historians like Thucydides and Arnold Toynbee and political scientists like Thomas Hobbes and Samuel Huntington (who died in 2008) influence my thinking. To them, no single event matters more than another event. Human behavior unfolds within a larger pattern or recurring theme. These patterns or themes are shaped by deep currents of nature, social forces, and cycles of history. This view might be seen by some as outdated, simplistic or dialectic: That everything fits together, into this type of explanation, is nonsense. But so much of today's economic injustices and inequality stem from this long view and big idea of history and society.

A GRAND AND GLOOMY THEORY

For better or worse, allow me a few precious moments of your time to present a "grand" theory of society and how ordinary people have existed over thousands of years while I skip over details and counter arguments. For American eyes, the theory is a little more alien and ominous because for centuries the oceans have protected us and we have been spared much of the grief and misery of the rest of the world. Since the beginning of civilization, the theory goes, the political masters of society became the economic masters, and the master group controlled the social order—and its institutions. The political and economic elites never understood the need nor cared to include, in any sense, the millions who were kept at the margins because of squalor, famine or disease. There was no perceived concern to reduce poverty or inequality; in fact, poverty and inequality were not issues, rather expectations—part of the normal conditions of society. The custom was for those in power or position to exploit the situation in the most expedient way. This would lead to unlimited domination and gain by a tiny minority and utter subordination and misery by the vast majority of the population.

For more than 5,000 years, since the ancient Hebrews to the rise of the British empire in the eighteenth and early nineteenth centuries, the expectation remained in Europe, and the rest of the world (except America) that the masses were destined to live at the brink of starvation, famine and disease. This was the way it had been since the dawn of civilization. The human condition was characterized first by chaos and then misery—as the strong plundered the weak. Economic life was a struggle, pure and simple.

The idea of a social contract between government and the people or that people had natural rights, including the ownership of property, or could live a descent life or have opportunities for improving their condition was considered illogical and contrary to norms of all societies. It violated the customs and traditions of the relations that abounded the Church and the faithful, Prince and subject people, property owner and peasant, master and servant, husband and wife, parents and child. Equally disturbing was that in the normal course of events ordinary people might expect anything but misfortune and privation, or that they might expect significant improvement in their social status or standard of living. From the beginning of recorded history, the workers and weaker members of society expected to be pressed down and exploited. The majority opinion was that the passions of men did not conform to the ideas of reason, fairness or justice; hence, there was the uncritical acceptance of the selfish nature of man.

A slightly more optimistic current took hold in America, spearheaded by political leaders who were influenced by the humanitarian ideas of the Age of Enlightenment. Still, the concepts of slavery and indentured servants existed and were woven into the social order during the colonial and post-colonial era. The platitudes of the natural rights of men (Voltaire's idea), a social contract between government and the people (Rousseau's dictum) the notion of "life, liberty and prosperity" (Locke's familiar statement) and the substitution of prosperity for "pursuit of happiness" (Jefferson's modification) were all abstract ideas that went against the tide of opinion and the dictates of reason prior to the American Revolution.

In Europe Locke, Rousseau and Voltaire were considered extremely radical among their contemporaries, promoting ideas based on a false and untenable conception of human nature. In some ways they were the mouse that roarded. Few people of power and property took them seriously, but eventually their writings began to seep into discussions at the taverns and coffee shops of London and Paris. Despite the American and French Revolution, the upper classes in both the Old and New World did not subscribe to these doctrines, nor did they have faith and/or respect in the common people. In fact, Thomas Jefferson was considered a traitor to the class interests of Southern plantation owners and northern bankers, similar to way Franklin Roosevelt was viewed by the Brahmins and business class when he implemented work programs and Social Security for Americans during the Great Depression.

During the Industrial Revolution which started in merry-old England around the time of the American Revolution, special skills and special abilities of people resulted in slightly higher wages than the norm. But the fixed economic system and social traditions of prior societies directed toward the past remained intact, rather than toward a future which men themselves might shape. The amount of people who rose from pittance to what might be called middle class was miniscule in numbers compared to the masses who remained poor and destitute.

Actually, the Industrial Revolution increased inequality between the mercantile and manufacturing class and the labor class because the vast portion of wealth attributed to economic growth went to the economic elite, not the masses. To be sure, a rising tide does not always lift all boats in the water, not when the surrounding environment or custom is fixed nor when man's position in society is considered from a static position as viewed for centuries. No doubt the new industries allowed a tiny number of entrepreneurial people to accumulate capital and equipment. Thus a few people endowed by nature, that is by strength and cunning, were able to take advantage of the fruits of their power and abilities.

This new concept of competition and productivity led to nineteenth century Darwinist and Spencerist thinking, that is "survival of the fittest."

Such thinking could be viewed as an outgrowth of the ancient world which set man against man in the pursuit of power, prestige and wealth—and left the masses to fend for themselves relative to their state of nature. This idea was slightly modified in the New World, whereby common people could successfully compete and fit well into the American landscape, largely because of the frontier experience, the abundance of free land and natural resources, the constant flow of immigrants, and long-favored notion of progress and change. Moreover, there was no history of warlords and family lineage; the land had not been carved up by centuries of war and strife.

The point is, there was so much land and resources for the taking that it did not create a zero-sum game between the power elite and the common person; the people with new powers and property allowed the masses to accumulate their own riches because there was so much land available for anyone who was willing to risk the unknown and work hard. "Survival of the fittest" eventually blended into the folklore of the West and the customs of the Gilded Age and picture of the self-made man of the nineteenth century, as well as the free market system of corporate America and the wizards of Wall Street in the twentieth century. For both centuries, the capitalist system evolved from the ancient world whereby the strong survive and the weak barely exist or perish. Life has always been a struggle in the Old World, as part of nature—where every group, every animal or human was always in a ceaseless struggle with its environment and its species.

Darwin's scheme of the social order, delineated in the mid-nineteenth century in *Origin of Species* and *Descent of Man* is an outgrowth of the brutal conditions of the ancient world—and forms the link to the "dog-eat-dog" practices of the Gilded Age I (1865-1900) and Gilded Age II (1980-Present). The notion of competition and free markets are expressed in animal and human behavior to survive, and that the industrial order (and now the global market) is little more than an effective instrument for accomplishing further evolution.

The outcome is that poverty and inequality remain part of the modern landscape, as it characterized all civilizations of the past, with perhaps one major difference. During the twentieth century, the idea of social programs and safety nets were introduced by democratic nations. But "haves" and "have nots," coupled with extreme inequality of income and wealth, still comprise the world order. The same theme of inequality has reoccurred through out history, with percentages slightly changing from the stand point of the century and society in question.

THE ANCIENT WORLD

Allow me now to back peddle to the beginning of civilization. For at least 5,000 years, until the mid-nineteenth century, the ordinary person (nearly 99 percent of the populace) lived on the edge of starvation, slightly above subsistence level. Economic growth would enhance the wealth of those who were already rich or powerful; the masses were little more than slaves, serfs, peasants, indentured servants or chattel—who worked until death or disablement and whose life expectancy was 30 to 35 years—depending on the century and society. Behavior was grounded in appetite, or desire and self-interest. Those with wealth and/or power sought to retain their position, and there was no opposition by working and subordinate people who lacked the ability to oppose what was perceived as the natural order. Nothing could be done to change it, and that is how the world existed for centuries. The idea that humans had rights is a relatively new concept—no more than 300 hundred years old.

Heredity privilege governed society and those fortune by birth were expected to benefit at the expense of the working masses who were limited by their unprivileged birth. Intelligence or any other human strength had to be extraordinary before it could count for much in comparison to heredity privilege. Each person, relying on traditions of birthright and background, and his own resources, labored for the good of society. But the rewards went to the rich and powerful while the ordinary person labored from dawn to dusk and lived in poverty and squalor. The superiority of civilization over barbarianism, in terms of philosophy, art and science, did very little to change the miserable conditions of working people, and in some cases it was more cruel in terms of how the masses were controlled by those who ruled.

With the exception of the Greeks and Romans, all the great civilizations of the ancient world would fall under the aristocratic rule of monarchs and emperors, supported with an entrenched and corrupt nobility or property class, where the "massline" were either slaves or manual laborers and peasant farmers who toiled until their death. The vast majority of people were nothing more than disposable units of production kept alive at the subsistence level. Their function was to keep the system running. Their wages or economic rewards would mainly cover the cost of their daily existence so they could produce the next generation of children who would till the land. They lived by war and conquest, and this is how the ancient civilizations developed: first from warlike families who grew into clans and tribes, cemented by blood, which then grew into small villages and settlements and then city-states and monarchies and kingdoms.

The warlords who commanded armies were paid by monarchs in gold, property and titles in exchange for their loyalty. These warring leaders obtained heredity titles and land, and thus were transformed into the "gentry" or nobility class. They gained recognition for possession of goods and people, as well as military valor. The masses—whether they were slaves or serfs, peasant farmers or laborers—surrendered their rights and freedom to those who could provide security and protect them from plunder and facilitate their survival needs. People were willing to live in a society where government had a heavy hand, even in an authoritarian order, so long as they knew they could live in relative safety; they would not be raped or brutalized by stronger people or roaming groups and there was food on the table.

This is one reason why people today are willing to live under authoritarian rule, even a system run by former gangsters or warlords. Government needs to maintain order and limit chaos. What we are describing here is a brutal world—and why people are willing to give up their political rights and economic opportunities. Civilization brought a degree of peace and security for the masses, compared to the age of barbarianism. In a nut shell, the emergence of civil society, a social order accompanied by a freedom of fear, plunder and rape, takes precedence over economic possessions and prizes. In the Hobbesian world, there is no moral high ground. People of power and property seek their own self-preservation and combine by marriage and alliance to obtain more power and property. They act as a force for change at the expense of less powerful people who are just trying to live day-to-day and feed themselves.

Now ancient Greece and Rome was a slightly different story. Their development was a variation of this theme, from barbarianism to civilization. But their political system was cemented by human agreement. Citizens had a political voice among ruling elites, rather than the simple bloodline and hereditary succession and the complete domination of the masses in the ancient civilizations that preceded them.

Our Western Heritage: The Greeks and Romans

Equality and inequality can be discussed from social, philosophical, economic, and educational points of view. The issues concerning the idea of equality are rooted in our Western heritage: Details which flutter down to us in tantalizing bits of information about the ancient Greeks and Romans. In the Greek era, a distant mirror of the politics of our own age, it was believed that the citizens had certain rights and civic duties—and could argue for or against any proposition in the marketplace of ideas—the courts, the public arena, etc.

Plato's *Republic* fashioned a plan for a perfect state ruled by an intellectual elite of philosopher-kings—not a money elite or hereditary aristocracy. Society existed to cultivate truth and virtue in its inhabitants, based on assumptions that only knowledgeable men should rule and that all inhabitants should contribute to the general welfare according to their intellectual capacity and particular aptitude. Education, not privileged birth, was the major agency for defining the social and economic relations of the residents of Plato's *Republic*. The educational system played a selective role as it rated intellectual aptitude and sorted children into categories: philosopher-kings, auxiliaries and soldiers, and workers. Once assigned to a class, individuals received the appropriate education assigned to the social-economic role—and mobility was frozen. Plato believed that each class would fulfill a necessary function and contribute to the common good. Such a society, he believed, would be harmonious.

Even now, both liberal and conservative thinkers, love to make comparisons between the ancient Greeks and our Western heritage. To some extent, we are all Greeks—at least in terms of our culture and political beliefs. Americans, I believe, are more likely to agree with a dead Greek than the best known lawyers or social scientists of the modern world to bolster an argument or advocate a point of view. We think the ancient scholars from the Greek countryside and islands spoke with less spin (and more virtue) than modern politicians and policymakers. This view is especially seen in the writings of traditional educators and philosophers who advocate the classics and great books approach to education.

We compare American education to Greek education, to their cultivation of knowledge and rationality, and overlook their elitist traditions in education, which focused on philosopher-kings and distinguished between a liberal education (for the elite classes) and a technical education (for the common people). The same issues haunt us today about who should go to college and who should be tracked into vocational programs—who should work with their minds and who should work with their hands.

We overlook the fact that Greek (and Roman) society, like all the previous ancient societies, were built on the back of slaves, and only a minority of Greeks (and Romans) had the rights and privileges of citizenship. We love to trace our philosophical thoughts to Aristotle and Plato, but we ignore that they both resisted democracy and believed it led to mob rule. In the final analysis, both men believed in a government run by a well educated and property class—nothing more, if I may add, than an oligarchy and what later would be called the European nobility.

Today, the American society is approaching a financial oligarchy, similar to the European nobility. Moreover, money and blood are becoming intertwined in American politics. The U.S. Senate is fast paralleling the House of Lords in England with lineage becoming a crucial factor for election as in the case of Bush, Clinton, Gore, Kennedy, Rockefeller, and Udel, not to overlook the fact that more than two thirds of the U.S. Senators are millionaires. The only bright spot is that the political lineage in America is no more than one hundred years old, compared to our English cousins where it goes back to Camelot and King Arthur's Knights of the Round Table.

It would be nice to envision America as the sole heir of Athens—where democracy first flourished—and to be a champion of moral virtue, philosophy and humanitarianism. But we are also Romans; so let us turn to that golden age of Latin prose. Laborers were "generally held in bad repute," Xenophon wrote some 2,300 years ago. "Their work keeps them too busy to be good companions or good citizens, so the men engaged in [labor] must ever appear to be both bad friends and poor defenders of their country."

The notion of class was paramount in the pride and terror of the gladiator's world, for only those accustomed to a hard life with muscle, speed, and agility could expect to survive in the arena. Manual laborers, slaves and prisoners of war lured by the prospect of prize money made up the names of those who fought to the death, while well-born Romans flocked to the arena to witness Rome's most popular "sport." The upper class sat on marble benches in front and the working people sat on wooden benches in the rear, watching and cheering as more than one hundred thousand humans perished in the arena over four hundred years. This was the Roman form of television, a super-sporting event, to amuse the masses; only the violence and blood were real.

The gladiator life was brief and brutal. As the lower ranks on the Roman totem pole, they were easily discarded and considered more dispensable than slaves (who at least kept the system running), while citizens with soft hands and flabby midsections sat on the sidelines, some on cushions, and were entertained. The same land that gave us Cierco and Virgil, and forged the foundations of our Republic, forced humans to square off against wild animals.[9] It is true that Cierco had climbed from a relatively humble surrounding to the highest offices of the Roman Empire. With Cierco's death, however, more precisely his assassination, the Empire lost its most staunchest legal advocate and political conscience—and soon fell under the autocratic rule of a series of notorious and corrupt emperors who brought ruin and decay to Roman society.

In his last years of life, Cierco warned the Senate about political cynicism and divisiveness, patrician greed, and class warfare. Cierco tried to shame his colleagues in the Senate about growing inequality between the patrician and plebian classes. The orator's words ring loud today: "A belief has become established—as harmful to the Republic . . . that these courts, with you senators as the jury, will never convict any man, however guilty, if he has sufficient money." We must also read Tacitus in terms of "diminutive rivalries." Strong men will trample weak men in war, politics or business affairs "as long as there are prizes to contend for which move their avarice or their ambition."

Edward Gibbon's *History . . . of the Roman Empire*, originally published as six volumes, was condensed to one volume in 1960 to reach a wider audience. Originally published between 1776 and 1788, it took more than 150 years to be appreciated as the most important book about Rome, serving as a bridge from the ancient world to the modern: "A narrative which began when Rome was revered and the reign of Hadrian and Antoninius Pius offered the prospect of universal peace" to the fall of Rome and the "triumph of barbarianism and of religion." Riddled by prolonged political corruption and moral decay, and exhausted by military overreach, the barbarians were able to bring down the most modern and powerful society of the age, something to think about if we consider today's low-tech world and jihad movement with the high-tech, modern Western world.

In the end the Greeks and Romans built a society based around family comfort for its citizens, along with laws and expectations for duty to the nation-state. Citizenship was limited to 15 to 20 percent of the populace, and differences in citizenship and noncitizenship, wealth and poverty, led to resignation of inequality and a major gap between the patrician class and plebeian class (or common people). Even among the citizens, there was a wide differences between the career politicians and property class, characterized by wealth and powerful friends—and the artisans, shopkeepers, and small farmers, starting out with neither wealth nor political clout. And, here is the rub, the link to our Western heritage, the eerie relevance: No more than 1 percent of the populace comprised the privileged, powerful, and property class—considered the proper guardians and patrons of Greek or Roman society. The rest of its citizens—the common people or the artisans, shopkeepers, and small farmers—irked out a living and existed on a day-to-day basis, very similar to the way most working Americans live today paycheck to paycheck. As for the noncitizens and slaves—they had no chance, only to toil, procreate, and die, not much different than how millions of Americans and billions of people around the world live in a "culture of poverty," trapped by generations of squalor and misery.

The Tragedy of War

There was a period in which the Roman Empire was "governed under the guidance of virtue and wisdom. The armies were restrained by the firm and gentle hand of [four successive] emperors . . . who delighted in the image of liberty, and were pleased with considering themselves as accountable ministers of the laws of the Caesars," wrote Gibbon. But absolute power leads to arrogance and avarice, to folly and failed virtues. The "restraints of the senate and laws . . . could never correct the vices of the emperor, and the corruption of Roman manners would always supply flatterers eager to applaud, and ministers prepared to serve, the fear or avarice, the lust of cruelty of their masters." A series of all powerful emperors, with no checks and balances of any substance, proceeded to abolish Roman liberties and laws and plunged the empire into a series of unnecessary and costly wars. Rome was exhausted; and, by the end of the sixth century, the barbarians were at the gates and sacked the City. A once prosperous and potent Rome, the seat of the empire and the center of the civilized world, was reduced to a second-rate power and subsequently during the next five hundred years became a third-rate power propped up by the increased strength of the Catholic Church.

Gibbons description of the decline of Rome is a classic story of hubris and military overreach, the same kind of political nuances that described the Bush doctrine; namely, that the U.S. could impose its will on belligerent nations while it spread capitalism and defended democracy. As in the case of Rome, it has drained American resources, costing American taxpayers between 2 to 3 trillion dollars, plus $7 billion a year for the next 45 to 50 years for military disability and health payments which will be financed by adding it to the federal debt.[10]

According to Victor Hanson, in *A War Like No Other*, hubris was also part of the Greek world. Athens and Sparta and their respective allies fought for 27 years, from 431 to 404 B.C. and ended with the surrender of Athens and its occupation by Sparta. As in the case of Rome and the U.S. (which must now learn to share power and form multi-national alliances in lieu of waging war alone), Athens was the richest city in the world. Its navy was omnipotent. The city-state was a democracy, attempting to export its political customs and cultural ideas throughout the Mediterranean world, and if necessary by force—similar to the U.S. imperialist position in Iraq, and Afghanistan and other parts of the Moslem world and third world. To be sure, as early as the eighteenth century, when our nation was young and politicians wanted to stir the hearts and minds of the crowds, America's greatness was described as the "City on the Hill" and linked to ancient Athens. Of course, Herodotus, the Greek scholar who invented history, would have snickered at the conceit of the Americans and all the other nations of the world that claim to follow the Greek classics or represent Greek civilization.

Athens also engaged in military overreach as Rome and the U.S. While fighting Sparta, it also invaded Sicily in 415 to 413 B.C. and lost a greater percentage of people (1 out of 25) than did the U.S. lose in the Civil War (1 out of 50)which was its most costly war. Financially, Athens was drained by the Sicilian invasion as hundreds of ships and thousands of naval crews were lost in battle.

Athens went to war repeatedly, partially to export its political system and other times to defend its way of life. The Peloponnesian War lasted 15 years, between 461 and 446 B.C., and the war against Persia lasted on and off for decades, until eventually Alexander the Great, only 25 years old, defeated its armies at the Battle of Marathon. Not only were great political leaders like Pericles bogged down by war, its philosophers and poets wrote about the achievements and folly of war—divided they were about the wisdom of war. Alexander the Great, was one of the first globalists, pushing eastward and waging war against the so-called uncivilized world. Influenced by his teacher Aristotle, and guided by the oracle who convinced him he was the son of God, he thought he was spreading democracy and Greek culture to the barbarians—only to experience military overreach and meet his match on the plains of Northern India in 326 B.C. His defeat can be described as the ancient version of Mad Max—whereby his legions were exhausted, depleted, and defeated by those with milliliters of brown, black, and yellow blood. Despite its Golden Age, and the wisdom of its philosophers, its democratic system of government and self-confidence, the Greek super power took on more than it could manage. Like Rome, it became a second-rate power, then shriveled up into a third-rate city-state and descended into the vagaries of human memory.

At the turn of the twenty-first century, American's intervention around the world rested on the same hubris and military overreach that considered the nation's hegemony to be desirable and sustainable without limitations. But America's rise in power and prosperity may have reached its pinnacle. Compared to how old and vast the rest of the world is, its super power status may be no more than a blip on the screen of human history. As with the Greeks and Romans, we must now contend with several emerging powers and learn to share power with other nations. To the extent we must recognize our own political and economic limitations, it is at this fault-line where the truth begins to restore our sense of reality. It is at this point where we would like to believe that we have learned the lessons of history. Or, we can take the position that the timelines are too long and we can rely on A.J.P. Taylor, the preeminent British historian of the twentieth century, who warned: "The only lesson of history is there are no lessons of history."

HISTORY—AMID THE DESPAIR

In the comparison of civilizations, Greece and Rome (like the U.S. today) were highly seculized, freed from religious dogma and governed by politics and philosophy. The other civilizations, from the ancients to the modern world, were driven by the power of kings who were allied first with high priests (a heredity class), and later with the church and religious doctrine. The early high priests before the Catholic clergy, Buddhist monks and Islamist clerics gave advice and offered spiritual hope and eternal life in consideration for gold, property and material possessions.

Now it doesn't matter if we drive over the bones of the dead in ancient Babylon, Egypt, Persia, the Aztec and Inca ruins, or the bleak stretches of Siberia and Mongolia prior to or after Confucius. It matters little if we travel through the Middle Ages or Renaissance period within or beyond Western Europe—to the great empires of the Ottomans or Slavs, to India, China, Africa, and the Middle East, or to the unification of Europe under Charlemagne or Napoleon. The conditions of life remained static; control over economic life continued to remain in the hands of the few, those privileged by heredity.

Power, authority and wealth were derived from ancestry, birth, and caste. The "massline" went along with system quite naturally without questioning the inequality between the dominate and subordinate classes. No one seemed to question the social and economic order—the entrenched wealth of the top 1 percent, people of privilege at birth, and the humble background of the bottom 99 percent.—the unprivileged by birth. Human life was not valued. Conditions for the masses were brutal and exploitative, as they struggled against long odds to survive. Nothing could be done about it. That is the way the world was, and how the system operated and perpetuated itself. Any person who questioned the social order was considered eccentric at best, sought of nuts, and sometimes disappeared in the dark of the night. Questioning the logic and presumption of the social and economic order as it existed was like swimming upstream. This is how it was before and after Christ—during and beyond the feudal age down to the nineteenth century, when the social and economic structure began to slowly change as a result of the Age of Enlightenment and Industrial Revolution.

In barbaric society, the people are concerned with surviving on a daily basis and satisfying basic needs of food and shelter. In his classic book on *Politics*, Aristotle argued that the evolution from families to tribes to monarchs as city-states made a race of people self—sufficient and civilized them; moreover, it reduced the number of wars between families, class and tribes. In civilized society, the people could develop social, moral, and intellectual abilities—and attain the "good life." But Aristotle and other philosophers of the Greek and Roman era, as well as after the fall of Rome, failed to appreciate that the good life was limited to the ruling elite as well as a small minority of philosophers, orators, and military commanders. The growth of civilization did very little for the ordinary person who toiled their entire lives, living at subsistence levels, while the ruling elite and property class sought honor and glory, more titles and property, and other possessions.

The very government that encouraged leisure and the arts and science, traditionally thought to be a superior way of living, ignored the labor class who had to work under the coercive powers of a family and hereditary class called the nobility or aristocracy. No matter what golden age we reference—Persia, Greece, Rome, China, or India, etc.—where the arts and sciences flourished and where some resemblance of ethics and law prevailed, the working person basically was a nonperson, laboring 10 to 14 hours a day and living in dark hovels and amidst famine and disease. There was no expectation of hope, growth or progress among the masses. Not only were they resigned to their fate, but also there was no one to show them how to claim their basic rights because there was no assumption of rights. Whatever wealth or growth that was achieved was not for the many but the few. And this is how society was organized right up to and beyond the Industrial Revolution into the mid-nineteenth century in Europe.

Life was depicted as a gigantic struggle whereby most people succumbed. This was the outline of history and society depicted by British economists David Ricardo and Thomas Malthus (to be elaborated later in this chapter) as well as by American economists such as William Graham Sumner, E.L. Godkin, editor of the *Nation*, and the Christian preacher Henry Ward Beecher. The three Americans expounded their theories of capitalism, laissez faire doctrines, and the efficiency of the profit system and sanctity of private property. There was no hope for the masses, certainly not by most thinkers of the mid nineteenth century.

It was Marx who predicted the eventual demise of the system—and on theoretical, moral, and ethical grounds he was right. His idealistic notions was a reaction against centuries of feudal oppression and horrific working conditions for peasants and serfs, as well as the roots of an ossified and corrupt church, monarch and nobility system in Europe. But the intoxication of dogma and revolutionary doctrine, coupled with the desire for revenge, attracted a host of zealots and maniacs which stoked the fans of fanaticism and led to ruthless authoritarianism and mass murder. Still, one of the most common strategies among proponents of capitalism in the United States is to label critics, including liberals, socialists and union organizers as unpatriotic.[11]

It is hard for middle-class Americans, as well as our friends in the western world, who eat three squares a day and have a roof over their heads, to understand the economic plight of the rest of humanity—much less the anarchic violence rippling around the world. Growing up against a back drop of Anglo-American model of capitalism that has largely gone unchallenged by ideological alternatives, and was successful in a fight to the death with totalitarian Communism, its hard to accept any other economic system, even if the present free market system is detrimental to the vast majority of ordinary people. Here we are referring to the masses in America and around the world that have no real chance to participate in the growth and prosperity in the United States or elsewhere. The capitalist system is accepted in the G-20 world, even though a sizeable chunk of people—more than 50 percent—do not share in the wealth of their respective nations. For thousands of years, the gains have gone to a relatively few at the top of the pyramid. The explanations have changed over centuries—hereditary privilege, entitlement, survival of the fittest, law of the jungle and now personal responsibility.

Thomas Hobbes, the English political scientist and moral skeptic, argued in the *Leviathan* that civilization was just as miserable and degrading for the common people as it was in prior barbarian history. The nature of the human condition was subservience, suffering and death; the strong trampled the weak and the landed upper class maintained its holdings from generation to generation while its workers lived in squalor and perpetuated the raw misery of their lives. The division of classes within society was ferociously unequal, caused by desire and appetite; the profits went to the property owners and workers were paid a subsistence wage—what future economists would call the market price.

The history of civilization, according to Hobbes, was supposed to reduce the coercive powers of the strong over the weak, substitute plunder and piracy for established laws and replace natural force with the influence of philosophy and science. But the political and legal institutions grew out of conquest and hereditary succession, producing European monarchies and gentry who distinguished themselves with symbols of honors and hereditary titles such as Duke, Count, Earl, Baron etc. The emergence of civil society brought peace and geographical consolidation among warlords and small kingdoms, but did very little to improve the status of the masses or nonprivileged people. For a thousand years, the pleasures and the extraordinary extravagance of the warlords and then the European aristocracy perpetuated until the storming of the Bastille in 1789, followed by the Napoleonic wars that consumed Europe for nearly twenty years. And, it was the French peasants that sparked the liberal revolutions throughout Europe during the mid-nineteenth century.

Hobbes in *Decive* was clear about the predicament of the masses: To work, be pleasant to powerful people, and remain subservient. Despite their liberty to think, subject people clearly were not at liberty to express their opinions in public, especially if they ran counter to prevailing opinion of their sovereign or for those who they worked. Even if subjects could judge for themselves, they were not in the postion to act. To be sure, his observations of the grand feudals, with their estates and peasant workers, closely parallel the bargaining strength today between farm laborers and property owners, factory workers and manufacturers, tenants and landlords. Besides, when Hobbes developed his theories of society, freedom and liberty were luxury items. The basic human need for survival (sufficient food, water and shelter) and security was a struggle. The preoccupation with food production and freedom from plunder and rape in many parts of the world today is a sad testimony to the long-view and accuracy of Hobbes' description of ancient and feudal civilizations. Stop to think of the bottom billion (possibly 1.5 billion) people in the world in parts of Africa, Asia, and Latin America who currently live on less than two dollars a day. They are small holding farmers and farm laborers who depend on two things for survival—rain and land. Even small climate blips or delays in rain or a cold spell can have devastating effects on food production and survival.

Agricultural and Climatic Conditions

If crops failed the people starved; the medieval farmer or serf lived on the edge of doom—subject to weather conditions, floods and soil erosion, disease and hunger. Often plagued by periods of great famine, the average life expectancy in the mid 1300s, at the end of the Medieval period, was 35 years and infant mortality by age one was one out of two or 50 percent.

By the mid-fourteenth century, the beginning of the Renaissance period, a shift in climate occurred—with conditions of wind, cold, and rain. Food production became extremely vulnerable to the weather. These conditions lasted for 500 years, into the mid-nineteenth century and was called by Brian Fagan as *The Little Ice Age*. The cereal crops of Europe—wheat, barley, oats, and rye—were dissemated because the plants were top heavy and grew above the soil. People across the European continent and Russia were weakened by frigid weather conditions and lack of food. They became subject to cholera, typhoid, tuberculosis—and then plague in the fourteenth century. The latter resulted in the death of 25 million people or one third of the European population. The result was mass hysteria—blaming and lynching some 100,000 Jewish people and burning some 50,000 women as witches. Passions were so strong during the plague that parents sometimes killed their children to eat—as reflected in the story of Hanzel and Gretel.

Michael Montaigne captured the pulse of the period in his description of religious doctrine in his best known essay, *An Apology for Raymond Sebond*. "Man, naked, empty, aware of his natural weakness, fit to accept outside help from on high more able to lodge the divine within him, annihilating his intellect to make room for faith." Montaigne's description of the fallibility and weakness of man is described as a "humble, obedient, teachable . . . He is a blank tablet, made ready for the finger of God to carve such letters on him as he pleases." Judgement for Hobbes did not have a religious flavor. He meant for man to exercise self-restraint and to follow the wishes of the powerful, whether it was his sovereign or employer. However, for Montaigne, religion served as a check on passions and plunder—as people became partisans for or against the Roman church.

Putting aside the doctrine of religion and the Church's resistance toward cultivating potatoes because it grew underground, the conditions of European history up to the 1850s was an unrelenting assault on crops.

To some extent, crop failure (and the search for food) was the cause of Thirty Years War in the seventeenth century, the French Revolution in the eighteenth century, and Manifest Destiny in America during the early nineteenth century. The potato was more popular in Latin America than Europe according to John Reader in *Potato*; it was keystone crop of the Inca Empire. The potato, was less vulnerable to flooding and climate conditions, because it grew underground. But it only became popular in Europe in the eighteenth century, and coupled with agricultural innovations of the English and Dutch, rescued the continent from crop failure. France held on to cereal crops well in the eighteenth century and famine was a factor for the eruption of Paris and the storming of the Bastille during the French Revolution. And, of all things, when the potato crop failed in Ireland during the middle of the nineteenth century, the result was massive starvation, the death of 1.5 million peasants or 25 percent of the Irish population, and the great Irish migration of more than one million to America.

In fact, throughout Europe for more than 500 years, famine and epidemics were common, as was rioting in the capitals of France, England, Switzerland, and the German, Austrian, and Italian city-states and provinces. "Bread or Blood" was a common slogan, as millions of Europeans threatened their sovereigns or emigrated to America. Poverty, famine and disease had been man's normal companion for thousands of years before and after the fall of Rome, and any other condition was unimaginable. Insecurity and inequality were the twin hallmarks of society. It was not until the rise of industrialization, coupled with agricultural innovations and the burning of coal which resulted in warmer climate, did Europe begin producing sufficient food for the masses to consume so they could live above subsistence levels. Not until 150 years ago, a wink in the passage of time, did the labor class of the world possess the knowledge and tools to produce sufficient amounts of food—and potentially break from the legacy of doom and gloom.

Still Marx did not expect the system to survive for he was convinced, like many of his followers, that the masses were exploited by property owners and capitalists. The masses could not rise above minimum levels, whether in agriculture or manufacturing. The governments around the world failed to provide needed land reform and labor reform, even the most basic health care and education needs or legal rights for ordinary people against their bosses. Avenues for a descent standard of living, or for any economic or social advancement for the poor and working masses did not exist. The only hope was revolutionary action—a reconstruction of society. Marxism was acclaimed in widening historical, economic and sociological circles as the new gospel in Europe and America, especially after the Russian Revolution.

Although the Industrial Revolution began to slowly change the iron-clad doctrine that the working people of the world would always remain impoverished, and that a few entrepreneurial people could accumulate capital or equipment and produce goods for a profit, the overwhelming majority of ordinary people in the Old World were still condemned to a bleak existence, pure and simple. Working conditions were keenly described by the words of Charles Dickens in England and Victor Hugo in France—at the time Marx was preaching the overthrow of capitalism. The difference between Dickens, Hugo and Marx was the latter was more direct about the need to topple the prevailing economic system in Europe. Dickens and Hugo were more nuanced, and therefore, more acceptable by the Establishment.

Economic Conventional Wisdom

Three major economists of the era—Adam Smith, David Ricardo and Thomas Malthus—also believed in a world struggle against war, famine and misery, but the control of big business, factory productions and property ownership would be retained by the dominant group. Economic control by the mercantile (capitalist) class was necessary to promote the harmonious development of agriculture and manufacturing. There was no hope to overturn the system. There was no chance for wealth and power to succumb to poverty and weakness.

It was Adam Smith (1723-1790) who might be considered the first major economist whose work centered around the idea of economic progress, competition and relationships between the wealthy class (merchants, manufacturers and property owners) and the working masses. His work *An Inquiry into the Nature and Causes of the Wealth of Nations* is still considered a classic analysis for describing the mercantile or capitalist system and the nature of free enterprise. In the natural course of events, the wealthy class had all the power and advantages over the working class, and the latter would always be pressed down.

How far down? The masses would be pressed to the level of subsistence, to ensure the workers would procreate otherwise "the race of work men could not last beyond the first generation." Although his interpretation was dreary and despairing, Smith was merely describing a system that had existed since the age of the Pharaohs. He did argue, however, that under conditions of rapid growth, workers would be in greater demand and their wages would increase, but only for a short period of time since the market would correct itself.

Believing in *laissez-faire* economics and the market system of supply and demand, he felt that in any conflict between the manufacturing or property class and labor class, the bargaining power was one sided. The first group would always be at an advantage, and the latter group always at a disadvantage. Those who lived by work were no match against those who lived in wealth and had the control of property, equipment and capital. So long as these three elements remain in the hands of the capitalist class, if I may add, the working class have only muscle and sweat to offer and are always treading dangerous waters. They are unable to accumulate necessary capital to invest in land or equipment; and, therefore are unable to rise above minimum levels of subsistence.

Although Smith strongly believed in the capitalist system as having unlimited upward potential to increase the wealth and productivity of nations, it would not lead to the wealth of the masses for they were unable to accumulate capital. In periods of growth or stagnation the wealthy class would still retain their power and privilege so long as they retained control of their land or equipment. A nation found its true wealth in the full development of its commerce and industry, rather than in its moral or social values for sharing its wealth with the common people. To be sure, this is how the system worked since history had been recorded and there was little expectation that the system would change. As for the masses, they were expected to live in a hell hole, with little chances for escape, and nobody expected them to live long.

In the world of Adam Smith, and the established order of business, the interests of the few (merchants, bankers and property class) prevailed at the expense of the many. Although the rising entrepreneurial class disliked the restrictions imposed on them by the mercantile class, Smith's economic theory was rooted in Newtonian logic of the physical universe, a rational and secular scheme in lieu of a supernatural explanation of the world. Greed and excess were now considered good because they were supposed to fuel economic growth—and not recognized as "semi-criminal, semi-pathological propensities," words used by the economist John Maynard Keynes in describing the extravagance of the capitalist class and accumulation of wealth in 1930—just prior to the Great Depression.

As with all free-market pundits like Smith, it matters little that economic inequality increases. What counts is that in the pursuit of self-interest, and with the individual's desire for power and status and the accumulation of wealth, the nation's economy grows. If you are a true believer in the theory of self-interest, and that gains should go primarily to the few at the top of the income scale who take risks, then the nation's growing inequality is acceptable. Here, then, are the roots of the modern-day "trickle down" economics.

The theory also leads to a perverse kind of logic, in which each person is supposed to compete, based on his or her own resources and abilities. The idea is also rooted in Smith's formula for economic progress. Given this scenario, however, we know that the strong will trample the weak; the rich have all the power to tip the scales against ordinary people; and the rich will remain as the dominate class and the workers will remain in a subordinate status. And, if you think this is Marxist philosophy, then you are fooling yourself—falling hook-line-and sinker into the conservative, free market model. Just look in the mirror. How much better off today are you relative to the super rich (top 1 percent) as the 18th or 19th century peasant was relative to the aristocracy? Actually, the spread in net worth, that is total assets minus liabilities, is greater now between the classes than it was 200 or 300 years ago.

American free-market advocates, since the epic days of Alexander Hamilton, the first U.S. treasurer, have rekindled Smith's ideas to trumpet the wealth gap and rise of economic inequality. While Americans may be unhappy that the rich are getting richer while they are not, most aspire to be rich and think they or their children have a chance to become rich. They fail to recognize or admit that the cards are statistically stacked against them, which Smith implied when he pointed out which class had all the advantages in the pursuit of wealth. Although the scale of opportunities world wide is open to debate, it is much more lopsided than we are willing to admit, even in America.

David Ricardo (1772-1823) was more pessimistic than Smith, whereby massive poverty, despair and inequality were basic ingredients of society. *On the Principles of Political Economy*, he argued that the production rate and profit depended on the amount of labor required to farm the most barren land. The most fertile land naturally produced the most food with the least labor and yielded the highest rent. As population increased, less fertile land had to be cultivated to feed the people; the poorer land required increased labor to maintain minimal output. But as the population continued to grow, demand for food increased. Rent would also rise and profits for workers would decline. The rising cost of rent led to flat wages or lower wages, but those who owned the land or equipment would realize more profits. Any increase in wages was viewed as reducing profits for the owners. As competition increased, pressure to keep wages low, not much different than the present-day Wal-mart model. In Ricardo's world, as well as in today's world, the property class had to prosper if there was to be economic growth, even at the unfortunate expense of the workers. It parallels the perverse idea put forth today by Republicans and big business interests that tax cuts for the rich will stimulate the economy.

For Ricardo the interests of the property class opposed the interests of the people. But the theory supported the idea that the economic condition of society was based on the status of agriculture, an idea which was whole heartily accepted by southern planters during the colonial and post-colonial period. Although Marx identified *capitalists* as the source of social and economic grief, he was influenced by Ricardo who saw *landlords* as the problem and a rationale for the working-class to revolt. Ricardo's ideas provide a basis for Marxist thought, but his economic theories coincided more with Adam Smith who viewed the market as imperfect but best left alone by government. Tampering with the market, for both Smith and Ricardo, would bring more headaches and economic problems—similar to the views of today's free-market pundits.

Do safety nets such as unemployment insurance and health insurance or government work programs cause economic disruptions? The free-market advocates and "trickle-down" theorists would say yes, more often than no, and thus unwittingly foster a Hobbesian society. They would argue the best government is a small government and the best economic system is an unregulated one. As for bubbles that burst and cascading events that turn into recessions or depressions, they are inevitable. The free market will modify the "delicate machine" and correct whatever errors exist. But the theory fails to consider the human condition—the existence of greed, stupidity and corruption. It fails to embrace that millions of people suffer from the errors of those in charge of policy and politics. When real life avalanches occur, such as the 1929 crash or the 2008-09 meltdown, the economic pundits merely junk a lot of their theories and come up with new excuses or interpretations to cope with the changing social order.

In Ricardo's view of the market, delineated in *Public Debt*, supply-demand was affected by the free movement of resources and the fact that wages normally exceeded subsistence levels. When the economy ceased growing, however, wages would level off and there was the threat of starvation among workers. The best case for the labor class was to work as many hours as possible to at least sustain themselves and to feed a family. The capitalist class was not expected to help the non-working person—regardless of whether they were old, sick or disabled. The prevailing notion was that the working people were not entitled to have health insurance, vacations, or pensions. They were condemned to toil until their death, unless disabled and then their family could attend to them.

Thomas Malthus (1776-1834) was a man of the cloth who rarely preached because he had a speech impediment, but held the first chair of economics in England and had several debates with Ricardo whom he held in high esteem. In his classics book, *Essay on the Principle of Population*, Malthus envisioned the eighteenth century world population, if unchecked, would start doubling every 25 years while the capacity of the land to produce food would increase arithmetically; the outcome would be world-wide famine and starvation.

Simply adding more labor or fertilizer to cultivate the land would not keep up with population growth, because the capacity of land to produce food would be reached and the law of diminished returns would set in. In reverse, any increase in the supply of food would only lead to more people who would consume more food. The consequence was that the masses would always live on the brink of starvation and in poverty.

Only the property owners could prosper under these conditions because their rents would increase. They would accumulate more capital which would lead to more inequality, somewhat similar to what is happening today on a global basis when you compare property ownership with those who work. You would hope things were different in America, and they are to the extent that Ricardo's iron law of wages and Malthus' iron law of population (and limited resources) have been slightly dented by safety nets and social programs, as well as by government regulation and labor unions which both economists had rejected as interfering with free markets.

The flaw in Malthus' argument was that it assumed flat growth in machinery and horticultural techniques and did not envision the impact of the Industrial Revolution and the breakthroughs of agribusiness and genetic engineering of the twentieth and twenty-first centuries. During the twentieth century the world population grew from two million to more than six million and food was adequate to meet word demand. Although the ratio of rich to poor nations produced sufficient food, the distribution techniques of rich countries eventually became bogged-down with political and protective nuances. Moreover, poor countries have been constantly plagued by political corruption, civil strife and anarchy. The privileged upper class have kept their holdings while the workers have suffered and remained subservient. When landlords are forced to flee, warlords and militia groups often replace them but the masses remain subordinate to their new bosses. The outcome is that today more than a billion people are malnourished, hungry, or living at starvation levels, although not nearly at the levels of catastrophe assumed by Malthus.

In short, the three economists were in some ways all influenced by Hobbes and the society he described in which there was a system of power and powerlessness, 1 percent against 99 percent, with limited justice and unlimited inequality. By the natural order, objects of desire were in short supply and competition among individuals for those objects (goods and services) were powerful enough to lead people to compete, fight, and plunder. Laws had to be adopted for those enriched by politics, land ownership or business to secure themselves and prevent attacks from the working masses. People of power and property combined to secure such laws in order to obtain more power and property at the expense of less powerful people. In a free-market system, a few people would succeed but the masses were still doomed to toil and suffering.

AMERICA AS THE PROMISED LAND

Much of the gloomy and fatalistic aspects of the classical economists of England and older ideas of Europe were rejected by American intellectuals as unrelated to American society. By the turn of the nineteenth century, the United States had rejected much of the political, social and economic thought of the Old World and went to great lengths to differentiate itself from Europe. Noah Webster, the father of the American Spelling Book and the American Dictionary, put it succinctly by urging Americans "to unshackle their [minds] and act like independent beings. You have been children long enough, subject to the control and subservient to the interests of a haughty parent . . . You have an empire to raise . . . and a national character to establish and extend by your wisdom and judgment." By the act of revolution, the American people had declared their political independence from England. Now they needed to declare social and economic independence as well.

There was also widespread belief that a benevolent God had blessed America with vast land and unlimited resources beyond the Alleghenies and that the common man could realize his full statue and potential as a person. Never before was there such optimism among the ordinary people. With buoyant optimism, and faith in the common man, the American dream was born and became part of the American character. So long as capital and labor led to economic growth and productivity, so long as the economic pie was expanding, the American dream was a reality. But it was not morality or compassion that fostered the American dream. It was a vast amount of land and natural resources available for common people to claim, work and develop—even if it meant plundering or killing other groups of people, nothing different than what had been going on for thousands of years.

Such opportunities for ordinary Americans did not challenge or upset the existing patrician class in America. It was not a zero-sum conflict where the opportunity for one person would lead to lack of opportunity for another person who already had power or wealth. Land was free for the taking so long as you were willing to confront hardships and put your life at stake; in later years the government sold hundreds of acres to a person for a few cents per acre in order to encourage westward settlement. The unique American circumstance deviated from the doctrines of the three classical economists. It made little difference to them or their economic orthodoxy because they were Englishmen who were more concerned with Europe and the English empire. America was merely an aberration, a series of policy errors that led to revolution among old cousins.

In the meantime, the increasing importance of the American West in the first half of the nineteenth century promoted the concept of a unique national character and unique opportunity for ordinary people. America was blessed with an abundance of animals, forests and rivers beyond the mountains—the subject of romantic legend, hope and prosperity. The American wilderness, the primitive conditions, and the picture and sounds of nature traveled across the Atlantic and bolstered the ideas of European romanticists such as Blake, Byron, Goethe, and Herder. The cult of simplicity and the notion of equality gave rise to American romanticists such as James Fennimore Cooper, Washington Irving and Herman Melville. The old pessimism that assumed calamity and was always around the corner gave way to an optimistic mood, both at home and abroad, in describing a place called America.

The bickerings and class distinctions of Old Europe, the gruesome hardships and squalor, and the wars, famine and disease of the feudal age were all obscured and left behind in the New World—and with it was the rejection of the old economic doctrines of Europe. "The picture of the West as a Utopia for dreamy idealists had little influence in the East, according to Merle Curti, in The *Growth of American Thought*, but the glamorous picture of the West and the "ever-beckoning finger of opportunity lured many a men across the mountains." They went West, to seek their fortunes and break from the cramping and restrictive conditions of the Old Order—or the Hobbesian world. And, so a place had been discovered where the ordinary person—the "rabble," "mob" "herd," "wretched," etc.—and all the other labels used by the favored class for describing common people—could prosper.

The doctrines of the natural rights, man and social progress had been set forth by the Enlightenment and were familiar to Americans through the writings of Ben Franklin, Tom Jefferson, Tom Paine and other leaders of the Revolution. Their ideas were interpreted to justify the elevation of the most unfortunate members of society and emphasize the basic rights, dignity and opportunities of the individual. Human nature was no longer viewed in Hobbesian terms, nor as the classical economists described—full of misery, squalor and the power of the strong over the weak. It was now imbued with moral sanctions and economic opportunities. America was the place where dreams came true. Newly arrived immigrants wrote home; the streets were paved with gold!

For the rest of Europe, where land and natural resources were limited, and in other parts of the world where the political discourse was dominated by brute power, monarchies, authoritarian bureaucracies, totalitarianism, and/or religious doctrine, the classic economic architects remained relevant as power elites attempted to defend manufacturing and property rights, free-markets, and even famine and disease as part of the natural order. In the Old World, the accumulation of wealth was seen for the sake of power, possession and status—not much different than today's gilded age in the New World—and not meant for the world of working people. Refusing to abandon the economic orthodoxy of the day, it was normal for society to invent perverse rewards and penalties for enriching the few at the expense of the many, for trying to hold on to an aristocracy based on heredity privilege while taxing labor to the maximum and keeping them from occurring capital, equipment and land.

Although some observers might criticize the American character and comment about our flaws and failures, we are the lucky ones. According to Walter McDougall, the historian and author of *Freedom Just Around the Corner*, the formation of the "United States is the central event of the past 400 years." Imagine some ship flying the Dutch, English, or French flag in the year 1600 and then being transported to the present. The difference would astound them. From a primitive and vacant land, we have become "the mightiest, richest, most dynamic civilization in history," exceeding the achievements of not only the European world but also the entire world. We are the most revolutionary country, a society that is constantly changing and reforming and revitalizing itself. To paraphrase Joseph Perkins, a famous orator of Harvard in 1797, we are "the Athens [and Rome] of our age," and until recently "the admiration of the world."

Shrinking the time capsule to the last 250 years, this nation has grown from a small cluster of colonies, with a ragtag collection of people and a makeshift army, to a free, mighty, and wealthy nation—the most influential one in the history of humankind and people on the present world stage. How was this possible? Does it boil down to accident, luck or design? I cannot give you a precise answer—why Americans are the chosen or lucky ones. The answer, to some extent, comes from the heart, from the feelings and emotions of plain people, immigrant people and working people who inhabit our landscape and who know they are free—free from the yoke of oppression—and therefore strive, innovate, and invent. Despite that we are a nation of many nations, with different customs and folklore, we all speak the same language as free men and breathe the same free air. The answer is echoed from all the people around the world who clamor to come to our shores to escape their nations' rulers, tyrants, and oligarchies—to find the pot of gold that can only be had in the New World.

James Weaver, a Populist philosopher at the turn of the twentieth century, identified with the Founding Fathers of 1776 and put it this way "Throughout all history we have had ample evidence that the new world is the theater upon which the great struggle for the rights of man is to be made." Or, could the answer simply be what Otto von Bismarck, the Prussian chancellor, once muttered? "God has special providence for fools, drunks, and the United States of America." Or, might it simply be that the world order requires at least one country to toss away old assumptions and embrace the poor and allow people of different blood, skin and bones to melt as one people, one nation, and grapple with the challenges and circumstances of life.

The United States has been blessed, indeed, although probably not in the way of the word, meant by Bismarck. Alex de Tocqueville, perhaps the most influential visitor and profound observer of America, put it in more realistic terms in his classic book *Democracy in America*, published in 1835: Whereas a "permanent inequality of condition prevailed" in the Old World, where the social conditions tended "to promote the despotism" of the monarchs and ruling class on the masses, the "principle of democracy" prevailed in the United States. Almost fifty years later, in 1888, a British scholar and barrister, Lord James Bryce toured the country and subsequently wrote a mammoth volume, *The American Commonwealth*. He claimed the United States had reached "the highest level, not only of material well-being but of intelligence and happiness which the race has yet achieved."

A little more than 100 years later, another foreign gentleman and immigrant from the far-off land of India, Dinesh D'Souza (someone much more conservative but just as idealistic as Weaver, de Tocqueville and Bryce) commented in *What's So Great About America*. "America is a new kind of society that produces a new kind of human being. The human being—confident, self-reliant, tolerant, generous, future oriented—is a vast improvement over the wretched, fatalistic, and intolerant human being that traditional societies have always produced and . . . produce now."

Then there is the recent book *American Vertigo* published in 2006 by French writer Bernard Levy who traveled across America and inserted Tocqueville in the subtitle to move his book up the ladder in sales.

Proclaiming to observe and listen to the eyes and ears of America, its ordinary people from small towns and big cities, he characterizes the nation as a land of paradox. America is magnificent and mad; greedy and modest; capable of facing the future but obsessed by its past; existential yet devoid of direction; libertine yet conventional; held together by strong bonds and minimal ones; run by power elites but built by people of all classes.

As with most French men, Levy has the tendency to exaggerate and flatter and rely on the superficial. He says that America will endure. "No matter how many dysfunctions [and] driftings there may be . . . no matter how fragmented the political and social space may be, despite [its] nihilist hypertrophy of petty antiquarian memory; despite this hyperbesity . . . of the great social bodies that form the invisible edifice of the country . . . I can't manage to convince myself of the collapse, heralded in Europe, of the American model. "In short, the Frenchman reaffirms that America will retain its place and force in the global village we inhabit. And, if you are fascinated by or embrace Levy's thinking, but need to be guided by religious truth, then allow me to add: God is watching us from a distance.

Now comes David Reynolds, a Cambridge don, and another lengthy history of the U.S., entitled *America, Empire of Liberty*. American contractions are described, this time between our lofty ideals and practices—keenly exemplified by the Bush administration which led to our intervention in Iraq as a grand policy for spreading democracy in the Middle East while the people of the Middle East, if not most of the world, saw us as occupiers. Mr. Reynolds rejects the ideal version of America and sees the nation in Hobbesian terms—as an empire pieced together by conquest much like other empires of the past. The oceans have protected us against invasion for centuries, but it has also limited our role in colonizing other nations as European nations have in the past.

In the end, Mr. Reynolds marvels at our diversity and sees America as a "miracle," a country bound together better than any other of comparable size and mixed blood. Only in America is there successful integration of white, black, brown, and yellow people which in turn makes for a land of burgeoning bourgeoisie, innovation, and diversity of thought. Out of the earth and from various parts of the earth, faceless and unknown, lacking heredity privilege and unprivileged, people come for a new life, a fair chance, a future that is offered no where else on earth.

As a new culture and society, the humblest and poorest have been able to lift up their heads and face the future with confidence; we have increasingly relied on education as an integral part of this process of becoming. On the negative side, this forceful, driving, and imaginative American characteristic has led to political excesses and abuses—nearly wiping out whole civilizations and extracting land from other people and places in order to further and/or protect our "interests." It has also produced some ghastly business ethics—based on greed and creative corruption—highlighted by the Gilded Age, the Panic of 1907, the Wall Street collapse in the 1930s, the dot-com bust and the era of "Euronism" in post-2000 and the financial and mortgage collapse of 2008 and 2009.

With all its mistakes, weaknesses, and eccentricities—and regardless of all the foreign observers from Tocqueville to Reynolds who have commented on America, we are unlike any place in the world. A nation of many nations, and a place where people come from the four corners of the world, it is the heart and soul of the world; it reaches out to the world and beckons the poor and wretched. People don't come to America to hold on to their identities; they come to our shores for opportunity and a better life than in the place they left behind. America is the only place, on a grand scale, where people can dream unimaginable dreams. Hierarchy, elitism, class distinctions, title, and heredity privileges are unacceptable and fall to the wayside—far different from the Old World and the dysfunctional and oppressive description of Hobbesian society.

I cannot fathom, and only fear to think of, a world without the United States. Without this land, there would be no asylum for the wretched poor, little hope for the masses from distant places to escape from their oppression and misery, and the world would be possessed by one or more of the great evils—Nazism, Japanese imperialism, Stalinism, and/or Maoism. In fact, most of the civilized world would be "subject people" or puppets of some foreign political order. Sadly, however, many Americans take our human rights and blessings for granted. We tend to be ignorant of the history that shaped America, lacking the barest concept of hopes and dreams of millions of early immigrants, many who were illiterate or semi-illiterate peasants and laborers, making the perilous journey, often on unseaworthy and fever-ridden "coffinships." The spirit of freedom and opportunity that has guided the American political and social order, the country that welcomes the wretched of the earth and provides asylum for refugees, is an America that some of us take for granted and/or fail to appreciate.

Today, I write from the perspective of a third-generation American, proud and thankful that I am an American. Had Europe been a different place, I might have spoken a different language and had a different set of experiences and relationships. To this extent, I am a citizen of an ideal land because of the cruelty of other lands that my ancestors were fortunate to escape with three or four bundles on their backs. As uneducated peasants, they never read Plato, Locke, or Rousseau nor the writings of Jefferson and Madison, but they understood that America was an asylum for the oppressed, regardless of their background. They realized what other immigrants from other places understood; what foreign and French observers like Tocqueville and Levy eye-witnessed and translated into magical words; what recent immigrants like D'Souza captured in his conservative voice; and what artists such as Irving Berlin, George Gershwin, and Rogers and Hammerstein have put to music in Broadway hits and movies.

Had my ancestors not understood the story of America, I would have no story to tell, no existence, no children etc.—one out of many millions whose ancestors were reduced to nothingness by racial and ethnic cleansing, plunder and war in Europe. I would have died before my birth in some mass grave or oven. And so some small event, some seemingly insignificant decision by some ordinary people to leave the security of their extended family and homeland behind and make the unknown journey to America had momentous consequences for the author. This is how the world works for people—in highly unpredictable ways. In fact, many of us reading this book would have no existence had their ancestors not made the long, treacherous journey across the ocean that once took several months. I don't think modern multiculturalists or advocates of the American dream, including Harvard's Nathan Glazer and Oscar Handlin or Michael Novak of the American Enterprise Institute could say what I just said with any more appreciation, conviction, or passion toward America and our way of life.

AN UNSTABLE, CHAOTIC WORLD

I would argue that the world is a paradox, full of misunderstandings and subjective and contextual interpretations of people and nations. Let me explain. While some Americans worry about whether the steak they are ordering in some restaurant will come out medium rare, or whether they will have time to shop at the next Gucci sale, there are billions of people worried about their next meal and whether the cloths on their backs will suffice for the winter cold. Depending on which countries you include, one-third to a half of the world, or two to three billion people in the third world, can be radicalized by a political or religious zealot who feeds and clothes them and is intent on using this new force to challenge our way of life or to try to bring us down.

Allow me another comparison. In 1900, a nickel did not make you rich, but it gave you a sense of empowerment. If you were living in New York or Chicago, for five cents, you could buy a beer, a cup of coffee, a hot dog, three donuts, or an ice cream cone. John Rockefeller, the world's first billionaire, tired to improve his image by handing out dimes to children on the streets of Cleveland during his Sunday walks. One hundred years later, in parts of Latin America, Africa, Asia, and the Middle East, $1,000 can turn an impoverished teenager or young adult into a human bomb. The larger sum may have something to do with inflation or reduced value of life among "true believers."

Consider that there are some 1.5 billion people marginally existing on less than $2 a day, and another 2 to 3 billion people earning between $2 and $3.50 a day and the number is growing because of the "population bomb." In 2000, the bottom half of the world's population owned 1 percent of the globe's wealth. The typical person of the world whose wealth was at the 50th percentile had assets worth $2,200, while the average American had a net worth of $144,000[12]. As a nation, we comprise 5 percent of the world's population but consume 25 percent of the world's resources. When we hiccup, the rest of the world hears and feels it. This kind of inequality only increases resentment toward America and adds to a wider set of threats that we must face.

How much of a divide between "haves" and "have-nots" can the world tolerate without instability? What role does the United States play? Should it be the world's policeman and moral compass? Based on whose values? Should the American president decide who is qualified to possess nuclear weapons? Why India? Why not Iran? Can our nation afford to remain isolationist? Distant, or indifferent? How much of our resources should the average American be taxed to hopefully gain friends or converts abroad? Do the spoils of the Cold War mean that the U.S. should adopt the role of "global cop"? Can educators prepare the next generation, for the world of 2050 and beyond, in which it is estimated that the world population will reach about 10 billion? Can people living in a tent in the desert or on a mountaintop, distant from modern civilization, be expected to understand why American jets have invaded their sky?

Back to the Hobbesian Perspective

The world has become a gigantic muddle, the workings of which the vast majority of us do not fully understand. Americans are traveling in mostly unchartered territory with only a faint idea of the destination that lies ahead. Most countries of the world are in the midst of unraveling. They are run by former warlords and guerilla armies or torn apart by civil strife and ethnic cleansing or corrupt and nonfunctioning governments. The threat to these failing states, once seen as a local or regional problem, is increasingly seen as a potential threat to the larger world because of nuclear proliferation, lack of cyber security, porous borders and the air we all breathe which knows no borders. If we pause and train our eye on the darker aspects of the world, then there are enough signs and subtleties to conclude that we live in a broken and unstable world, a post-Hobbesian place.

George Will, the conservative historian and news pundit is quite explicit. "One manic with a small vial of small pox spores [or anthrax] can kill millions of Americans . . . About 30,000 trucks cross our international borders" daily. It doesn't take a rocket scientist or genius "to smuggle in a football-sized lump of highly enriched uranium sufficient to make . . . a nuclear weapon" and blow up Manhattan or Washington D.C. Some of Will's prose may be construed as jingoism, but there is enough truth in the statement to get people's attention on 42nd Street and Broadway or on DuPont Circle.

Then there are the modern-day barbarians—today's terrorists, Islamic Jihadists and the soldiers of Hamas, al-Qaeda and the Taliban—plotting attacks against the democratic and civilized world. There wars are not locally limited to Afghanistan, Pakistan or Palestine, rather they threaten the U.S. and Western world under the guise of attacking the unjust imperialist order. In many parts of the Moslem world, governments have failed to provide land reform and even the most basic forms of education and healthcare. In the Middle East, where there is oil, government jobs dominate which leads to corruption (the buying and selling of jobs) and nepotism, and oil money has remained in the hands of a few and not filtered to the people. Avenues for opportunity for the vast majority of rural people and even educated youth do not exist, leading to huge inequality of income and wealth; the value of cattle and goats are considered higher than women. Fighting against the long odds to bring their societies into the modern age, Shariah law and rulings based on the most extreme interpretation of the Koran have been frequently imposed—allowing clerics to dictate daily life and ferment anti-American sentiment and even sanction the killing of anyone, including fellow Moslems.

Can the U.S. afford to be isolationist, distant or indifferent? Should it act as a force of change in the Moslem world? Or, should it even try? Must we be concerned that pro-democratic government officials, journalists and intellectuals have had their heads cut off and throats slit—that when family honor is at stake women have been disfigured and stoned to death, or that secular schools that compete with the mosques have been burned down? Can we afford to ignore these issues—or the existence of any radical Islamism threat whatever? In traditional Islamic societies, any attempt to promote democracy, women rights or secular thinking is seen as western interference that goes back to the Crusades. What really drives Americans, according to Columbia Professor Rashid Khalidi in *Sowing Crisis*, is the desire for economic control of the oil-rich Middle East, a policy that has guided Washington for nearly three fourths of a century. Our meddling has kept political and civil conflict boiling in the weaker states—whereby the princes, imans or warlords rule the multitude and prevent reform. Even in the stronger states, because of past colonialism, there is the habit of denying basic rights and blaming the West for its problems. But the dangers to the West are real. As an open society, the U.S. (and Europe) are unable to guard all places and defend against all forms of terrorism.

In almost everyplace where modern-day barbarians flourish, there are weak governments, no governments, or corrupt governments which rely on security forces to maintain power. Armed militias, gunrunners, and drug smugglers terrorize the country side in many weaker nations of the world—just like they did prior to the rise of civilized society. We fail to recognize that military upheaval, misrule or nonrule, characterize much of the world today. Military rebels and guerillas roam the countryside in many parts of Asia, Africa, and Latin America—paralyzing governments, burning villages, raping and kidnapping children. More than half of the 53 nations in Africa are governed, or actually misgoverned, by former warlords. These horrows are reinforced by world-wide poverty and disease and the lack of essentials (food, water, and sewerage) which translates into human misery and suffering in more than 50 percent of the world's populace. In all these ungovernable places, the economy is stumbling and the vast majority of the people live in squalid camps, urban hovels or shacks—perfect places for recruiting militias, drug runners and terrorists.

Most third-world nations are either ungoverned, under governed, misgoverned and contested areas. All this misgovernance leads to a lack of security—that is a moral foundation, faith in the law and freedom from fear—all required for human growth and development. This lack of security, coupled with shortages of clean water, food and health care, high unemployment and population explosion is a source for why so many countries outside the Western world have been held back for decades, if not centuries. Roughly, this is why governments continue to be corrupt, unstable, and autocratic and people in these places are easy prey for criminal activities, militia recruitment, terrorist cells, and various forms of extremism—much of it directed at the West who they blame for their problems. There are bizarre places, what Robert Cooper in *The Breaking of Nations*, called "zones of chaos," that average Western citizens with a college degree cannot fathom, not to overlook the fact they are unfamiliar with the Hobbesian interpretation of society.

An index of nation-state weakness in developing countries, based on 20 political and social indicators, reveals 27 "critically weak" nations, including many in Africa (such as the Congo, Liberia, Mozambique, Rwanda, and Somalia), former Soviet Union (Abkhazia, Georgia, South Ossetia, and Transelniestria) and the Middle East (Iraq, Lebanon, and Yemen). These are countries or "failed states" characterized by "misrule, violence, corruption, forced migration, poverty, illiteracy and disease," according to the *Economist*. Many of the regions, in Africa, are dominated by warring tribes and clans, fueled by war, genocide and plunder—a world not to distant from *Blade Runner*.

To add to the grim list of unstable places, the U.S. State Department has also identified 100 (out of 195 nations) of the most "ungovernable" places in the world; they overlap with the Brookings list of 27 "critically weak" nation-states. The top 100 most wretched places include such countries as Columbia, Haiti, Indonesia, the Philippines, Peru, Mexico, North Korea, Liberia, Nigeria, Sri Lanka, Sudan, and Uganda. The people in Columbia, Peru and Mexico—and parts of Central America have been wrecked by drug smuggling; Haiti and Liberia by government misrule and extreme poverty; Indonesia, Sri Lanka and Philippines by corruption and terrorism, and most African countries (some 53) were never functioning states.

Here we have nearly one billion people living in what is often called the "dark" continent, largely ill-governed and burdened by the shadow of colonialism, ethnic history and political corruption. When the colonists left, so did the government structure, which in turn led to civil war, plunder and rape, incompetence and rotten government leadership, nepotism, racism, racketing and military terrorism. More than half the continents people are living at starvation or malnourishment levels, seeking food and shelter as well as safety and security. The search for these basic needs dominates the daily existence of most Africans.

High-Tech vs. Low-Tech Nations

The cell phone, internet, and cable TV that we are accustomed to are apparitions to the population of poverty, a world of color that is growing rapidly, and represents the gulf where danger resides. Put simply, the low-tech/ disconnected world could overwhelm the high-tech/ connected world. So long as these poor remain docile, they remain invisible to us, and we remain unaware and unconcerned about billions of people running through heaps of garbage and sleeping in the streets, places where the majority of children drop out of school by the sixth or seventh grade and are called "street children," "beggars," and "no-hopers." Our media and education system is divorced from this global reality; yet this world (the third world) may weigh down the world we know—what most of us would call the Western World, or industrialized world. [13]

Despite the world increasingly speaking English and drinking Coca-Cola, most of the inhabitants in developing areas of the world are rural immigrants and urban refugees within their own countries, many living in streets, drinking poisonous contaminated water, sip by sip, people adrift and yearning for a better life and a little dignity. These poor and wretched people are the new proletariat—possessed by a growing dislike, jealousy, and even hatred toward Western values. These are the same kinds of people Europeans, and to a much lesser extent Americans, have exploited through colonization and capitalism. It is the world depicted by Hobbes—characterized by misery and squalor, where life has little meaning.

In economic terms, "third-world" countries comprise (the Hobbesian World) zones of chaos, the threat to the West (or nonHobbesian world). Even among emerging nations, part of the functioning world, most parts of China, India, and Brazil—are still characterized by poverty and third-world living conditions. However, it is the third-world nations that are now trying to pull themselves in the world market by selling their agricultural products, only to come upon the rich nations' insistence on subsidizing their own farmers, creating rock bottom prices. Poor people, often farmers, are unable to compete on a global basis and continue to struggle on a daily basis. The developed world's (or G-8 nations') annual $320 billion in farm subsidies dwarf its $75 billion in assistance to the undeveloped world. A 1 percent increase in Africa's share of world exports would amount to $70 billion a year, some three times the amount ($25 billion) provided in aid in 2005[14]; this "rigged game" of keeping agribusiness afloat in wealthy nations fuels world poverty and is sowing great hostility toward the United States, as it is viewed as the principle architect of the world economic order. In short, poor nations are unable to expand their agriculture markets, which would shift hundreds of billions of dollars from the rich to poor nations of the world. By rich countries imposing tariffs and eliminating the farm competition of poor countries, they have added to malnutrition, as well as illegal immigration to Europe and a movement of rural poor to third-world cities—increasing worldwide, urban squalor and sowing the seeds of radicalism and anti-Western movements.

Adding to the agricultural woes of poor nations, the U.N. estimates that by 2050, when the world's population is expected to reach 9 billion people—global food production will need to increase 70 percent because of population growth and rising incomes. But a 70 percent increase in food production means increased rates of habitat destruction—including the acceleration of the extinction of annual species and deforestation for producing food and fuel. This in turn, has serious implications for climate change which was created by the industrialized nations (with the U.S. being number one culprit) and whether there will be enough land and water to produce the food needed in the future.

So here is the rub: Billions of people, about half to two-thirds of a growing world population worried about whether they can feed themselves, squashed by economic imperialism and envisioning the United States as the chief villain. These billions of bottom people, represent an inevitable force with a reason to rebel and bring down our way of life—not by invading armies but through social breakdown, health problems and viruses, rebellion from mountains and jungles, as well as overpopulated cities, taking advantage of our dependence on fossil fuels and threatening us with nuclear terrorism, and/or cyber warfare.

Conservatives might argue that our nation has never been so misunderstood by the world, but I would argue that the world knows us much better than we know the world. They would also argue that globalization will eventually lead to a trickle-down economic benefit that over time will help the poor and make production more efficient and less expensive. Such an argument is rooted in the idea of a free-market economy, whereby consumer demand and efficient production win the day for capitalists while benefiting the masses with lower consumer prices. I guess the argument works on paper, if you believe in American-styled capitalism and it's O.K. for one country, the U.S.A., to run the world's economy. Try telling that "hokum pokem" to the members of the E-20 nations, who are now insisting on global regulation of Wall Street and the world's banking system, or to the bottom half of the world, who are struggling on a day-to-day basis and living in the midst of turbulence.

Depending on the benchmarks we employ, about seventy-five to one hundred countries are caught in a "poverty-trap," a term used by Columbia University's Jeffrey Sachs in his book *The End of Poverty*, to describe a combination of poor geography, poor infrastructure, poor health care, and limited educational resources and if I may add, poor transportation links, a shortage of skilled labor, and nonexistent credit. Moreover "dirty" money and money laundering, as well as the smuggling and trafficking of people, drugs and weapons, make up half the economies of nations in Africa, the Middle East, and Latin America. About the only thing holding the world's poor populace together is their government, and we are forced to support corrupt leaders and dictators and hope these governments can restrain the extremist part of the population that wants to cripple the West.

These impoverished people are to some extent the people we once called barbarians who brought down Rome. The world has not changed much in the last one thousand years, at least not when it comes to counting powerful people and powerless people, except maybe the scales are more lopsided and there are more poor people in the world willing to sack the place where all financial roads lead (no longer to Rome, now New York, London, Zurich, and Tokyo).

Is foreign aid the answer? Will money solve the "poverty trap?" Sachs believes that, if rich countries increased their annual foreign-aid budgets between $135 to $195 billion for the next decade, extreme poverty in the world would be eliminated. That said, the World Bank alone committed $105 billion to poor countries between 2008 and 2010, to help them unvest in agriculture and infrastructure.[15] Conservative critics would argue that Sachs needs a reality check—that political, social, and cultural conditions prevent economic improvement in the foreseeable future. Even if oil or other resources were discovered in these countries, political and business corruption would prevent the vast majority of the populace from receiving benefits. The money would wind up in the hands of a tiny group of families or politicians, nothing more than a mirror of the history of most third-world, poor nations. Sometimes the problem centers around European businessmen protecting their investments, sometimes it is home-grown mercenaries or rebels, and sometimes it is government officials or the country's ruling class hatching plots and stealing the riches from the county's oil fields. Typical cases where political corruption, family conflict, or mercenaries steal or squander oil revenues or prevent oil production are countries like Azerbaijan, Kazakhstan, the Congo, Nigeria, Sudan, and Yemen.

Given our wealth and resources, and our belief in the rule of law, how do we prepare our children and their children for this age of uncertainty, for what endures around the world, and for what might be. All around us there are ghettos and genocide, starvation and malnourishment, sickly and starving people living amidst rampant political waste, fraud, and corruption, a pending global apocalypse. Do Americans understand that we are no longer the source of "cool," that our movies, music, and art no longer win friends, but make enemies? In the past (and even today), Americans have been unable to make the leap the other side of the tracks, one or two miles away to understand, what sociologists have called the "invisible poor." How are Americans expected to make the global leap to better understand the world around them, when 60 percent of college-age Americans do not know where the United Nations headquarters is located and cannot find Iraq on the map.

Economic Insecurity: The Growing Proletariat

The world's poor are a forgotten people; few people know or care to know their plight. About 40 million third-world people are infected with HIV; 300 to 500 million people are infected with malaria every year; 20 million children in third-world countries die of starvation each year, while another 800 million to one billion people suffer daily from malnourishment and hunger; and one fourth of the world's population lives on no more than two dollars a day. ironically, in ten years, between 1987 and 1998, poverty (defined by the World Bank) increased 20 percent in Latin America, 40 percent in South Asia, and 50 percent in Africa. In Eastern Europe and Central Asia, it increased more than 1,000 percent. [16]

Whatever economic gains were made in the twenty-first century among emerging nations, most has been battered by the slump in Western consumerism—as exports and jobs have gone into major free fall in countries like Brazil, China, India, Taiwan and Vietnam. Falling exports have squeezed jobs and reduced domestic spending—adding to move unemployment in these export dependent economies. In twenty third-world countries (ten in Africa), the life expectancy is expected to dip below forty years. In Sub-Saharan Africa, children under five die twenty-two times the rate of children in industrialized countries, and also twice the rate of the entire developing world. According to economist and Professor Gregory Clark of the University of California, Davis, in *Farewell to Alms*, living standards in almost half of Africa have fallen below hunter-gatherer times and 40 percent below the living standard of eighteenth-century England.

An angry urban proletariat is growing around the world as poor populations—namely, hundreds of millions of rural migrants—flood to grimy, overpopulated urban areas. There, they are assaulted by what is perceived as Western culture: luxury cars, nightclubs, sex and drugs, porno movies, gangs, and prostitution. Their daily existence is plagued by electric blackouts, unsanitary drinking water, overflowing sewage, and an assortment of five killer diseases—tuberculosis, typhoid, malaria, measles, and AIDS—annually killing some 54 million people worldwide. It is not uncommon for more than half of this new proletariat to live on roof-tops, street alleys, and the outskirts of the cities by garbage dumps. This is the world, the real world, that Americans do not understand or know, given the paradox of American prosperity.

As America preaches the gospel of freedom and democracy, and romanticizes market globalization, high-tech gadgets, and entrepreneur capitalism, there is a growing post-Cold war proletariat class that infests, digests, and surrounds the cities of the most populated, underdeveloped and developing countries. Whatever their language, whatever their skin color, religion or tribal descent, they resent the national government that often rigs elections, if there are any, and is corrupt and unable to provide basic necessities of life.

Dealing with global poverty is essential if capitalism is to continue to prosper; otherwise, the growing world poor may tip the scale and its weight may eventually bring down capitalism. At the present, capitalism is basking in its victory over communism, unaware that, as global poverty increases, radical and fanatical elements of third-world countries gain in power and the potential to challenge the existing system. This trend is compounded by the Western and civilized world being pitted against the terrorists and the fundamentalist nature of Islam, under the guise of a so-called attack against the unjust, imperialist and colonialist order. Islamic jihad is not a local conflict, confined to the mountains of Afghanistan and Pakistan or the streets of Palestine and Somali. Not only are their neighbors threatened, but also moderate Moslem nations such as Saudi Arabia, Jordon, Egypt and Indonesia are possible targets. And, if the Taliban is successful in Afghanistan or Pakistan, the jihadists will likely threaten India—the largest democratic country in the world. In fact, it can be argued radical Islam is an attack against the Western world similar to the way the barbarians attacked imperial Rome. We may have stock piles of nuclear bombs (that we don't want to unleash), but they have suicide bombers which are used almost on a daily basis.

The people of third-world countries are not burning the American flag, nor are they rioting in the streets on a regular basis. Their anger toward the west and rich nations is loosely articulated, because these people, for the greater part, are working and struggling on a daily basis to exist and do not have time to take part in demonstrations. The third-world people we do see demonstrating on CNN are riveting to the American audience, partially because of their anger toward the United States, partially because of their zeal, and partially because they seem to exist in another world so different from ours. The world is more fragile, today, because the nation's economies are globally interconnected. For the most part, the world's poor believe, or are led to believe, that the United States is the cause of their squalor and misery, that their government cannot function efficiently because of the U.S. dependence, and that the recent global financial meltdown, and the concurrent loss of hundreds of millions jobs in emerging world markets, has been caused by the American capitalist system. We have become the military and economic bully of the world.

America Faces A Defiant World

Then there is China, India, Brazil and Russia, part of the G-20, which have been not only criticizing the U.S. free market system and lack of regulation, but also pondering the degree to which U.S. economic power has declined and that the U.S. is no longer in position to dictate economic policies to other industrialized nations. These four countries, along with Venezuela, have introduced the idea of a new currency to replace the dollar—which, if it came to pass, would have immense downspin on our own economy.

Even our closest allies have become critical of the U.S. At recent summits, French President Nicolas Sarkozy and German Chancellor Angela Merkel called for the regulation of global banking, targeting the U.S. economic system: CEO salaries and bonuses, hedge funds, credit agencies, and tax havens were labeled as part of the problem and reason for the world economic crisis. Both Sarkozy and Merkel argued that the poorly regulated free market system in the U.S. created the 2008-2009 international meltdown and that the U.S. must now recognize the European model (characterized by progressive taxation, safety nets and a central regulatory bank) is superior, "and a foundation for this new financial architecture [that] must be laid now."

At a recent G-20 summit, Britain's Prime Minister Gordon Brown was quick to point to America as the chief villain for the world's financial woes. Without mentioning the U.S. by name, he argued that moral decay had descended on the capitalist system, running counter to the European belief that "economic progress and social justice advance together, or not at all." To be sure, the American economic system was severely criticized and blamed for the recent global meltdown. Instead of lecturing our allies or defending the U.S. economic system, President Obama was humble and summed up that America has "learned the lessons of history." Really? In two or three years, given our short memories, most of us will forget. Greed, arrogance, and malpractice will vault back in the saddle—and then off to the races with these three horses in the forefront.

Even before the economic meltdown, many of the governments of emerging and undeveloped countries were sensitive to Western imperialism and colonialism. These nations rejected any international pressure from the U.S. or their allies as an affront to their independence and national sovereignty. The trouble is so many of the undeveloped and poor countries, do not have a national sovereignty because they are splintered by internal strife and lack national institutions and governmental instability.

According to Oxford's Paul Collier in *The Bottom Billion*—or the world's 60 most impoverished countries—he argued that Western styled democracy and capitalism were a farce. Violence, fraud, graft, and rigged elections prevailed in these countries, and therefore an array of sophisticated and do-good policies had minimal impact. A natural identity with national institutions did not exist in these countries. Ethnic and tribal affiliation influenced political and economic policy making—who won or lost elections, who went to college, who got what job—in short, how money and opportunities were parceled among different groups. To be sure, the world is a mess. Nearly all the gains in growth among poor countries in the last decade that lifted hundreds of millions above a $2 a day poverty line was lost in the last global dip and downward trickle.

In this new Hobbesian world, eventually, the capital-rich nations of the West, may be challenged by "no-hopers"—people who have nothing to lose since life means very little in a society characterized by squalor and misery (for which they believe America is to blame because of the way capitalism exploits). This "no-hopers" concept partially explains why it is easy to recruit guerilla soldier's intent on battling American-sponsored dictatorships who are anticommunist and/or pro-American; it also explains why terrorists are easily recruited from poor rural villages and urban hellholes. The old elite, the wealthy in third-world countries, live a life walled off from the masses who are poor and who have migrated from rural shanty towns to urban squalor, where children die from starvation and disease, a world ripe with catastrophe that has lost much of its meaning to wealthy nations. By 2015, more than fifty cities in developing countries will have populations of 5 to 10 million in which the poor have no land, no business, no machines, no tangible assets to create wealth—only the labor and sweat on their backs to offer, at a minimum wage for twelve to fourteen hours of work per day.

It is these places, the rotting cities or urban garbage heaps of the world, where a new proletariat is being created—one in which the present governments are unable to provide basic necessities. While some of these governments have been celebrated in the West and in the United States as pro-American or "democratic," this new and growing proletariat, sees their governments as corrupt, elected by ballot-rigging or overrun by military coups, and supported by U.S. dollars, which get diverted to the pockets of the politicians and military at the expense of the inhabitants. The paradox is that, as government authority is weakened or overthrown, the people of the third world are being organized by regional guerilla, drug-smuggling or religious groups at the expense of national, progressive, or secular ones.

The governments in power must contend with, and in some cases to survive work with para military-rebels, extreme religious and left-wing political ideologies. In the meantime, the third-world proletariat grows larger—fostered by increasing poverty, illiteracy, and birthrates, and it is being fueled by anti-American and anti-Western sentiments which are easy to induce because of the growing gap between the rich and poor in the world, between the West and the third world, between modern-day rationalism and medieval irrationalism.

When *Good* Times Disappear

On a global basis, and even within emerging nations such as China and India, inequality has grown and the rich and super rich continue to follow historical trends (since the dawn of civilization) by acquiring most of the wealth and gains of economic productivity. Even during the 2008-09 global bubble, the bankers and financial "wizards" made off with public and private money at the expense of ordinary people who now need to work harder and longer to offset their losses. Then the same people who put us in this mess were bailed out by taxpayer money, under the guise they were too big and too important to fail.

Unemployment around the world is soaring at a dangerous rate and leading to world instability. The International Labor Organization, a U.N. agency, estimates that the jobless rate will top 225 million within the industrialized world or G-20 by the end of 2010, (with China experiencing the highest number, some 20 million migrant workers and another 20 million knowledge/information workers. These figures do not count under employment (probably another 250 million) and people who have given up looking for jobs. The breadth of the problem tends to underestimate the real threat to world stability, since it is different to obtain accurate data from nations outside G-20—where migrant workers, farmers and rural townspeople, and small business people working out of their homes make up most of the population. The unemployment outlook of the U.N. is limited to factory, construction, government, and white-collar workers—people the ministries can easily track and report. A good guess is that unemployment outside the G-20 was another 250 million at the end of 2010.

Many countries that moved out of the Soviet orbit, or moved from communism to government regulated capitalism, or prospered because of oil exports have known only boom years since the early 1990s. The ripples from the world's economic slowdown in the industrialized and emerging nations are felt in third world and undeveloped countries in Africa, Asia, and Latin America—as migrant workers and immigrants find themselves unable to find jobs. It's a delicate global machine, and laid-off workers in China, India and Indonesia have few or no rights and can only look across the horizon to America as the country that created this mess—increasing anti-American attitudes around the world. Indeed, the "masters of the universe," the people who move money around and believe in the virtues of capitalism (which boils down to their own economic interests) have helped create civilization's instability and strife—reminding us of an old Hobbesian world, where the strong take advantage of weak. The world has become "flat," (Thomas Friedman's notion) and interconnected by banking, trade, and cyberspace. Without proper checks and balances, without stable and accountable governments, without laws and rules to protect women and ethnic minorities and without international legitimacy to curb nuclear proliferation and fossil fuel consumption, our existence is bound to degenerate into "a life-and-death" struggle. We are entering a contemporary world of Darth Vader, where the dark forces become part of the natural landscape and cascading events lead to misery, if not catastrophe, for hundreds of millions of people.

It is nice to suppose that the great economists of the day, who possess a natural ability to see through the forces of despair and depression, will find the moment and marshal the public and private tools in an appropriate manner to prevail against the notion of doom and gloom. How many years it will take to fix the world, no one can be sure. In the meantime, with the current forces of uncertainty and instability, the delicate world economic machine is sputtering—adding more chaos to a very fragile world.

According to the sociologist Hernando de Soto, in *The Mystery of Capital*, Marx was right in claiming that capitalism strips workers of their assets, except their labor. They are unable to accumulate capital legally because they don't own property or other tangible assets, such as businesses that create capital and permit people to accumulate wealth. So the market is restricted, mobility is inhibited, and wealth is limited to those who control the property and other tangible assets. The only way for the poor in these countries to accumulate money is to deal in drugs, arms, sex trafficking, or some other black-market product or become a corrupt government bureaucrat and provide some service for a fee. In short, world corruption and criminal behavior are rampant within most emerging and undeveloped countries. Greed is not an American invention, but it is rather part of the human condition. Adam Smith's theories of profit were read by more than Americans and our English cousins, and a lot more people around the world saw Michael Douglas's movie *Wall Street*, which glorified money and materialism.

The United States cannot police the world, nor does the United States have a fiduciary duty or capability to economically support it. In short, there is no easy answer to this growing tide of world discontent, which is continuously boiling. Similarly, the United Nations lacks the status, flexibility, and powers to serve as a moral authority or react to military challenges. Their own audits point to mismanagement and fraud in their global operations. Even worse, the power of America has been exhausted; we are in slow decline—and there is a redistribution of wealth taking place in front of our eyes. The American people are going to have to learn to live with less while other parts of the world gain from our decline.

On still another level, for the first time, we hear people at international conferences wondering if the U.S. is politically or economically unstable. To be sure, critics enjoy poking fun and criticizing America. Plagued by partisan politics, the near—collapse of the banking industry, high unemployment and huge deficits, as well as by issues related to poor education, poor infrastructure, and poor health care, it appears that we are now the ones who need help. In the meantime, there is the growing reality of the rise of China, India and other emerging nations—accompanied by a shift in importance from the G-7 to the G-20.

CONCLUSION

We fail to recognize that we are surrounded by a Hobbesian world, a world of consisting of failed states, corrupt governments, civil strife and war, poverty and disease. We would like to think we have escaped from this world, that we are on top of the economic heap and have a solid middle-class populace, and that we are governed by laws. Face the facts. The world around us, has become broken and chaotic—a dangerous and dysfunctional place.

The ice cap is melting, the air we breathe is polluted, our energy resources are being depleted, drinking water is in short supply, sexual slavery and AIDS are a fact of life, kidnapping and drug smuggling are booming businesses, and the worldwide landscape has been continuously plundered. In most parts of the world, including the U.S.A., big business people and politicians are often corrupt and drain off resources from their nations. Most Governments are unstable and some close to home in Mexico, Columbia and Peru are facing potential collapse. Their drug cartels and gun trafficking problems are spilling over into our borders, already operating in 230 U.S. cities.

An emerging kidnapping and ransom industry is flourishing—illustrating the growing number of nonfunctioning governments. Mexico now has the most kidnappings (tied to the drug industry), with some 7,500 in 2010, replacing Columbia as the world's kidnapping hot spot. But kidnapping has spread to the Middle East and Africa, highlighted by Al Qaeda and the Taliban—using it as a political weapon and to spread terror. Then there are Somali pirates seizing dozens of ships annually from wealthy countries, and Nigeria and the Congo rivaling Mexico as the number-two and three kidnapping spots—coinciding with their rebel and gun-running movements.

The world we inhabit is further plagued by a growing population bomb that is projected to reach 10 to 12 billion by the end of this century, depleting resources, especially clean water, causing rising food prices and climate changes that can lead to global chaos. A parade of grim environmental realities makes for a long list, with the loss of large portions of forests, vegetation, top soil, natural resources, and animal life. You don't have to travel to the top of the world or dive to the bottom of the ocean floor, and you don't need a Ph.D. in marine biology, to recognize that the world's ecosystem is in jeopardy. The good news is that they third world understands that the environment is globally connected; the bad news is that the United States is considered the worst culprit, the biggest user of world resources, warming the earth with carbons. China and India are no longer growing at 10 to 12 percent per year, but despite their slower growth rates with their combined population of over 2.5 billion people still comes chemical plants, metals and mining, cars and refrigerators—increasing carbon emissions, elimination of the protective ozone layer and destructive climate changes.

Most of us in the Western world feel the global recession and are forced to reduce our conspicuous consumption. A few of us are still buying new cars and larger houses, and others are visiting shopping malls and purchasing the latest cell phones, iPods, and computers. But the apple cart is bound to be turned over by the growing imbalance of world economic scales. We are bound to have rogue nations that possess "the bomb" and others that have access to biological and chemical weapons.

Given today's era of computers and satellite communication systems, nuclear plants, and a high-tech infrastructure, it is almost impossible to speculate the damage and ripple effect of a major terrorist attack on fragile utility, transportation and high-tech sites. No government can prepare its populace for all potential terrorist attacks. The next attack, which statistically is bound to happen, could be much worse than 9-11. In the meantime as we try to fend off the inevitable, the nation is in slow decline and all around the world there is misery and chaos. All we need to do is to open up our eyes and ears. Thomas Hobbes has come back from the pages of history to haunt us.

Chapter 3

QUESTIONS TO CONSIDER

1. How did the American distribution of wealth in 1776 (the year of the signing of the Declaration of Independence) square with the distribution of wealth today?

2. How did the class structure in the U.S. compare to England during the colonial period?

3. How does U.S. inequality of income and wealth compare today with other industrialized countries?

4. What percent of the American colonialists were considered eligible to vote? What criteria were considered essential to qualify for voting?

5. How did General Washington get along with and view the rank-and-file soldiers he commanded? In what ways did his attitudes and behaviors coincide with patrician norms or royal elitism?

6. In what ways was John Adams, the second president of the U.S., more aristocratic than democratic? More like a philosopher-king than a yeoman farmer? More distrusting of the common people than the English monarchy?

7. Why did James Madison, the fourth president of the U.S., devise a representative form of government with checks and balances and separation of powers, rather than a democratic form of government, whereby people had more direct influence and power

8. Why did Adams, Madison, and Hamilton believe that the masses could not be trusted with political power? What was Hamilton's view of the masses?

9. Why did Madison believe in limiting both government and the church? In doing so, how was he helping the property class?

10. In what ways do the gloomy views of Thomas Hobbes coincide with the views of Adams, Madison, and Hamilton? How do they differ from Thomas Jefferson's view of the common people?

11. Why did Hamilton reject the ideas of the "rights of man" and that "all men are created equal"?

12. Why was Jefferson considered radical by many of his contemporaries?

13. How does the colonial Tory party compare to (or differ from) today's Republicans (Democrats)?

14. How do the Federalists of the colonial era compare (or differ from) today's Republicans (Democrats)?

15. How were our Founding Fathers influenced by Greek and Roman society? Age of Enlightenment? In what ways did they socially and economically reject the Old World?

16. To what extent does Hamilton represent today's conservative views about business and society? To what extent does Jefferson represent today's liberal views about working people and society?

Chapter 3

THE SPIRIT OF 76: PATRICIAN THOUGHT AND ELITISM

While America has never had the well defined classes or estates that have existed in Europe, we have always been a nation of unequal's, originally in terms of who went to college (children of the rich), who could vote (only white males who owned property), and in terms of income and wealth. In 1776, for example, the richest 10 percent owned more than 90 percent of the property of New York, Philadelphia, Baltimore and Charleston.[17]

Nearly two hundred years later, the poorest one-fifth of the American population owned 2 percent of the wealth and the richest ten percent owned 70 percent of the wealth; the top 1 percent owned nearly 40 percent of U.S. wealth.[18] Optimistic readers would say there is more equality today; pessimists would argue that the economic pie is much bigger so the gap between rich and poor is wider. If we take the long view and consider two hundred and fifty years of political and economic spin (America is the City on the Hill, the foundation of hope, the land of opportunity, etc.), then the record is less than impressive. If we confront the facts, the U.S. inequality gap is tops among the twenty industrialized countries, except Switzerland, that records such disparities.

REVOLUTIONARY ICONS

Prior to the Revolution, America was in flux. Henry Adams, a descendent of the Adams' family and one of America's first historians, described the land as a backwater, uncultured place, consisting of parochial wrangling and treasonous and scheming people. But this remote, miniscule, and provincial place was to meld into a new nation, based on the principles of the Enlightenment, that was to lift the social level and souls of the average man to the most favored position—a free man endowed with certain inalienable rights and liberties, The nation was to be guided by a government of the people with safeguards built into laws against unlimited despotic governments. This new faith in people, founded on egalitarian and humanitarian principles, would become translated into the idea of *democracy* and subsequently serve as a beacon of light for transforming the Old World.

Because of immigration and geographical expansion, it was much easier for those in the thirteen colonies to move up the social and economic ladder, or to fall down, than in England where the population was static, the national boundaries limited, and a paternal monarchy had existed for centuries. Although a class structure evolved in the colonies, it was socially and economically based, not ascribed heredity; there was no aristocracy based on birthright or bloodline. Americans felt more equal in social and economic status than their English counterparts. Despite the deference for privilege, power, and rank among the manufacturing, banking, and plantation class, the vast majority of Americans had a sense of independence and freedom not expressed by the average Englishman. The Revolution that was to come was intellectually based on Enlightenment theories, but the military struggle was to be fought by an emerging working—and middle-class populace—a refinement on the historical class struggle. The battles on the field were to be fought by common people, from the village and farm, from below, and not by a professional army, not by paid warrior-masqueraders wearing shining suits and emblems and carrying shining swords and guns.

The Founding Fathers as a group never thought of the coming Revolution as a fight for democracy. All men were not created equal, so was the majority opinion. Some people by birth of intellect had more talent than others and a government based on truth and virtue (Plato's dictum) would put the "natural aristocrats" (philosopher-kings) in charge of government. Pulling on the other side, in the background, was the thirst for equality, ideas that had plagued ancient Greece and Rome, and later most of Europe, what was to be defined as part of the Old World. Royal patronage had dominated early colonial government affairs, defined in terms of Tory positions and rank. Ultimately, the coming Revolution would lead to a schism within the colonies, or battle between "monarchs" and "radicals," "courtiers" and "patriots," over the hearts and minds of the American people.

Eventually what would emerge in the colonies would be an aristocracy of the talented, based on merited rank and performance, rather than ascribed, based on birth (and bloodline) into an aristocratic family. That's the traditional historical interpretation of America, the one we learned in school. This view excludes factors such as who in colonial America enrolled in the Latin Grammar Schools (rich children) or the Academy, for those not going onto college, (working-class children), who attended Harvard and Yale (rich children); or, who could vote (the property class or about 10 percent of the colonialists) and who were free citizens (not black slaves nor native Indians).

The fact is that the majority of the Founding Fathers feared "excessive" democracy and sought to frame a government less by egalitarian principles and more by autocratic beliefs so that well-bred and well-educated gentlemen would run the government. The so-called working class (bakers and bricklayers) and middle class (artisans and tradesmen) were unable to vote since they did not own sufficient property. The best known Founding Fathers, including John Adams, Alexander Hamilton, and James Madison, gave us a Republican form of government and capitalism, but they had reservations about the rights of the common people (who Jefferson defended) and about taxing the property or manufacturing class.

Washington: the Nation's Leader in War and Peace

Class differences have always counted. When Washington took command of the colonial army, according to David McCullough in *1776*, he repeatedly complained that the men he led were "exceeding dirty and nasty" and "afflicted by an unaccountable kind of stupidity." At times, he felt he was in "command of an armed mob" who were often drunk and ate like slobs. The slave-owner, then commander-in-chief of the Continental Army, took offense at the presence of many of his officers who he complained were "indecisive, incompetent," and uneducated compare to the British officers who were more disciplined, more tidy and neat in their uniforms, and more refined.

Washington was not a superior tactician or strategist, and many of his soldiers found him cold, distant and aristocratic. Repeatedly, he had to be rescued by his so-called "mob-like," working-class soldiers and "inept" subordinates. The British generals, all from the upper-class ranks, originally likened the rebellion to a fox hunt in which they were to "bag" their prey when they had the chance first at Lexington and Concord and then at Fort Ticonderoga and Saratoga. The colonialists didn't play by the rules of war! How unsportsmanlike! They hid behind trees and fought and ran instead of marching on the battle field, standing firm and dying like "good little soldiers."

Washington took command of the Army to fulfill a "consuming passion . . . to gain honor and respect," writes Richard Brookiser in <u>The Genuine Article</u>, and to be "the best known and admired man in the colonies." He fed patrician needs for rank and fame, to project the image of a great military and political leader, just as he wanted to be known as the "most graceful ballroom dancer and finest horsemen." It all had to do with a feeling of superiority and snobbishness and desire to show he was above the common stock and represented the best virtues of Roman republicanism, elitism and fashion, as well as the patrician view of serving the public and pursuing the public good (a little like Carnegie, Rockefeller, and Kennedy). To be sure, there was a class consciousness that filtered through Washington's personality, as well as many of the Founding Fathers who envisioned they were superior to the common stock, and thus more than equal.

I realize there have been many attempts to debunk or criticize Washington. When events called for it, however, he rose to the occasion and led the nation in war and peace at a fragile period in its history and at the creation of the United States. He was the most respected man in the colonies, later considered by many to be the Father of the Country, the most influential president, and the greatest American. Washington gave power away, when he could have seized power like Caesar or Napoleon. When the war ended he told his troops to disband and go back to their farms and shops. After the war, he "held the government together until the people could learn to be loyal to the government itself." Then, again he stepped down and gave power away, when many Americans wanted him to stay on as president, or even become king.

As historical analysis goes, Washington was motivated by the desires for honor and glory, and recognition first for his military prowess and then as President; and in both positions to show his wisdom and control the actions that govern armies and nations. He was patrician in the strictest sense with a vast accumulation of land, goods, horses and slaves. To be sure, the most powerful form of elitism and vanity among military commanders and patriarchs is the desire to win battles and to be esteemed as wise and learned later in life by having one's ideas and doctrines recognized as the ruling or authoritive opinions of society. Washington was the embodiment of the Greek and Roman patrician warrior, philosopher and politician who managed to arouse the common people, control their actions, and sway their thoughts by skillful exercise of power—and then be popularized and institutionalized.

Adams: Not So Liberal

The idea of democracy and equality at no time engaged unanimous approval among the Founding Fathers. Even John Adams, our second president, a staunch believer in liberty and the principles and rights of the Revolution, had his doubts and suspicions of the people. Although he came from blue-collar and modest surroundings and needed financial support to attend Harvard, and although he was described as an abundantly humane person and idealist by David McCullough in the recent work *John Adams*, he believed in a natural aristocracy of property and intellect. Such people were entitled to cultural and economic privileges and should direct the affairs of the new nation. "The people of all nations," he wrote, "are naturally divided into two starts, the gentleman and the simple men . . . The poor are destined to labor, and the rich, by the advantages of education, independence and leisure, are qualified to superior stations."

With the exception of a few radicals, Jefferson and Paine being the most famous ones, the vast majority of the Founding Fathers had little intention to share government affairs or property interests with the common people, as they considered themselves the proper guardians. They likened themselves to be more like philosopher-kings, right out of the pages of

Plato's *Republic*, with the right to govern the common people who they felt, according to University of Wisconsin's Merle Curti, were "ignorant" and dangerous." In this view, Adams attacked egalitarian principles of government and property as a "false and untenable conception of human nature."

Even James Madison, an intellectual elitist and moderate Federalist, labeled Adams as a *closet monarchist*. When it came to class differences, Adams stressed the inequality of men. From this starting point, he deduced that certain people are destined to rise to the top and others to sink into poverty. Biologically, individuals were physically and intellectually unequal. Society cannot keep a strong man or educated man down, and it cannot prop up a weak or uneducated man, unless through artificial means. Here than lie the seeds of "Social Darwinism" and "survival of the fittest," a defense for future robber-barons and the basis for the principles of heredity and IQ in determining the outcomes of life. Even worse, Adams argued in the *Essay on Davila* that society had the right to "establish other inequalities it may judge necessary and good." Here then, lies the future rationale for promotion business interests at the expense of the common people, shifting the burden of taxation on labor instead of wealth, and expounding "trickle down" theories of economics, which favor the rich under the guise that they provide jobs for the masses.

John Adams was good friends and sometimes on the same political wave length with Boston radicals like Sam Adams (his cousin), Sam Otis, and Tom Paine. Still, in his early volume, *The True Sentiments of America*, he expressed concern for mob action and the Boston "rabble," similar sentiments expressed by the more conservative minds of colonial America. Despite that he spoke in favor of justice, both as a lawyer and a politician, he believed (like many of his contemporaries who signed the Declaration of Independence) that the common people were inclined to be shiftless, vulgar, and unreliable and had to restrained and disciplined by legal and judicial authority. To his credit, however, he rejected kings and queens, and maintained that "the love of power is insatiable and uncontrollable . . . The only maxim of a free government ought to be to trust no man living with power to endanger the public trust."

His solution was to devise a system of checks and balances in government, a view similar to James Madison's, not only to curb the instincts of the powerful but also to curb the instincts of the mob. Although Adams feared the rise of an unprincipled financial oligarchy if the rich were allowed full reign, he supported property interests and naively believed the "well-born, and educated and disciplined to be free from the crudest temptations for self-advancement." He failed to understand that kind of reasoning, if unchecked, invites massive abuses and inequality.

In the final analyses, Adams believed (like most of the Founding Fathers) that democracy (one person, one vote) would ultimately lead to anarchy. Property rights must be preserved and government must be devised to ensure that the common people, who Alexander Hamilton would later call the "mob" and "herd," do not strip the upper class of their wealth and assets or interfere with their economic enterprises, which he felt was part of a sacred social contract. Adams was skeptical of the lower and working classes, feared mob rule and used the French Revolution and Jacobin radicalism as a example of the dangers of egalitarianism.

Despite his working-class and humble start in life, Adams lacked the ability to appreciate and communicate with the small farmer, shopkeeper, and soldier—each who shared their own common experiences and who put their lives on the line for the birth of the nation. Adams forgot the spirit of the Revolution and retreated into the arms of his wife, Abigail, for the advice and consolation. On the other had, Thomas Jefferson, our third president, despite his upper-class upbringing not only understood but also folded himself into the arms of the people and pushed the principles of the Revolution into practice. Adams saw the masses' potential breath of violence, especially as the French Revolution unfolded, whereas Jefferson knew they were grunts but welcomed the power of the people and appreciated their creative endeavors and loyalty to the new nation. The outcome is Adams was defeated by Jefferson in his attempt for the second term as president, and retreated to his farm in Massachusetts to live out his life, whereas Jefferson continued to affirm his greatness as a thinker and president for two terms.

During this period Adams and Jefferson rekindled their old friendship built around 1776 and the framing of the Declaration of Independence, and fermenting years before, and wrote hundreds of letters to each other describing their personal feeling and political views. For those of us who believe in fortunate cookies or fate, they both died on the same day, July 4, 1826.

Madison: A Roman Form of Government—A Republic

It rested on James Madison, the chief architect of the Constitution, to devise a republican form of government that would protect property interests and curb the ignorance and dangerous behavior of the masses. Madison is considered by many historians to be one of the two greatest statesmen of the revolutionary period, the other being Jefferson. Both were good friends who wrote thousand of letters (1,250 have been preserved) to each other over fifty-year period, lengthy discussions about political affairs and government.

Madison was concerned that the government, under the Articles of Confederation, could transform into a monarchy as it lacked a bill of rights and rotation of the office of president. His main purpose was to establish stability in the government, with checks and balances to prevent political mischief and corruption. But he rejected all proposals that would enhance power to the people, which he felt would substitute disorder for tyranny. In a republican government, fashion by Roman ideas, the people would delegate their power to a few to exercise for them.

As the liberal historian Bernard Bailyn reminds us, the advantage of a representative government over direct democracy (a Greek idea) would allow "people to delegate power to persons as unlike most of themselves . . . to persons distinguished by their abilities and talents, by the very talents that would lead voters to favor them." Hereditary privilege and power was a bad thing, agreed, but it was the "people with greater virtue, greater talent, and perhaps incidentally, greater wealth than their neighbors . . . whom the people should trust their government." He sincerely believed that this intellectual and economic elite would not be overcome by "irregular passion" and would resist popular pressure "until reason, justice, and truth [could gain] authority over the public mind." Along with other conservative minds, he believed that "the only thing the people by themselves could do about government was to destroy it."

Madison did not trust the common people and thus rejected the idea of direct democracy. He sought a representative republic, a larger electoral process with fewer representatives to make it "more difficult for unworthy candidates to practice with success the vicious arts, by which elections are to often carried." All well and good, unless you believe the common people are irresponsible and stupid and unable to discern the personalities and policies of one candidate from another.

Madison failed to recognize that not only are smart, refined, and wealthy people corruptible, but they cannot always connect closely to the interests of the poor, working and middle classes. In the end, people most often vote according to their self-interests, not the common good as Madison thought. People donate money to elected officials, not to promote democracy, but to promote their own agenda. The experience of the Roman Empire with the patrician and the plebian class, and the experience of the British parliament with the property class and the common class, are good examples where the rich and powerful draw a line to protect their own interests and where political power conforms to economic power (the same process exists today).

Like Jefferson, Madison believed in the natural rights of man, and in order to govern himself he must form a government of the people. But the people who hold power are capable of corruption and evil, and so government must be limited. "If men were angels," he wrote in the Federalist, "no government would be necessary. If angels were to govern men, neither external nor internal controls on government would be necessary." His method for limiting and constraining government was reflected in his view of the separation of powers, and by a host of checks and balances.

Government should be powerful enough to make laws and protect its people, and according to Madison (and his good friend Jefferson), the church and state must be separated to protect civil and religious freedom. Religion was construed as another form of politics, to be avoided because it would most likely arouse dangerous zeal. Although government was to be limited (and balanced) to protect the people, so was the church in civil matters, and thus individual rights could be protected in society. The idea was to cut down on all forms of political and religious zealousness and ideology of which many of our Founding Fathers were fearful, based on the history of the Old World. However, never forgetting his favorable sentiments toward the property class, Madison also maintained that, by limiting both the government and the church, there would be room left for the people to accumulate property and wealth without having to forcefully surrender it to the government or church. In a free society, people had the right o prosper by the fruits of their labor which would later be translated by modern-day conservatives as part of the theory of "free-market systems," "property rights" and "ownership society."

For Madison, the rights of ownership of property and the accumulation of wealth were considered inherent rights, by the new natural order, along with "life, liberty, and the pursuit of happiness," words embedded in the Declaration of Independence. Such *pursuits* involved property and wealth, and both were to be protected by the Constitution and Bill of Rights, which Madison was instrumental in framing. As the Fifth Amendment maintains: "Nor shall private property be taken for public use without just compensation."

Although Madison was not a Federalist, but a member of the Republican/Democratic Party, he helped write the *Federalist Papers*. Like the Federalists, Madison urged that a strong national government be formed that could put down rebellious movements that defied government. In this regard, Madison believed both the Shay's Rebellion in 1786 and the Whiskey Rebellion in 1794 were both populist rebellions by the debtor class and small farmers against the creditor class and property owners. He labeled the rebellions as "distressing" and "odious" and the rebels as "enemies of Republican Government." He described the participants, who had to be suppressed by the government troops, as "nothing more than riotous."

Jefferson, in one of his famous letters to Madison, argued that "a little revolution now and then is good . . . and necessary [to express] the rights of the people" and to prevent government from becoming too entrenched. (The reader must understand that Jefferson was a champion of the small farmer and states' rights.) Madison, always looking for national stability, would have certainly put down most future populist, labor, and civil rights movements that threatened the political and social order or the authority of the government. But in the end, to his credit, he managed to rescue the American Constitution from the hands of the conservative wing of the Federalists, who were intent on preserving privilege, rank, and inequality, as well as class differences between the manufactures, bankers, and property owners and those who were destined to labor and live off their sweat. Along with his good friend Jefferson, he drafted the Virginia and Kentucky Resolutions during the Adams administration (Adams tried to censure the newspapers), which protected freedom of assembly and the press against the Federalists.

PATRICIAN PRINCIPLES AND PROPERTY RIGHTS

The critics of democracy enjoyed a significant measure of influence before and after the signing of the Declaration of Independence in 1776 and the Constitution in 1787. The natural rights of man and the principles of liberty were constantly under attack by the ideas of past, English legalism and American theocracy, by property rights and the landed gentry. These conservative ideas were rooted in well-known British theorists of government such as Thomas Hobbes and David Hume, who were *absolutists* and who set forth a traditional interpretation of human nature, condemned democracy, and associated the rise of the common man with an increase in anarchy. Both men felt that chaos and civil strife would grip society if the new barriers of rank and heredity were broken down. Hume, in particular, sought to check the lower classes, fearing that they would become a beast or mob that would destroy the government.

The doctrine of natural rights of man, "the right of life, liberty, and the pursuit of happiness," the idea that "all men are created equal," a belief in a government consisting of checks and balances to help prevent the abuse of power, the equal right to own land, the right to assemble, the protest and express opinions, the devotion (and right) to education and self-improvement for plain people—all these principles that we take for granted today—did not come easy, and it was an uphill battle of ideas and for the minds of people. To be sure, the nobility and clergy had always felt superior to the common folk. It was the abstract ideas of the Enlightenment, with its emphasis on freedom, liberty, and tolerance, that broke the control of these twin classes and orthodoxies.

The eighteenth century in America saw the sweeping change from an *absolutist* conception of government, controlled by the aristocratic and theocratic class, to a *republican* ideal of government, based on democratic principles, representative government, and the "natural rights of man." In the process, the outdated concept of loyalty to the Crown and the notion of special rights of inherited nobility and property were overthrown for a government of the people. During this century, three political groups emerged: (1) aristocratic *Tories* with loyalty to England, who felt the "gentlemen" class who owned property were superior beings and should control government affairs, and in doing so maintain social stability; (2) *Federalists* and *Whigs*, conservative business people and professionals who supported the Revolution, but opposed a wide extension of democracy and were more concerned about their own businesses and entrepreneural interests than the interests of people; and (3) *Republican/Democratic* party who were concerned with expanding the natural rights of all white men, as well as the potential for education opportunity and self improvement. They were able to translate their ideas into stirring calls to action such as "Give me liberty or give me death."

The Tories

Tory thought was extremely conservative, linked to the spirit of the Anglican Church, the monarchy, and feudal vestiges of landholding. They were an influential minority who resented the growing body of farmers, mechanics, and other folks who were struggling for liberty. They were well bred, educated, and rich. They believed in the monarchy and envisioned the Revolution as a revolt against the mother country and against the Crown's authority. They had little respect for democratic principles and the notion of equality, or that privilege and power could or should be eliminated or checked from the natural order of society. In philosophical, political and social matters, they felt they were more English than American and sought to preserve the special status of the American colony in the English empire. According to historian Merle Curti they had no inclination to share wealth or property, or even "the intellectual and aesthetic values of which they considered themselves the proper guardians and patrons."

The Tories favored a two-tier system of education based on class, not necessarily on merit, where the sons of property owners and the wealthy commercial class would be favored for Harvard, Yale or William and Mary and the multitude would receive the rudiments of an elementary education, so a literate workforce would be available for an expanding economy. The Tories were obviously instrumental in squashing the democratic plans of Benjamin Rush and Thomas Jefferson, who favored a state plan of free education to ensure the education of *all* children in their respective states, Pennsylvania and Virginia.

The worst and most infamous of the Tories were Thomas Hutchinson, the last royal governor of Massachusetts, and Daniel Leonard, a Harvard graduate and lawyer, who like Hutchinson allied himself to the Crown, English Constitution, Bible, and divine authority of God and the church. Hutchinson was a descendent of Anne Hutchinson, but there was not the faintest spark of liberalism and idealism left in him. The historian Vernon Parrington in *The Colonial Mind* describes him as a "cold, arrogant, dogmatic, unimaginative, self-righteous individual," marked by reactionary politics, and with all "the enthusiasm of Mistress Anne washed clean out of the Hutchinson blood." He was the spokesman of New England gentry, always on the side of the monarch, resented liberal forces, and saw no reason to compromise or change. He realized Parliament did not represent the people, that it was controlled by the aristocratic and landed gentry, and espoused the Tory interpretation of the English law for the colonialists, which he knew was a sham. But that's the way he wanted it, and that's the way it is with people who have excess power. "He knew what was at stake in America—whether political control should remain in the hands of 'gentlemen of principle and property . . . or whether it should pass into the hands of the majority,'" which he labeled as the mob and unfit to govern.

Hutchinson's goal was to remake and merge the colonies into the British Empire along Tory lines, which would foster a "nobility appointed by the King for life." This, he felt in the end, "would give strength and stability to the American government." As royal governor, he often dispatched mail to England. Here is one of his memos written in 1770, just before the Revolution, cited by the historian J.K. Hosmer in the *Life of Thomas Hutchinson*. He describes a town meeting as a source of democratic dissatisfaction with the Crown, organized by "inferior people [who] meet together" in a mob-like atmosphere. "This has given the lower part of the people such a sense of their importance that a gentleman does not meet with what used to be common courtesy, and we are sinking into perfect barbarism . . . The spirit of anarchy which prevails in Boston is more than I am able to cope with."

The more the people of Boston petitioned and organized for their freedom, the more letters he wrote complaining about his fellow countrymen; the more political ground he lost, the more he pleaded for help from the Crown. He was convinced that the future welfare of America was linked to the subordination of the colonies to the mother country and the subordination of the multitude to the few. Boston radicals like Sam

Adams, John Hancock, Sam Otis, and Tom Paine would ruin the country and their petitions and acts represented "the madness of mobocracy."

To the end, Hutchinson held to his feudal beliefs, ingrained with aristocratic snobbery: Gentlemen with good manners over good wine resolve all matters of the state. When bricklayers and carpenters, vulgar in their appearance and habits, discussed such matters over their beer or cider, the atmosphere was ripe for anarchy. Hutchinson could sense the coming Revolution but he refused to compromise or recognize the fresh air of freedom. He was out of step and out of place in the new world; he grew more frantic, with fits of rage, as his feudal world collapsed.

In his own letters Daniel Leonard saw the rebellious spirit of the colonialists as unlawful, wicked and groundless, "dangerous to the peace and well-being of society." Influenced by Thomas Hobbes, who saw man in state of anarchy, in need of government to protect both person and property, Leonard felt that the ferment of rebellion was "the mischief-maker that unlooses all the evils of Pandora's Box." For Leonard, in letters that he wrote, "rebellion is the most atrocious offence, that can be perpetrated by man," which he saw as a cruel act against God and the Crown. The goals of the Federalists and Whigs were clear treason, he argued, and "postage . . . and duties imposed for regulating trade and even for raising a revenue to the crown" were appropriate.

Leonard, until his death, argued that "the king and Parliament" had only purest "intentions of justice, goodness, and truth . . . . They can only repeal their own acts, [and] there would be an end of all government, if one or a number of subjects, or subordinate providences . . . refuse obedience." By such logic, Leonard opposed all natural rights of the common person. He left the colonies in 1774, was rewarded with a post as chief justice of Bermuda, and died in London in 1829, as one of the last of the Loyalists.

Federalists and Whigs

If the Tories were a "10" in their belief of a natural aristocracy, a class structure based on a hereditarian principles, a reverence of good upbringing and good manners, and a belief that the masses were stupid, vulgar, and destined to toil and had limited use for an education other than the ABCs, then the Federalists were "8" or "9" and the Whigs were a

"6" or "7." Now that is a harsh analysis of early America, but it is rooted in thousands of years of history where in every society power has always been concentrated in the hands of very few people. The more man has struggled to sweep away his bondage, the more resistance he has encountered from the people who already have power and privilege.

The Federalists, led by Alexander Hamilton and John Adams, was the opposition party to the Republican/Democrats, the party of Jefferson. They disintegrated in the early 1820s, to be replaced by the Whigs who had gained increased influence by the turn of the nineteenth century and eventually became the opposition part to Andrew Jackson's Democrats. The Federalists and Whigs were gentlemen, perhaps not as well-bred as the Tories, but they were well-educated professionals and / or businessmen—who preferred a good political jingle or verse to the preaching of a sermon and a smooth glass of wine to a hearty beer. Their politics ranged from moderately to clearly conservative, not liberal or progressive, but many were willing to join with the Republicans/Democrats in the struggle for independence to protect their own economic interests. They were driven not by political idealism, but rather by their opposition to the stamp taxes and British trade restrictions because such polities interfered with their commercial and merchant interests. They attacked aristocratic Tory philosophy, the British imperial government, and the notion of royal and landowner superiority, which attempted to keep them from owning their own property and restricted their businesses and their ability to accumulate wealth (by imposing taxes). They accepted the traditional interpretation of man, a mix of Thomas Hobbes and Edmund Burke, in the context that democracy could lead to mob rule and that social class differences were largely based on innate intelligence and family background.

Most Federalists and Whigs felt the political writings of Sam Adams, John Hancock, Sam Otis, and Tom Paine were too radical, and they were concerned that he plebian mass might vulgarize government. Whereas radicals like Adams appealed to the yeoman, tradesman, and mechanic—the multitude of people—both the Federalists and Whigs rejected the concept of equality. They were in favor of overthrowing the monarch, and separating the church and state, but they wanted to limit democratic ideals by imposing a strong national government that would maintain order, limit taxes on profits, and favor business—sort of a stepping stone to the Republican platform of the twentieth century.

Whereas Thomas Jefferson and the radicals from Boston were concerned about expanding democratic principles, the Federalist and Whigs were more concerned about economic class interests and how the new economy would support business interests and function within the new government apparatus.

The two classes—Federalists/Whigs and Republicans/Democrats—might work together to overthrow British rule, but they were pretty much on opposite ends of the political and economic platform when it came to property rights, voting, education, and opportunity. The merchant and commercial class (Whigs) and aristocratic planters and seaboard manufacturers (Federalists) might welcome the support of the shopkeepers, artisans, and mechanics against grievous taxes, but the "high-born" would try to hold on to their accumulated wealth by ensuring no taxation and protecting free market systems—and by preventing the working class from voting, holding office, or sending their children to the Latin School and Harvard. Thus Sam Adams, who worked closely with Jefferson in securing the Bill of Rights, welcomed the election of his friend as a return to the democratic principles after an unhappy period of Federalists/Whigs control of the government, which he dubbed as the era of "prejudice and passion." In a letter, written to Jefferson in 1802, he warned: "You must depend upon being hated . . . because they hate your principles."

Colonial liberalism is hard to define, simply because there was such a wide group of diverse geographical and economic interests, social and religious thought, and political ideas—just like twentieth-century progressivism and liberalism are hard to define because of so many competing wings, subgroups and interpretations. Only a small group of Revolutionary leaders was consciously democratic. Our Founding Fathers were from gentlemen stock and mainly from the Federalists and Whigs class. The politics that united the southern planter and yeoman farmer and the Boston seaboard manufacturer and fisherman had more to do about British imperialism than political idealism.

In works like the Declaration of Independence, the Federalist papers, the Constitution, and the Bill of Rights, our Founding Fathers laid the foundation of the nation's freedoms and liberties. In doing so, they purposely separated religion from the public sector while providing a respectable place for morality and ethics in its place. Their intention to curtail religious ideology and dogma was based on European history and respect for Greek philosophy and the Roman legal system, as well as ideas of the Enlightenment that underscored the need to design institutions and laws based on tolerance, pluralism, and respect for the common good. Kings and priests would not be allowed to influence the public sector in the New World.

More to the point, our Founding Fathers were influenced by the Greek notion of truth, virtue, and justice, the Roman political system of checks and balances, and the seventeenth—and eighteenth-century British ideas of science and reason (Francis Bacon), commerce and industry (Adam Smith), property rights for common people (John Locke), protection of both individuals and minority rights in the face of the tyranny of the majority (John Stuart Mill), and separation of church and state as designed to protect the government and people from the power of religion (John Milton).

CROSSING SWORDS: HAMILTON VS. JEFFERSON

What follows is a brief survey of the ideas and thoughts of the leading Founding Fathers. Their secular humanist dispositions, abstract and radical voices about natural rights, and ideology of reason and morality reflect the best of European ideas. Raised as British subjects, they combined ancient Greek and Roman thought about human life and intellectual liberation with British social virtues of reason and progress to form a new nation, a new government, and new laws.

From the beginning two sets of ideas would emerge, ideas that would form the basis for modern life's ideological balance sheet consisting of the political Right and political Left: the federalist and anti-federalists, intellectual elitists and egalitarians, and conservatives and radicals. The battle lines of the "best and the brightest" were drawn. As the nation plunged into debate about its place in the world and its moral obligations to its people, the two opposing camps quickly emerged, dividing as to whether the new nation should be run by an aristocracy of the smart and well-bred money class or whether decisions should rest in the hands of the general mass that could not fully understand all the abstract and radical ideas being proposed and debated.

Each of the opposing camps had its champions, with Hamilton (and, to a lesser extend, John Adams) emerging as the chief spokesman on the political Right and Jefferson along with Paine (who was much more radical and controversial) representing the ideas of the political Left. Somewhere in the middle of the intellectual divide, that slippery and elusive center, were the likes of Ben Franklin and John Hancock. Whereas most historians would place Madison somewhere on the Left/Center, I would push his label more to the Right/Center; however; I am somewhat of a contrarian when it comes to the Founding Fathers.

The conservatives put their faith in the elitist ideas of statesmen, bankers, and manufacturers—the powerful and prestigious—in linking voting to property rights and in gradual change. The radicals wanted to push "the spirit of '76," insisting on an egalitarian agenda—a nation run by the working class and yeoman farmers, exactly what Hobbes and Hume and later Hamilton feared, a quasi-Marxist polity. The debate came down to whether the new nation should create and foster an economic pyramid with inherited privilege at the top or create and foster a sociology of virtue and egalitarianism. The promise of America for the radical or left wing of our Founding Fathers was that the Enlightenment, with its stress on human rights and human dignity, could emerge and fully blossom in the New World.

They believed there was a *natural order* of rights and freedom, as well as liberty and equality (words that sparked the American and French Revolutions), that had been hijacked for centuries by the monarchy and church. Metaphorically, we were "the chosen people." The natural order of the rights of man, as embodied in the principles of the Revolution and the framing of the Constitution and Bill of Rights, could gain a new birth in the New World. But the conservative wing had an affection for property, commerce, and competition, and in the modern world they represented the birth of corporations that rendered Jefferson's small businessman, shopkeeper and yeoman farmer powerless. Jefferson would have opposed the Wal-Mart and Kmart landscape, not only because it conflicts with nature but also because these giants threaten small businesses and shop owners.

To be sure, the American Right has always drawn its inspiration from Hamilton, and to a lesser extent from Madison and Adams. The American

Left has always drawn its inspiration from Jefferson, and to a lesser extent from Paine. In fact, it can be reasonably argued that the roots of American utopians of the nineteenth century and intellectual radicalism at the turn of the twentieth century, still common today in academic circles, can be traced to the ideas and vocabulary of Jefferson and Paine.

But history sometimes makes strange bedfellows. In the last forty-plus years, since the Barry Goldwater era right up the Newt Gingrich, Dick Cheney, and George Bush, the conservative side of the political aisle has selectively paraphrased Jefferson and Paine to vent their suspicions of a highly centralized government and support their claim that democratic values are universal and are to be defended throughout the world. The ideas of Jefferson and Paine were so radical and forbidding among the Tories and Federalists; nonetheless, they have gradually become part of the common coin of academic discourse and among some conservative thinkers today. Two cheers for Jefferson and Paine!

When it comes down to who's on first or second, that is whose ideas were most favored or most influential, it boils down to Jefferson and Hamilton. Henry Adams, perhaps the first American historian to work with archival documents, and Richard Hofstadter, perhaps the premier liberal historian of the twentieth century, both saw Jefferson as the early champion of democracy whereas Hamilton "considered democracy a fatal curse." Jefferson was human and thus flawed. Based on his Southern roots and political ambitions, he mildly supported slavery despite the fact that he sensed it would become a curse on the American landscape. In metaphorical terms, he wrote: "We have the wolf by the ear, and we can neither hold him, nor safely let him go." The remark is not forgotten by his critics, but is also reflects the predicament of the Old South; the South could not or would not free the slaves and the North would not permit them to hold on to them. Nonetheless, Jefferson had faith in the people to govern themselves, a radical and revolutionary idea at the time, whereas Hamilton wanted to hold on to the past and hold down the people, who he considered ignorant and did not trust.

Jefferson is also considered to be "the author of America," the most influential polemicist in shaping the nation's ideas and opinions. Hamilton is considered to be the first and foremost American banker and chief proponent of centralization and business efficiency, as well as critic of state governments (Jefferson's position), which he believed would lead to political problems and fragmentation. For conservatives, today, states' rights is another way of expressing their libertarian view of economics and disdain toward big government, fearing federal regulation. Conservatives also reject a strong federal government, fearing federal regulations, audits, and checks on big business. In varying degrees, America's political Right are partial-throated Jeffersonian-style political populists.

Alexander Hamilton: Limiting the "Mob"

Alexander Hamilton was perhaps the most influential Federalist; he had significant influence on the early birth of the nation because of his friendship and military staff relationship with George Washington. He believed in the worst of man, and supported the *Leviathan* state, Hobbes's theory that supported aristocratic and property interests over democratic interests. He was against local government such as town meetings, agrarian legislatures and village politics, for he felt they would reduce the power of the federal government. He sought a strong central government to enhance business and financial interests, at the expense of the masses, and to keep the common people in check who he labeled as the "anarchistic forces unleashed by the Revolution."

Hamilton is best known for establishing a national banking system, borrowing and credit system, and tariff policy to help expand business interests—all of which he associated with the growth of America. As a champion of manufacturing, he welcomed the idea of taxing the farmers and backwoodsmen, rather than taxing the business class, (sounds like echoes of Bushism) to raise money for the nation, thus precipitating Shays' Rebellion, which was a revolt led by farmers against the government. He encouraged long hours of labor, from sunrise to sunset, as well as child labor, arguing that the mills and factories were "nurses of virtue for lower-class children and women." He also proposed the idea of a militant Christian society to check the "Jacobian" influence on "American towns."

For Hamilton, if there was no rank, no authority, then there was no order; when there is no order, there is no society, and no government. Hamilton believed in the principle of hereditary and class domination; historically, the strong dominate the weak and they form into a master group. (The next leap is perhaps a little excessive, but the Nazis would call it a master race.) The master group will come to control the social, economic, and political institutions, "not only to further their interests, but to prevent the spread of anarchy which threatens every society." In the old days, according to Vernon Parrington, the "master group was a military order," then it "became a landed aristocracy," and in modern times it rests with commercial interest groups. "The economic masters of society of necessity become the political masters." It was unthinkable for the government to go against the wishes of the property class, for historically it would destroy government and lead to anarchy, for "no man or group of men will be ruled by those whom they can buy and sell." Here, then, is a perfect description of how money and politics are intertwined, and how people who control both the purse and political apparatus will resist the popular will and promote their own self-interests. Thus we have a near perfect storm—a rationale for Karl Marx to later advocate the worldwide revolt of the proletariat against the capitalistic class.

Hamilton argued that government must serve the property class and the interests of big business and capital; otherwise, who would invest, how would labor find employment, and how would the multitude in the cities feed themselves? "If the economic masters do not organize society efficiently, how shall the common people escape ruin?" His explanation was that the common people possessed limited human capacities and were stupid, and, therefore he had no faith in them. While practical businessmen, Federalists and Whigs bought into Hamilton's philosophy because it promoted their interests, the Republican/Democrats strongly opposed his ideas. For such opposition to big business, America remains thankful it had a sufficient number of political leaders who believed in the democratic process and were willing to curtail some of its abuses.

Here are Hamilton's own words in *The Federalist* papers: "All communities divided themselves into the few and the many. The first are the rich and well born, the other the mass of people." The Republicans (Jefferson's party) think God represents the people. Nonsense. "The people are turbulent and changing; they seldom [can] judge or determine right." For government to function, "the first class [must have] distinct, permanent share in the government body . . . to unsteadiness of the second." Coming close to the idea of an oligarchy, Hamilton argued that the masses would never pursue the public good, and "nothing but a permanent body [of bankers and industrialists] could check the imprudence of democracy. Their turbulent and uncontrollable disposition require checks." In a nutshell, Hamilton's views are pretty scary and mean spirited, dividing society in a way that the vast majority remain outside its borders and creating a permanent division between high and low humans. But, then there has always been economic divisions in society, a dominant class ruling a subordinate class. As the centuries unspool, there has always been class warfare—the rich against the rest of us. That has been the way of the world, since the beginning of civilization.

Thomas Jefferson: Natural Rights and Humanitarianism

If there is any one person we have to thank, for his wisdom and writing ability, it is Thomas Jefferson, who was the ultimate Renaissance man—a violinist, surveyor, architect, gentlemen farmer, expert horseback rider, wine connoisseur and collector of fine art and figurines, intellectual, lawyer, writer, and reluctant politician with a voice so soft you could hardly hear him from the podium. At thirty-four years old, he was entrusted by the Founding Fathers (who were putting their lives and fortunes at stake) to draft the Declaration of Independence.

Jefferson's basic thoughts were revolutionary: "We hold these truths to be self-evident, that all men are created equal." Here is the man that found the words to express the greatest aspirations of humanity, a few hundred words that are still debated today and inspire people around the world to rise up against monarchs, dictators, and tyrants. Here were the sentiments that expressed the most important truths about civilization—a philosophy of freedom rather than of predestination, one which believed in the basic rights of man and assurance that reason and natural law enabled man to control his universe and mold his destiny, as opposed to being coerced by government or religious doctrine.

Indeed, the ideas of the Enlightenment were congenial among the American common folk, the farmers, traders, and merchants—largely working class and middle class in composition. The ideas saw the good of the human spirit; they preached a freedom of the mind, not to obey the dictates of the church or state without considering the rights of people, to consider the moral implications and other rational choices—what democracy is about, at least from a liberal vantage point. But it was Jefferson who put it all together, who put his trust in the people, maintaining they had the most to gain or lose in the final analysis. In his notes to the people of Virginia, he maintained that the man with the plow had more "common sense" than members of the natural aristocracy of intellectual elite. Similarly, he felt the common person and small farmer, what he called the "yeoman," had an intense sense of *morality* and *justice* and could distinguish right and wrong just as well and "often better than the [political leader], because he had not been led astray by artificial rules," and, if I may add, political compromise and temptation of power and payoff.

Jefferson was the most intellectual and best-read American president; his library consisted of 6,500 books, an immense number for the period and equivalent to hundreds of thousands today if we consider the number of books now available. He was fluent in Latin, Spanish, and French, and he had the advantage of being influenced by both Locke and Rousseau, who were the driving force of the Age of Enlightenment. Both Locke and Rousseau had disdain toward the aristocracy, and both believed that the political order should be based on a contract between the people and the government, which would rule by the consent of the majority. It was Locke in the *Two Treaties of Government*, in 1689, who first argued that all persons possessed inalienable rights of "life, liberty, and property," and it was Jefferson who used the first two words and changed property to "pursuit of happiness" to frame the Declaration of Independence.

Rousseau argued for a secular society against an established church, which became one of the cornerstones of the U.S Constitution and the driving force for a secular system of public education. It was Rousseau who objected to distinctions based on wealth and property and preferred "noble savages," or common folk, free and uncorrupted by urban strife and social inequality. Although Jefferson would put greater faith in agrarian society than urban life, he would not condemn the accumulation of wealth and linked it to the establishment of government and national prosperity. He would also argue, as Locke and Rousseau had, for the national rights of citizens.

Jefferson's ideas went against the grain of many of his contemporaries who were politically influential and determined to limit the rights of the people, the masses who they felt could not be trusted. In the South, where plantation life and social elitism prevailed, and where there was emphasis on private schooling, the idea was to keep the black population ignorant and maintain a white working underclass. The libertarian and prevailing view was illustrated by Virginia Governor William Berkley, who in 1671 argued in a public document to the authorities that educating the poor would result in "disobedience and heresy" and bring conflict and "sects into the world . . . aimed at bringing down the government and property classes."

Few Americans in colonial America were qualified to vote at that time, with voting limited to those white males who were of the property class. Jefferson was willing to turn the prevailing system upside-down, emphasizing the natural rights of man and noting that human nature was not, as Thomas Hobbes insisted, egotistical and selfish, but on the contrary imbued with moral sense, humanitarianism, and the dignity of individual thought. Make no mistake, these ideas were revolutionary, given historical precedent of lack of universals that protected the common person and concentrated power in the hands of small elites with preservation of wealth and property uppermost on their minds (not much different than today).

And, in the North, there were several conservative thinkers—a mix of Tories and Federalists—who felt Jefferson's ideas of equality written in the Declaration of Independence and the Articles of Confederation were high-sounding, unrealistic sentiments that contradicted common knowledge and puritan scripture. Obviously, some people were not and never had been equal to others. So John Adams in *Essays on Davila* "attacked equalitarianism of both American and French leaders as unrealistic and based on a false and untenable conception of human nature." Democracy, for Adams, was "unworkable and considered a step toward anarchy." In *The Federalist*, Hamilton defended the need for "a strong central government to better serve the interests of the bankers and industrialists" against what he called the "mob." James Madison, another political giant and "Founding Father," stressed the innate diversities in the faculties and "the accumulation of property by the wellborn and educated." Indeed, Jefferson was often playing defense, trying to explain and defend his ideas.

Some fifty years later, even Alexis de Tocqueville, the champion and author of *Democracy in America*, qualified its merits and had a basic reservation toward excessive freedom and rights of the people. His aristocratic upbringing filtered through his political and social lens, leading him to believe that equalitarianism tended to promote the despotism of the masses and had the potential to limit property rights. And Plato, who for many philosophers and scientists is considered the father of rational thought, more powerful in his ideas than Zeus, was suspect of the masses and relied on philosopher-kings in administering and shaping society. Plato did not believe the people had the knowledge or virtue to govern themselves; rather they should be educated as warriors or workers, depending on their temperament and abilities. He put his trust in the state (seeds of fascism), whereby the state would take children away from parents to be educated in state-run schools (similar to Nazism and Communism). Plato, like Hamilton and Voltaire (Rousseau's alter-ego in the sense that Voltaire was a rationalist and Rousseau was a romanticist), mistrusted the "herd" (Hamilton's expression) and believed that the spirit of a nation always resides in a small number who put a large number to work and tell them that what to do (similar to the thoughts of the robber barons of the nineteenth century and free-market economists today).

Jefferson, who read Plato, disagreed and went against the tide of the times. He forcefully argued in "A Bill for the More General Diffusion of Knowledge," introduced in the Virginia legislature in 1779, a plan to educate both boys and girls and both common people and landed gentry "at the expense of all, [and of the need] for the talented to attend college"—and so was born the seeds of universal education. In the final analysis, Jefferson had great faith in educating the common citizen as a means for promoting democracy, for it was "the people [who] are the ultimate guardians of their own liberty." It is the kings and queens and nobility that could not be trusted to promote the interests of the ordinary people, and it was Jefferson who understood that Europe was flawed by its aristocratic beliefs, and that the hope of a new Athens laid on the shores of a wilderness called America, with its new breed of people—diverse in religion, ethnicity, class, and occupation. Hence, the nation would become the starting point, the shining star, in a global struggle to replace worldwide tyranny and misery with the ides of freedom and hope.

Jefferson and Hamilton: Yesterday and Today

Although Jefferson's reputation has been rapidly sinking from the twin leaks of Sally Hemings (who he supposedly slept with) and the larger issue of slavery, his defenders and those who know him well enough need to throw away their gags and make sure the American people are reminded what they owe him. Abe Lincoln put it most aptly: "The principles of Jefferson are the definitions and axioms of free society." On the other side of the political divide were Hamilton and the majority of Tories (and some Federalists) who were monarchists in disguise but knew this type of royalty was unacceptable to their countrymen. Nevertheless, their polemics came from the antidemocratic side and were motivated by fear of the multitude and a conviction that the "riff raff" could not govern. If given power, the common people would tax the wealthy and destroy all rank and privilege throughout the country.

Whatever lessons humankind learned from the little band of revolutionists who we call our "Founding Fathers," Jefferson best represents the enlightened wing, not only Greek democracy but also the Age of Reason, the natural rights of man, and faith in a government by and for the people. According to the well-known American historian Bernard Bailyn, by condemning Jefferson for his human flaws we commit political suicide—tough words from an aging historian whose books on the origins of the nation are considered classics.

In mathematical terms, if I may venture an educated guess, without Jefferson there is more than 50 percent chance there would be less democracy and more oligarchyism, less enlightenment and more elitism, characterizing American history and society. Whatever habits or compromises Jefferson made as a person, slave-owner or statesman, there would be no America as we know it without him—possibly no Revolutionary victory in the first place and no Constitution with teeth to protect the people. Most important, there would be no lessons learned from it by and for the rest of the world. Without Jefferson's diplomacy and writing ability, the more conservative convictions of Hamilton and his Federalist/Tory friends would have won the day.

Democracy is more fragile than we realize, and all we need to do is look at Latin America, Asia, Africa, or the Middle East to fully grasp how difficult it is to plan, implement, and maintain. It does not take a great genius to understand that democracy involves continuous vigilance and both protection and participation of the citizenry. The liberal ideas of Jefferson favored an appreciation of the common and less educated people who Hamilton and his rich friends considered as "inferior species." Jefferson believed that a favorable environment, such as the American countryside, nourished the best virtues of humankind and was an important ingredient for a democratic society and greater opportunity for plain people. Hamilton, as well as John Adams, George Cabot, John Jay, and Chief Justice John Marshall—all dyed-in-the-wool aristocrats snickering at the idea that environment might be more influential than heredity in determining merit and talent—attacked the egalitarianism of both the American and French Revolutions as unrealistic expressions of the masses.

Jefferson realized democracy was a messy process and involved give and take among different people and the natural rights of people built around the spirit of the Enlightenment. He wanted to humble the aristocracy and wealthy class in the New World and eliminate all vestiges of absolutism of both monarch and church of the Old World. He wanted to free the common people from the rule of a few people despite whether they were kings or clergymen. Hamilton's friends "loathed the mob," believed democracy led to anarchy, and agreed with his remark: "Your people, Sir, is a great beast." Given the dark side of historical interpretation, Hamilton and his buddies would have divided America into "have" and "have nots," elites who own property, equipment and capital and lower echelons working for cheap wages and churning out new goods for society—what free marketing and profiteering is all about.

There were many more wealthy elites and conservatives than liberals who participated in the framing of the Declaration of Independence, Constitution, and Bill of Rights. But Jefferson was the grandmaster chess player, who with the help of John Adams, who was almost twice his age and who he never knew until they both arrived in Philadelphia in the summer of 1776, and later in 1787 with the help of his friend and neighbor James Madison, was able to outwit and outmaneuver the conservative Federalists. Madison was to the principle architect of the Constitution, but Jefferson was able to address the fears of his contemporaries and win their confidence by asking a simple question: Having thrown off one ornamental and onerous government, would the people who met in Philadelphia saddle it with another?

The Federalist papers, chiefly authored by Alexander Hamilton, John Adams, James Madison and John Jay, advanced the debate between the Federalists (who wanted a strong central government) and the anti-Federalists (who promoted the rights of the states and individuals) and who argued, as Thomas Paine did in 1788 (and as Reagan claimed in the 1980s), "that government is best which governs less."

The polemics came from the conservative (and anti-constitutional side), led by Alexander Hamilton whose members felt they were superior to the masses who they considered an inferior lot; checks had to be devised to restrain the "rabble." It was considered fitting and proper for government to favor the wealthy business and merchant class in order to promote economic growth; the more restraints on business, the less growth. (Sounds like today's Republicans are familiar with Hamilton's ideas.) Nearly all the convention delegates sent to ratify the Constitution were men of wealth and property. Thus, according to Wisconsin historian Merle Curti, John Adams, (one of the more liberal Federalists) argued there was a "physical inequality . . . and intellectual inequality of the most serious kind," and thus society had the right "to establish any other inequalities it may judge necessary and good." Madison, who gets most of the credit for writing the Constitution, also emphasized "the innate diversities in the faculties of men" and the resulting "reasons for inequality of property and wealth."

Jefferson labeled the conservative delegates at Philadelphia as "monarchists" and "pro British"; in fact, Adams at one point during the early ratification stages of the Constitution wanted to call the president "His Elective Majesty" and provide special titles for cabinet members of the government. Jefferson and other liberals were labeled as "pro French" and "Jacobins" (or radicals), ignorant of human nature and unrealistic in their egalitarian beliefs that man had natural and basic rights in legal, political, and social matters. In order to try to discredit Jefferson and his ideas, the Federalists and conservatives spread rumors and insulted him about his alleged intimacies with slave women (not much different than what the opposition did to Clinton's character and how his liberal policies became sidetracked).

Once his critics mixed race and sex, Jefferson knew his response would be a lost cause and he remained silent; the allegations continued into his presidency. Just as the clergy, mainly conservative, attacked Jefferson for his loose morals and vomitous behavior, the religious Right of the 1990s defamed Clinton. Jefferson refused to respond to his critics. Had he responded, he could have taken down two-thirds of the Southern aristocracy and half the Founding Fathers who owned plantations and "messed with women." Clinton responded and was almost impeached. Like it or not, Jefferson is the spirit of American democracy (and universal education). His legacy stands despite his alleged intimacies with one or more slave women or his position on slavery (which he repeatedly warned his neighbors and legislators was contradictory to democratic principles and would come to haunt future legislators and eventually lead to what I call the Second Revolution).

The republican form of government that emerged became a fight between aristocratic and patrician beliefs and much larger number of ordinary "yeomen" and plebian ideas; between gentility and civility on one end of the social ladder and vulgar routine people on the bottom; between those representing the business and money interests and those committed to the public welfare; between Federalists who sought a strong national government and the anti-Federalists who opted for states' rights and local interests. The political and intellectual conflict could be summed up as a sword fight between Hamilton and Jefferson.

As the Revolution gained momentum, and as the Founding Fathers filed into Philadelphia (it took about two weeks on horse to ride from Boston to Philadelphia) and formed the government, there was an assault on privilege and rank that had never been experienced in humankind and on the social bonds that characterized the early royal ties of the Tories with England and monarchial society. The notion of he natural rights of man, with liberties and laws and a sense of justice and equality, became embedded in the discussion of the new republic. It competed with the idea that the freedom won in the Revolution meant freedom to make as much money as possible and to restrain the irresponsible and plain people that Hamilton and other conservative Federalists and Tories feared would foster anarchy and bring down the republic.

Class differences did not die or evaporate after the Revolution; in fact, it might be argued by revisionist and radical historians that it increased as people competed for the riches of the country. But everyone had the opportunity, at least if you were white and male, to acquire property and improve one's station in life. Social distinctions (not necessarily economic differences) began to disappear. Every American citizen, including the most common and lowly, thought himself equal to the next person in terms of natural rights and before the law. Regardless of birth or rank, anyone who did not work was suspect and lost favor in the public eye. As the yeoman class worked and prospered (Jefferson's ideal American), the business and banking class (Hamilton's ideal citizen) realized that the new government had moved beyond traditional republicanism to a belief in equality that would transcend and become part of the nation's fiber.

Gordon Wood, professor of history at Brown University, summed up the new social and economic situation: "Equality became so potent for Americans because it came to mean that everyone else was really the same as everyone else, not just at birth, not in talent or property or wealth . . . Ordinary Americans came to believe that no one in a basic down-to-earth . . . manner was really better than anyone else." The dignity of the common man had been elevated to a status that was unknown and never as high that any other nation had ever had it.

The Revolution and new government did not do away with social and economic distinctions, but it gave the common man a new pride and power, new opportunities, and multiple chances to succeed. The new experiment, the United States of America, amazed foreign visitors who came to observe the social conditions and institutions of the nation. The two most famous were the French scholar Alexis de Tocqueville who between 1835 and 1840 contrasted the "nobility class and permanent inequality" of Europe with principles of democracy and equality in the New World and the British scholar Lord James Bryce who wrote fifty years later that the United States had reached "the highest level, not only of material well-being, but of intelligence and happiness which the race has yet attained."

CONCLUSION

The new nation was never supposed to be a perfect or utopian society; it retained a host of inequalities and inequities which have and still do shape the American populace. The ideas of Jefferson, rooted in the Enlightenment, could only go so far in a world where the human condition is susceptible to flaws, weakness and temptations, but it did generate a new form of equality and respect for talent, hard work and merit. It is these intellectual and social ingredients that have provided fuel for the American engine—and for the nation's optimism and hustle, invention, and innovation, productivity and standard of living which cannot be matched anywhere in the world or in history.

We shall never escape from the historical clash between Jefferson and Hamilton, for their opposing ideas still filter through today's sentiments and language in the political arena, the media and on college campuses—simply under the labels of liberal and conservative. Rather than try to sanitize the sentiments of Jefferson and Hamilton, and defend or praise liberal or conservative beliefs, it is safe to say that the Revolution and the government that was formed has had the most-far reaching effects on the world stage. It still does, as the Paul Krugmans and Robert Reichs of contemporary America cross swords with the David Brooks and William

Kristols in newspapers, on cable television, and in college classrooms. The compromises that resulted among the Founding Fathers represented by the ideas of Jefferson and Hamilton set in motion the most important series of events since the rise and fall of ancient Greece and Rome, affecting more people and more nations that any other nation in history.

One more thought, one more comparison between Jefferson and, this time, Lincoln, as these two presidents shaped American history more than any other president. Regardless of the version of the story you prefer and which gray-haired expert you listen to, I would say Jefferson and Lincoln rank among the greatest presidents—best agents of their time and America's destiny. Both men consciously sought power, possessed a rare sense of timing, and were able to accomplish their political purposes. Both presidents understood the complex feelings of common people, ordinary Americans, and both recognized and elevated the dignity of man and strengthened by reading such writers as Locke, Rousseau and Voltaire. Jefferson and Lincoln were against slavery, although Jefferson, in context with his southern roots, advocated gradual emancipation.

While Jefferson was concerned about forging a Union, free of the ancient inequalities of the Old World, Lincoln was focused on preserving the Union and came off much less likable to the enduring rural, agrarian South which was Jefferson's political base. Jefferson distrusted the urban centers of the world, as products of the inequalities of man. Lincoln accepted the cities and factories and reluctantly the inequalities revealed—all the dangers Jefferson as his cofounders of the Union had feared. Both presidents promoted the idea of progress. Jefferson saw it in the uncontaminated wilderness, beyond the frontier, the ideal setting for a new type of society in which poverty and the entrenched inequalities of a settled society would vanish. The final blow of the Revolution meant the end of the feudal relationships that existed in the Old World, exemplified by heredity privilege, the inequality of property ownership and material possessions and the subsequent selfish strife of the rich and the suppression of the working masses.

Lincoln saw progress of the human race by eliminating the evils that accompanied slavery. The Civil War, he felt would eventually make America the greatest land by reason of its suffering and sacrifices. America would be the land where all its people had the chance to freely work, to strike poverty and misery from their lives, and turn the ambitions of ordinary people into lofty ideals while striking down greed and avarice.

Although America was transformed into the world's largest and fastest growing economy after the Civil War, he failed to grasp the full force of the Gilded Age and the unchecked power of the "robber barons" who grew rich beyond imagination.

These captains of industry—the Rockefellers, Vanderbilts, and Goulds—would nearly overturn American democracy, as the cult of success and self-made man would turn into ruthlessness and corruption to create fortunes for a few, miserable working conditions for the masses and massive inequality between the rich and the rest of Americans. The advance of the capitalistic enterprise during the last thirty years, often labeled Gilded Age II by this author, would come to characterize the same greed, corruption and brutality of this early type of entrepreneur (robber baron) and economic period (Gilded Age I). Of lust for speculation and private gain, and with little concern for the public good, the new captains on Wall Street and in banking, now called the "masters of the universe," would wind up nearly crippling the American economy and turning the global economy into shambles.

As we close the chapter on the Revolutionary period, and the conflict between patrician thought and equalitarianism, we shall move our story in the following pages from the post Civil War period to the early decades of the twentieth century. Here we shall focus on the masters of capitalism and organizers of the nation's economy, as well as examine this bridge or period of time which links us to the present—Gilded Age I to Gilded Age II.

Chapter 4

QUESTIONS TO CONSIDER

1. What historical period characterizes the first Gilded Age? The second Gilded Age?

2. In what ways are the first and second Gilded ages similar? Different?

3. Who were the major robber barons of the Gilded Age I? Gilded Age II? In what ways are the robber barons of the early period similar to the current titans of industry and masters of the universe?

4. Which historians view the Gilded Age as little more than a political spoils system, whereby big business and big government are in cahoots with each other and where labor and ordinary people are exploited and victimized? How does this perspective coincide with the current view of Main Street vs. Wall Street?

5. Which historians view big business practices of the Gilded Age as ethical and essential to American prosperity and the robber barons as heroes and patriots? How does this perspective coincide with the current view that American business needs to be free of government restrictions

6. How do westward expansion and the taming of the frontier in the nineteenth century coincide with the notion of evolution and rugged individualism in business and the growth of America?

7. In what ways do critics view unfettered capitalism as exploitative and part of a class struggle that extends beyond Marx to the dawn of civilization?

8. In what ways do proponents view capitalism as essential to the growth of democracy, which also extends beyond the American borders?

9. To what extent do you believe (or reject) the notion that capitalism needs to be reformed, checked or regulated in order to protect ordinary people or the public from mischievous people or from the economic elite?

10. How do Henry Adams, Mark Twain, Thorestein Veblen and Scott Fitzgerald describe the wealthy class of Gilded Age I? In what ways to their descriptions coincide with today's super rich, that is, the wealthy class of Gilded Age II?

11. How do the ancient warlords, later the dukes and earls of Old Europe, and now masters of the universe, differ in their practices? Or, are their attitudes and behaviors similar?

12. How does the notion of the American dream restrain ordinary people from revolting against the super rich and the system today?

13. If people have unequal talents and abilities, does it automatically follow that entertainers, bankers, and corporate executives are entitled to their millions?

14. Should safety nets and social programs exist to provide orderly people (who cannot run a swift race) a chance to live a decent life?

15. Do corporations and Wall Street serve the public interest? Or, do they redistribute money from the bottom to the top of pyramid, from the worker to the money class?

16. In what ways have new inventions and technology increased productivity on a national level while lowering the standard of living for most Americans?

Chapter 4

GILDED AGE I AND II

The most persistent historical controversy in American business has centered around the Gilded Age, a period between the post-Civil War and turn of the twentieth century, along with the critics and defendants of the "robber barons" concept of big business. Far from being an academic exercise, this controversy has extended at various times to how Wall Street and banking applies its insatiable appetite for profits—and how government is either corrupted or remains indifferent to the predatory activities of modern-day robber barons.

The discussion focuses on some of the major issues centering around the Gilded Age. From this discussion, the writing will extend into the present which recently experienced the worst financial meltdown since the Great Depression, and what some commentators have dubbed as "Gilded Age II." Although finance and housing are different from railroads, steel and oil, there is today a striking similarity of speculation and quick profits, unethical schemes, looting of corporations, display of wealth, income inequality, special lobby interests and subsidies, and corruption of legislative bodies through donations and side deals that is reminiscent to the robber barons of the Gilded Age. Carnegie, Gould, Rockefeller and Vanderbilt were robber barons of the past, but their ruthless tactics have reappeared, much like "ghost riders in the sky," represented by different horsemen with new names, faces and accents. As in the past, we are told that the new robber barons were overseeing multibillion dollar companies and doing great things for the country.

Here we are not talking about a few "bad apples"; just about the entire system today is rotten—driven by unusually excessive fees, erroneous earnings and false profits, and the lack of independent audits and regulation. The only people consistently benefiting are today's robber barons—the executives of large firms and financiers with huge salaries, bonuses and retirement packages—regardless of whether their firms or financial institutions are profitable. The advance of business and the enormous profits obtained by a tiny few, to be sure, is associated with both economic periods, as is a corrupt or indifferent government, one that develops a rationale or justification for not restraining a capitalistic enterprise which puts a premium on speculation, get rich-in-any-way-you-can, and cheating investors and consumers.

We can use different names to justify this triumph of business—"law of the jungle," free markets or free enterprise, small government or "invisible" government—all which represent the seeds of self destruction since people cannot be trusted (to do the right thing or act ethically) when the emphasis is on materialistic and acquisitive values. This is an inherent problem with capitalism, and unless the players are regulated or actually fear the arm of the law, the people with power or political connections (and big customers who expect secret or inside information) will often exploit and fleece the ordinary worker, consumer, and investor. Greed corrupts, money corrupts, and power corrupts! It's American as apple pie, and it's world wide as time is memorial.

INTELLECTUAL ROOTS OF INEQUALITY

The division between social reformers and defenders of the Gilded Age is mainly reflected today in the differences between liberals and conservatives. If we revisit the skeletons of the American past, the differences can also be traced to the opposing philosophical views of Jefferson and Hamilton and even further back into time when the U.S. was merely an outpost for the Dutch and English trading companies. On one side of the coin is the moral argument for the rights and general good of the people as investors, consumers and citizens, and the need for a more equitable distribution of wealth. On the other side is a set of assumptions and a defense of the forces of property, capital and industry, despite the natural and immutable outcomes of inequality, and the persistent desire for power and money by a favored few under the guise of growth and productivity.

But just as there are two sides to a coin, or the Eastern notion of ying and yang, there are at least two opposing interpretations of history and human behavior. On the negative side, we have a bunch of hustlers, adventurers, and arrogant individuals who were born at the right time (call it luck) and took advantage of the period. They were able to successfully mix vision and brains with greed and hubris to achieve massive wealth at the expense of people without competitive spirit, and only labor to offer in return for wages. On the positive side, it can be argued that such men were great figures who were part of the last segment of the rise of industrialism, jump started by the textile, iron and coal industries in Britain in the early 1800s, which then spread throughout Europe and across the Atlantic in the mid century where there was more land, resources and opportunities for men of talent to invent and innovate. Here we must give credit where credit is due to a few individuals scattered in America and throughout the world who had the spirit, guts and intelligence to take advantage of a paradigm shift in society.

If we take a trip down memory lane, we might recall that our New England church leaders can be cheered for their humanitarianism, pacifism and charity, but they can also be chastised for their absurdity, mysticism and for imprisoning the minds of their followers with irrational thinking that was antithetical to the values of the Enlightenment. They can also be criticized for their economic precepts which proclaimed the ways of the rich and well-to-do were noble and the poor should be satisfied living their lives by deprivation and toil.

And so, Joseph Morgan, the self-proclaimed spokesman of the Lord argued in 1732 that the poor should be "content with their station" and that the rich had a "miserable life . . . full of Fear and Care . . . whereas a man that have but food and Raiment with honest labor, is free from the fears and cares." But then there was the social reformer and Quaker preacher John Woolman, who declared in 1754 the Christian virtue of a "just distribution of a man's worldly goods, that excessive riches and abject poverty led to endless ills" in society.

One hundred years later in 1859, Francis Bowen, the conservative Harvard philosopher declared that great wealth was a moral right, "following from Christianity and humanity." He recognized and accepted "the aggregation of immense wealth at the end of the scale, and the increasing amount of hopeless poverty at the other," so long as the rich exhibited personal virtues and "exercises of sympathy . . . common brotherhood . . . and [giving] largely to public charities." During the same period, the labor leader Thomas Skidmore of New York maintained the need to "redress the economic grievance of the working class," and that if we failed to reform the system of production and distribution of wealth, "the American worker would be in the same desperate condition that darkened the existence of his fellow worker in England" and the rest of Europe.

At the end of the twentieth century in 1896, the conservative E.L. Godkin, editor of the *Nation* maintained that he knew of "no more mischievous person than a man who in free America, seeks to spread . . . the idea that they [the workers] are wronged and kept down by somebody; that somebody is to blame because they are not better lodged, better dressed, better educated." In the meantime, the liberal counterpart and social critic, Charles Francis Adams, a descendent of John Adams, expressed general disdain toward the new money class and giants of industry who defined national destiny in terms of *laissez-faire* economics and self interest. "I have known . . . a good many successful men—'big' financially—men famous during the last half century . . . Not one that I have ever known would I care to meet again, either in this world or the next."

What we have here is a split that divides America on a philosophical and economic grounds, rooted in 250 years of history (before Jefferson's and Hamilton's day), and clouded today in cultural and faith-based differences and shades of Gray and Blue that go back 150 years ago. If you put history in perspective, despite the fact that some critics argue that history is nothing more than a struggle between the privileged class and the common people, there is a better chance to appreciate the reformers (liberals) and defenders (conservatives) of the period: The public outcry to expose the economic evils of the day and expect some opposing army of people or government to limit and possibly punish abusive and fraudulent practices of powerful titans in business and finance; and the conservative defense that ignores business and government abuses and welcomes free markets and free competition.

The $64,000 question is how many common people are willing to voice their concerns in public and storm the barricades—a constant struggle between those who are too busy or complacent and need to work in order to survive and those who have the power and money. This has nothing to do with Marx or any other type of "radicalism" or liberation movement. It's a daunting issue that goes back to the dawn of civilization and became part of a hopeful struggle during the Gilded Age. But here is the rub. In America, and a few other democratic countries, you would like to think there is hope. You can invite parties to the table, talk until you are blue in the face, offer heaps of pabulum and proposals, and produce a flurry of government reports. In reality, however, very little is accomplished until there is a major political or economic crisis, or until the system feels threatened. And, whatever is achieved rarely lasts once the crisis subsides; the wonks of greed, arrogance and corruption rear their ugly heads, as evidenced by the repetition of overheated markets, followed by fear and panic, recessions and depressions, and the breakdown of the broad public interest and overall growing inequality in America and the world. Anything in the name of social welfare or reform is trumped by market forces and the privileged class—and by the lack of power of the working class.

The social reformers of the Gilded Age were hopeful that their ideas would eventually be incorporated into the political and economic system. Their platform and starting point can be traced to post Appomattox, followed by the Westward movement and increase of population in the American heartland.

The Ebb and Flow of Ideas

The first Gilded Age can be analyzed according to the biases of authors (Chapter 1); in Hobbesian terms or the American dream (Chapter 2); and by socialist and progressive criticism or conservative and capitalist defense, which is rooted in the different philosophies of Jefferson and Hamilton (Chapter 3). These different broad themes help the reader because one explanation or variable to describe an economic practice or historical era lasting several decades is hard to defend or convince others that it represents the best interpretation. No doubt there are elements of truth in each explanation, but none by themselves offer a satisfactory interpretation of a politically changed and complicated period. Let me start with the biases of authors, since a liberal perspective filters through my own analysis.

As historians go, the best know criticism of the gilded Age is Vernon Parrington's *Main Currents in American Thought* and Charles and Mary Beards' *The Rise of American Civilization.* These historians view business people as greedy and manipulative, at best selfish, dishonest, and able to buy off politicians and to take advantage of the political spoils system, and at worst exploitative toward labor, fraudulent and corrupt with other people's life savings, piling up profits and engaging in monopolistic practices at the expense of the public. This analysis tends to coincide with the view on Main Street and the current thoughts of the *Nation, New Republic,* and *Dissent.*

As a side note Parrington used maritime metaphors to express his contempt toward the robber barons, describing them as "ruthless" and "predatory," comparing them to "capitalistic buccaneers," "pirates," and later injecting "Captain Kidd" into his description of them as villains. The Beards relied on medieval metaphors such as the "barons of business" and "the new capitalist baronage" who would "put on armor and vanquish [their competitors] in mortal combat [or] sometimes hire strong-arm men" to do their dirty work. In short, both expressed contempt toward American business practices and stereotyped business men as malefactors of society who had no interest in the great mass of people, who robbed them in the name of free enterprise, and who manipulated stocks, intimidated workers, and made secret agreements with corrupt politicians.

In defense of big business and the Gilded Age, we have Richard Hofstadter's *Age of Reform* and Alan Nevins' *Study in Power.* Their perspective is that we need businessmen in order for the nation to prosper. Most of them are respectable and ethical in their practices and the pressure for profit runs all through American culture and not just big business. Most of the robber barons were not robbers but American heroes, as well as forerunners and builders of America and prestige. This analysis would coincide with Wall Street and the current views of *Forbes, Fortune* and the *National Review.*

As another side note, Hofstadter and Nevins were expressing values dear to the hearts of many Americans of property and position, and many others (average Americans) who saw dangers in restricting free enterprise and in new formulas and proposals for reform. They were not concerned about their pocketbooks, because they had little money in them, but were hoodwinked about the harm that would come to poor people and working people through social planning and "general pampering." American business had to be free of restrictions. The moral fiber of the country and American initiative and individualism would be hindered; the American dream would be impaired.

If you want to laugh, two famous historians claim neutrality in their discussion of American business during the post Civil War years—Frederick Jackson Turner and Merle Curti. Both professors taught at the University of Wisconsin and adopted a theory of the frontier, and the importance of westward expansion—tied to the expression of equality, rugged individualism and the growth of America. Turner believed in laws of evolution, natural selection, and "survival of the fittest" as part of the development of American civilization and the new breed of businessmen who built America. Despite Turner's belief in neutrality, he was a major supporter of the robber barons that he saw as an extension of American nationalism and prosperity. In fact, I would argue that he envisioned the robber barons as an extension of the rough-riding and flag-waving Yankee man who fought for God and country and grabbed the Indian and Mexican lands, what most of us in school called Manifest Destiny and Teddy Roosevelt later called the *Winning of the West*.

Curti, who held the position of "Frederick Jackson Turner Professor of History" at the University of Wisconsin, thought he was also kind of neutral since he relied on primary sources such as letters, diaries, church sermons and newspapers to build his arguments. Nevertheless, he had an inborn inclination to criticize the robber barons as immoral and defend the rights of the laboring man and small yeomen farmer, and to see the rich growing richer and the poor and working people growing poorer—even in the midst of prosperity. To a large extent he conformed more to the Jeffersonian model of democracy than Turner's view of adaptation and natural selection—a Darwinist point of view.

Other than my working-class roots and my liberal education, I have no other conscious reason to see unfettered capitalism (with no restraints or controls) as exploitative and part of a class struggle that goes way beyond Marx and extends to the dawn of civilization. Of course, if I had come from the farm belt or a small auto town in Ohio or Indiana, I would have more good reason to feel the pinch of depression and disgust since the small farmer and small town resident have always been subservient to the rest of the economy. "It's nice to live in a rich man's world," to paraphrase the Swedish rock group Abba. Thanks to technology, the accelerated pace of communication and the rise of global markets, a few innovative corporations and financial institutions are able to take advantage of business opportunities—often by driving down wages, eliminating jobs, and impoverishing people and communities. To this extent, Wall Street and Wal-Mart have the same ability to bankrupt firms, crush opponents, and destroy people and towns, what Robert Reich calls "supercapitalism." Companies like Goldmen Sachs, Blackstone and the Caryle group have similar power to manipulate financial markets and destroy a person's pension fund, while top executives of these firms have became celebrities and their donations and parties appear on gossip pages and TV shows like "Squak Box" and the "Kudlow Report".

Although the notion of common good has disappeared from business practice, most barons of business and captains of banking are polite and preppy on a personal and social level. Their lavish parties have a certain cache, dress code and etiquette. Once in a while the conversation is about lineage, but mostly about safe subjects—school and community life, summer camp, gardening and golf. Their conversation, indulgence and genteel traditions parallel Scott Fitzgerald's *This Side of Paradise* and *The Great Gatsby*. As for the dark side, their disintegration of human character to a competitive and ruthless norm is well depicted in Theodore Dreiser's *An American Character*. In a democratic society, we should hope that everyone might expect a moderate well-being with reasonable chance of opportunity and success, and that capitalism not be the source of inequities and human injustice. We would hope that people making hundreds of millions and billions would be willing to pay higher income tax.

A Mini Digression

In a lesser known academic book, Thorstein Veblen, the economics professor from the University of Chicago (the University built by Rockefeller money) best described the new wealthy class in the *Theory of the Leisure Class*, published at the turn of the twentieth century. He dissected the norms and behaviors of the new moneyed class of Americans, characterized by enormous wealth amassed in a short time. The age of industrialization, accompanied by new markets and new jobs, allowed business people to accumulate huge profits, compete for prestige and mimic the habits of the European nobility. This class wasn't supposed to take hold in America, because there was little or no lineage and dynastic wealth. He coined the term "conspicuous consumption" to describe the desire for people to display their wealth, to intimidate and impress others.

And, 110 years later, Veblen's description is just as relevant for describing America's new rich (and even much of the old rich) who have a passion for big mansions and big yachts and are more than willing to drop $500 for a bottle of wine (while entertaining others), $5,000 for a Gucci handbag, or $10,000 for a polo watch—the latter sum which represents more than the annual earnings of 9/10s of the world population. So long as you are a Darwinist—or a believer in free markets and free enterprise—people who make money can spend it anyway they want and buy bigger and more expensive goods and services.

But Veblen analyzed the economy as a zero-sum game, "the accumulation of wealth at the upper end of the pecuniary scale implies privation at the lower end of the scale." That might seem too simple for conservative thinkers or the upper crust to swallow. If you believe that the wealthy class invest and create jobs, that there are sufficient safety nets such as unemployment compensation, welfare programs and social security, or that the rich and superrich donate and support social and educational institutions, then the economy is functional, fair, and efficient; it needs no government adjustment nor monitoring.

The fact is, however, people at the top of the pyramid are continuously redistributing wealth from the common people to their own pockets (This is the history of human kind.), allying themselves with those who run the political system, writing self-serving rules concerning investments, credit, insurance and banking. Even when the day of reckoning comes, and markets tank, the people in charge of corporate capitalism and finance manage to recover or get rescued by the system. When Washington bailed out Wall Street in 2008 and 2009 and spent billions to assist the "masters of the universe" who bankrupted the nation and created the economic meltdown around the world, it was the ordinary worker who paid the bill. Money was redistributed form the bottom of the pyramid to the top. The executives from Wall Street and banking had engaged in legalized thievery—and made off with hundreds of millions, while leaving the rest of the nation in ruin and putting the whole global economy at risk. The outcome in the U.S. was millions of homes in foreclosure, millions of jobs lost, and billions and trillions of savings and pensions vanished. The rest of the world saw a system of government, which was supposed to regulate, monitor and hold people accountable, that allowed the robber barons of the twenty first century complete immunity and placed the rest of the world in jeopardy. Inshort, no one responsible for the economic melt down was held accountable.

The people who should have known better did know better, but concentrated power of big government and big banking, as well as greed and arrogance prevailed over caution and morality. Money, money, money—the ringing of the till—was the paramount norm that drove the passions of the money-making people. But that's how it always has been, so why expect anything different from chief executives, bankers and brokers just because they worked in large "institutions" or wore pin stripe suits instead of military armor. What makes these people more civilized, more law abiding or more honest is only the fear of the law. Simply put, regulations and laws with teeth are needed to restrain super-capitalists; it is naïve to count on ethics, morality or self-policing.

These are people who evolved from the ancient warlords who once roamed the countryside, plundered villages and towns and collaborated with the monarchs for titles and possessions. Since the dawn of civilization, nations have swaped the rule of one tyrant for another, one group of warlords for another. Today the "masters of the universe" work out their deals with Congress, the Swiss banks and other power centers and institutions of the world—by bending the laws and hiring lobbyists and consultants to serve their interests. In the world of giant firms and financial institutions, it has reached a point when it is impossible to distinguish where policy ends and crime begins, where people should read the fine print and lies start, where robber barons compensate themselves with large bonuses and golden parachutes and books are cooked to paint glowing stories and defraud investors and stockholders.

Obviously not all Wall Street players, bankers and corporate CEOs are crooks and cheats. There are many hardworking, honest executives who try to do the right thing. Most of us, it is safe to say, would not finger all corporate chieftains and investment bankers and hedge fund managers as villains. There are some "good" guys (and now women) who consider the welfare of workers, stockholders and the public interest on the basis of equality, fairness and justice. Nonetheless, the history of civilization is a conflict between the predatory and industrious, a conflict in attitude and behavior which shifts in the form of brute force and fraud, to the talent and skills of those who are bound by ethical principles and hard work. In this contemporary moneyed culture, we would be hard pressed not to find more people who are corrupted by power and money than who are concerned about the general good. Few people who sit on millions and move it around in various transactions are worried about ordinary people who work for a wage and are just trying to earn enough for a descent life.

BARONS AND DREAMS IN COLLISION

It should be recognized that the robber baron image is an outgrowth of criticism toward big business during the second half of the nineteenth century that coalesced with Social Darwinism and stuck and became part of the historical and economic folklore. However, a case can be made that the image is an extension of the old European warlords who plundered the countryside, where the fittest would survive and the unfit would be eliminated. The warlord legacy later became part and parcel of the nobility class. In turn, bloodlines, breeding and eugenic theories led to the conversation of robber barons who often traced their lineage to Anglo-Saxon families and the European nobility class. Among the early New York and New England elite, class distinctions and family property was traced to the Old World.

What we have here is the bleak concept of the economic and social order which presumes that most of humanity, including Americans, exhibit the same behavior and live by the same rules. The strong and venturesome seek power and possessions and the masses merely try to survive. Why should America be different? From the earliest times ordinary people lived on the verge of starvation. They were handicapped by poverty, famine, and disease; they had no land, equipment or capital to improve their lot.

But America was "the Promised Land." The Declaration of Independence stated that all men were created equal. The Constitution provided basic rights and liberties for Americans, rich and poor. In reality, however, you have to ask yourself, when and where did that the labor class, small farmer and artisan have equal bargaining strength with the money class—the land lords, manufacturers, and bankers. Herbert Spencer, the chief architect of the phrase, "survival of the fittest," put it bluntly in his publication, *Principles of Ethics*: "What can be a more extreme absurdity than that of proposing to improve social life by breaking the fundamental law of social life."

For Spencer and the conservative base in American society, nothing had changed with the fundamental arrangement between the money class and the working class. Carl Schurz, the social reformer and husband of Margaret Schurz who established the first American kindergarten in Watertown, Wi, was the first person at a Harvard University meeting in 1882 to describe big businessmen, whose ruthless practices suggested a warlike method reminiscent of the feudal age in Europe—as a robber baron.

Henry Lloyd, another social reformer, made a similar reference the same year in an *Atlantic Monthly* article, likening the American businessman to the land barons and property class of Medieval Europe. He elaborated how small businessmen and small farmers were driven to the wall by large industrial ad railroad corporations. He was convinced that equal political rights could not compensate for the denial of equal rights to the resources and wealth of nature. He returned to the same theme twelve years later in his well-known book *Wealth Against Commonwealth*. Here he documented the rise of Standard Oil (and one of the most notorious robber barons, John Rockefeller) through ruthless and fraudulent practices which were ignored by the courts and buried in government commission reports.

The term "robber baron" was broadened with use and over time to describe most big businessmen of the Gilded Age, a wholesale indictment of the sweeping nature of their swindles and corrupt practices, as farmers, populists, muckrakers, and journalists described the unfolding social and economic order in America, including the conflict between business and labor. The image confirmed for the critics that very little had changed over centuries. It was not unreasonable for them to infer that the Hobbesian world was alive and well and had stretched across the oceans to the New World, despite the fact that most Americans—in their vague, naïve and uninformed belief—took stock in the expression of the American dream.

Business conditions steeped in the rhetoric of strength and survival had given rise to the robber barons, and instilled an aura of respectability while ignoring the shameless reality and link to corrupt business and corrupt politics. Oscar Cargill, in *The Social Revolt* warned about the "almost complete silence . . . of business rapacity and political corruption of the Gilded Age [and] demanded the wrath of Jeremiah [strike at] the vulgar wickedness of Vanderbilt, Gould, Fisk, Drew and Tweed." Mark Twain, in *The Gilded Age,* described the manipulation of spectators and swindlers in business and government in a wickedly humorous, old-rogue satire.

Stewart Denison's *An Iron Crown* pointed out politics and big business had become partners in crime and money; it was just as easy to "buy an alderman or congressman than to buy a watermelon." And, Henry Adams in *Democracy*, argued that American democracy was threatened due to the "onslaught of corporate power": Always consolidating wealth, "ever grasping new powers, or insidiously exercising covert influence" over government.

The same indictment, the same painful commentary, could be made by those who knew the knights and warlords, and later the dukes and barons of Old Europe—and how they advanced their desires for power, property and wealth by working out political arrangements with monarchs. The working masses, the unsuspected, and least powerful were caught in the gripes and force of strong men involved in increasing their share of land, resources and capital—not much different from the American robber barons who bribed public servants and legislators and lined their pockets with public money.

One protest book after another—Bellamy's *The Brenton Mills*, Davis' *Life in the Iron Mills*, Trowbridge's *Farnell's Folly* and Ward's *The Silent Partner*—delineated the same grim picture. Big business was a jungle. The capitalist and worker competed in an unequal battle, one for riches and wealth, the other for food and survival. It should be otherwise, at least in America, but landowners and big businessmen would need to concede basic rights to labor and the yeoman farmer—and they were not inclined to do so. Sounds a little progressive? Perhaps. But for others, it described the economic tenents of Richardo and Malthus who were conservative by ideology.

It also expressed the ideas of Thomas Jefferson who believed that the political and social institutions of society determined the laws which could be rationally attacked and improved—not the iron laws of nature or God's wrath, which were static and unable to be altered by man or sentimentalist dreamers. Of course, it's an argument that Alexander Hamilton had rejected, since he felt that the masses were ignorant and could not be trusted to make wise choices or govern themselves. Only a strong government run by an economic elite—the landowners, merchant and manufacturing class—could maintain order and defend property rights. Sounds a little conservative? Perhaps. But for much of humanity this is how the world has worked—and still works today.

As an offshoot to the American Dream, a host of "success" manuals and books promised to help men succeed and prosper. A list of do's and don'ts, coupled with little ditties on good conduct, manners and etiquette filled the pages. The essential message was that good morals and manners were the gateway to economic and social mobility. These materials were written by ministers, educators and publicists—remarks that were half quackery and half commonsense—and hawked by traveling salesmen in small towns and the rural countryside. At the height of their popularity in the 1870s and 1880s, the publishing houses employed 50,000 agents, a booming cottage industry, with annual sales of over $10 million. The prescriptions of success were the forerunners of twentieth century practical books on good housekeeping, gardening and medical advice and the salespeople were the forerunners of the traveling bible salesmen that soon dotted the American landscape.

More important, the story of the American dream continues today in the midst of modern-day business looters and Wall Street buccaneers, as it did during the Gilded Age. It still serves as a powerful antidote to mask and explain away the plight of ordinary Americans, to link strength and shrewdness with the law of the jungle (now called the principles of free market and free competition), why certain people succeed, and why the concentration of wealth remains in the hands of the few. Although the real story of life is supposed to take place on a spiritual level, according to defenders of the faith, exteriors are nevertheless a part of life. Since civilization began the rights of property have always been more important than the rights of people for the political and economic elite. People who question this arrangement, or seek the dubious ideals of freedom, opportunity and equality are branded as sentimental humanists or traitors.

The conservative ideal has always been to stifle concern for social values and social reform by labeling critics and protesters as ungodly, unpatriotic, or "radical." It is expressed in sharp language and often pseudo-scriptural, invective and tinged with the fear of immigrants, minorities, and labor. The modern-day conservative argument is no different, just as an alarmist, except the pundits have a larger platform because of their influence in media. They spew the same God-fearing, nationalistic, pro-business message mixed with a similar but updated alarmist message concerning socialism, terrorism and "over-paid" union workers who cripple the U.S. economy.

The broad aspects of human nature and distributive economics have not changed much in the last 5,000 years. It is similar to how the warlords once ruled in the Old World, then how the nobility and monarchy ruled, followed by the rising class of American robber barons and monopolistic capitalists, and now "masters of the universe" (Wall Street/banking crowd). Given their own platform, Fox News, *The Wall Street Journal* or *Forbes*, they label today's critics and reformers as liberals, socialists, communists, etc—or just plain naïve or stupid. They mount a defense for the prevailing economic order, with a mix of arrogance, corruption and exploitation, and explain the beneficence of capitalism that appeal to Wal-Mart stockholders and Reaganite Republicans.

If you buy into the conservative ideology, then the argument prevails that (1) people by nature are unequal and are rewarded for their talents and abilities, (2) ordinary workers have received their fair share of the profits and (3) yesterday's business titans and today's corporate executives are entitled to millions of dollars of compensation since they have earned it. Although the market place may need a lose screw or bolt tightened here or there, the system is basically sound and it can function the same way in the future. No major over hall is needed—and all the talk or need for reform is groundless and silly "puppy talk." As James Stewart would say, "It's a wonderful world"—and that is what Americans want to hear and want to believe in.

Mounting Criticism By Reformers

The post-civil war period saw an unprecedented growth in American commerce, business, and industry. A new social and economic order was in the making which pitted millions of farmers, miners and laborers against the titans of the new capitalist order. The social movement and organization of working people reasserted the older values of a democratic society, part Jeffersonian and part Jacksonian, in which the common people had an expectation of opportunity and success and the chance for a descent life—free from deprivation and misery. Focusing on the relationship between profits and economic exploitation and between power and corruption, the industrial capitalist was criticized for breaking laws, morals and basic human values.

Out of the Midwest came a host of populist and progressive leaders, among them James Baird Weaver who in *Call to Action* compared the fight against monopolies as a crusade that was fought by our Founding Fathers for the natural rights of the people. Corporate wealth had gained control of "the articles which the plain people consume in their daily life" and had deprived them of a life of well being. The people had to "rise up and overturn the despoilers" and rebuild a framework for democracy.

Edward Kellogg was concerned that the bankers and industrialists were allied together. They controlled and regulated the currency against the mass of people who were in debt—farmers, workers, small business people, even many professional people. He called for a new social program, whereby "wealth, instead of being accumulated in a few hands, would be distributed among producers. Products would be owned by those who performed the labor." The program would not abolish private property or free enterprise, he argued, but would alleviate poverty and provide more opportunity for the labor class.

It was Walt Whitman, among the reformers, who in *Democratic Vistas*, expressed sadness. The Civil War should have lifted the nation to new spiritual, moral, and economic heights. But the promise of America had not been achieved. Democracy was on trial because of prevailing materialism, consumption and superficiality. Appearing for a nobler race of people who would develop the full potentialities of a democratic society, he poured out his scorn in the "corruption, bribery, falsehood . . . and scoundrelism . . . of respectable and nonrespectable" government officials and business leaders. "In business the one sole object is, by any means, pecuniary gain." In the fable, "the magician's serpent ate up all the other serpents, and money-making is our magician's serpent, remaining today sole master of the field."

The flavor of political outcry can be felt by the Illinois farmers in 1873 who declared the need to publically control "any corporation [that] tends to oppress the people and rob them of their just profits." It was then resolved that railroad tycoons who "defy our laws, plunder our shippers, impoverish our people and corrupt our government be subdued and made to serve the public interest." The progressive wing of the Republic platform in 1872 was harsher. It appraised the money class—the corporations, trusts and titans of business "as sucking money out of the agrarian class [and labor] since the end of the Civil War." It sought to eliminate the "roguery and plunder, born of the multiplied temptations which the

[post] war [era] furnished, and stealthily crept into the management of public affairs." The party proposed radical reform, to rid government of the "scalawags and thieves" [and to] "emancipate [the nation] from the rule of great corporations and monopolies."

William Jennings Bryan represented the common people—small farmers and businessmen, as well as miners and urban factory workers, against industrial and financial monopolies which had crushed honest labor and individual enterprise. He sought to restore a measure of equality by reviving the defunct Civil War tax on the wealthy which was denounced by his critics as "socialism, communism and devilism." He ran for President and lost in 1894.

Journalists and Muckrakers

As the publishing industry expanded with more newspapers and magazines, the spirit of social protest became more vocal and began reaching a wider audience. Thomas Nast won instant fame with his cartoons against the corrupt Tweed Ring in New York. Publishers such as Hearst, Pulitzer and Scripps increased their circulation as they exposed corruption between business and government and sought civil reform for honesty and descency in the corporate and political world.

In popular magazines such as *Collier's, Cosmopolitan, McClures's* and the *La Follete Weekly*, radical journalists (called muckrakers) investigated the abuses of business titans, spoilsmen and politicians. The muckrakers were relentless in their commitment to scoop and splash the wrongdoings of the plutocrats—and boosted the circulation of these magazines. Given the moral tone and conservative values of the country, the journalists gained an influential megaphone that impacted middle-class Americans from coast to coast as they were outraged by the greed and excesses of big business and government. The evils of the day were also depicted in more scholarly magazines such as *Atlantic, Harper's, Nation* and *North American Review*. Intellectuals such as George Bancroft, George Curtis, E.L. Godkin, and James Russell Lowell wrote regularly about corrupt business tycoons and local, state and federal politicians—in formulating protest and reform thought.

Peter Cooper, a philanthropic industrialist and social reformer (sought of a modern-day Bill Gates or Warren Buffet), summed up the need for change in a letter to President Rutherford Hayes in 1877: "Billions of men and women, in this hitherto rich and prosperous country, have been thrown out of employment, or living on precarious and inadequate wages, have felt embittered with a lot, in which neither economy nor industry, nor a cheerful willingness to work hard, can bring an alleviation." What changed? Rutherford's response was zip. One hundred twenty-five years later, the same statement could be made about America—about the rich and the rest of us—about the conditions of employment, sweat and low wages for the majority of workers.

As the intellectual writings became increasingly apparent from the post Lincoln years to the Roosevelt years, methods of gaining wealth of a few by wronging the masses of people were examined. The reform movement sought to curb fraudulent speculation, illicit mining and railroad and oil schemes, the threat of pools, trusts, and monopolies, the unhealthy conditions of the meat and packing industry, as well as drugs and food and the corrupt relationship between big business and big government. By the 1880s, those writers were called *muckrakers* among the best known Henry Lloyd, Frank Norris, Ida Tarbell and Upton Sinclair. They were pioneers in journalistic exposé, written not only to inform but also to reform. One story after another described sordid labor conditions, social injustices and of people driven to the wall by the methods of the robber barons, the dealings and malpractices in business, manufacturing and government that were injurious to the health and living conditions of people—all justified in the name of the inequalities of nature, *laissez faire* economics, and progress.

The muckrakers were not jealous or envious of corporate and banking wealth for they were comfortably well-off and self-made. These reformers were driven by their convictions which centered around stopping the social injustices and enforcing the natural rights of the common man which were rooted in the Age of Enlightenment and the Jeffersonian belief in the yeoman farmer and the artisan. The little person was being hounded and exploited, kept from acquiring decent wages and a descent life. Government had to be recaptured from the interests of big business to save the people. (Today, it's the influence of Wall Street and banking that drives government, as evidenced by the bailout in the billions and belief that if banking goes so goes the country.)

Even James Bryce, the English scholar who was an admirer of American democracy, was highly critical of government and business corruption, including the spoils system and system of bribery. In 1888, Bryce's *American Commonwealth* described the nation's political system as morally and ethically bankrupt, serving the interests of wealth at the expense of the people. The two political parties had lost their purpose and usefulness because they failed to represent the American people. Both groups used their office to reward party hacks and business barons in an ever-growing spoils system: "Neither party has any principles, any distinctive tenants." The two parties "were like two bottles. Each bore a label denoting the kind of liquor it contained, but each was empty."

Property Rights vs. People Rights

In retrospect, most historians would agree that the political parties during the Gilded Age was void of leadership, characterized by one mediocre president after another whose thinking was that American individualism and the American dream went hand-in-hand with Social Darwinism and free enterprise. There was no need for government regulation of industry, and there was no need to read into the differences between Democrats and Republicans. The issue of social and economic reform were not on the minds of politicians who were often consumed by post-war sectionalism and regionalism. Neither party saw anything dramatically wrong with American life during this period in American history.

Business was as usual—highlighted by backroom deals between corrupt politicians and business titans, *laissez-faire* economics, and disregard for the social and economic conditions of people. The people cast aside by the system were immigrants of supposedly inferior stock (not from Anglo-Saxon or Teutonic countries), incompetent or incapable of independent action; or even worse, according to Elbert Hubbard in the *Message to Garcia*, "morally deformed . . . stupid . . . or fire-brands of discontent [who] are to be impressed only by the sole of a . . . boot." People who were failures deserved to be failures, and people who gained wealth were gifted and superior in business and deserving of their rewards, so Hubbard concluded.

In short, democracy had become subservient to capitalism, and the purposes of democracy and business became blurred. The ideals of Jeffersonian and Jacksonian Democracy, "a government of the people and by the people," was replaced by the business notion: "What is good for business is good for America." Lobbyists for labor, farmers, immigrants, blacks, women suffrage and other human rights were shunt aside. Business, and especially the railroads, mining and oil, were the most powerful lobby group in Congress; they basically owned the place through bribes, kickbacks and swindles that went unpunished.

Democracy in this period of history was linked to protecting the rights of business and property, not the rights of people—so the reformers who sought *change* (Obama's favorite word) were put on the defense and ridiculed as anti-American, utopian, socialist, radical, etc—similar to the labeling process today that goes on by the conservative right. It is true that the reformers were intent on curbing free enterprise and laissez-faire practices, but only to the point where abuse and corruption had become apparent and where conditions for ordinary workers and farmers were so bad that they had come to believe that some modification or restraint was needed to restore opportunity associated with the past.

It wasn't until the election of Teddy Roosevelt and Woodrow Wilson did historians come to believe that leadership had been restored in the White House and that reform was possible. As the twentieth century unfolded, the farmers and factory workers combined with the populist and progressive intellectuals—then called muckrakers, to cast a vote for both Roosevelt and Wilson for their promise to curb big business and monopolist practices, as well as to recognize collective bargaining and the rights of the small people.

So long as people thought the economy would continue to expand, they believed in the American system and felt they would get some fair share of the dream. Given this hoken pokem, they succumbed to the greedy and ruthless practices of the robber barons and free market. They saw the myth (or dream) as reality and reconciled their displeasure with the system as part of everyday life and as part of world history. However, the years from 1873 to 1896 witnessed a long wave of recessions and depressions, and the Panic of 1903 revealed the breakdown of an overheated economy and the deficiencies of the credit system—not much different from today's meltdown.

Once the majority of Americans felt they were on the short end of the stick, however, the differences became more apparent between Wall Street and Main Street, between New York's Park Avenue and surrounding slums, Chicago's Gold Coast and surrounding agricultural wastelands. Economic realities set in; the common people believed they were not going to share in tomorrow's prosperity. As the economic system began to breakdown, the wrecking ball of discontent got bigger and louder. Surprisingly, the American people did not take to the streets (although there were a number of labor riots), rather voiced their displeasure in the voting booths—by hanging their hopes on progressive presidents.

Eventually you must ask what has changed on Pennsylvania Avenue. Business is as usual, regardless of whether Democrats or Republicans are in office, as influence peddlers, lobbyists, and spinmeisters descend on Washington to forge backroom deals and funnel public funds to favorite firms and pet projects. Earmarks for "bridges that go nowhere" are merely the tip of the iceberg, if you stop to count all the stuffed shoeboxes totaling tens of millions of dollars, the corporate campaign "donations" in the hundreds of millions, and the swinging door between government and corporate America—high-paying lobbyist jobs and consultant fees that await former politicians from Pennsylvania Avenue. Now, instead of only big business, it is also the banking and Wall Street lobbyists that own Congress and have convinced political leaders they are too big to fail and too powerful to reform. Business goes on the same merry way, despite the trillions of dollars in stock equities and property lost by ordinary people over recent years.

Defenders Respond

Appeals to a more equitable distribution of profits and wealth fell on deaf ears among the political and economic elite; in fact, one of the most common strategies among conservatives was to label anyone who challenged the doctrines of private property, free enterprise and *laissez-faire* economics as un-American and un-Christian. The Social Gospel of the day was that God determined the success and failure of his children which resulted in and justified vast inequality among men. Needless to say, such inequalities never existed before on such a large scale in America, but it was reconciled by those who believed in the precepts of the American dream and had faith in the ways of the Lord. These abstractions and isms belied people and stood out in stark reality to an increasing long wave of inequality, and the struggling and suffering of ordinary people. Of course, you need to understand that most Americans were and still are true believers.

Listen to the words of Leading New York City preacher Henry Ward Beecher who asserted in 1877 that "God has intended the great to be great and the little to be little . . . I do not say that a dollar a day is enough to support a working man . . . and five children if a man insists on smoking and drinking beer . . . But the man who cannot live on bread and water is not fit to live." In 1875 Princeton University's President James McCosh defended wealth as a divine and godly right: "God has bestowed upon us certain powers and gifts which no one is at liberty to take from us or to interfere with. All attempts to deprive us of them is theft."

Inequality rested on the natural laws of God which were fused with the laws of nature, first expounded by classical economists such as David Ricardo and Thomas Malthus. Their doctrines described the nature of causes of wealth. Profits and wages were in conflict. Capitalists and landowners must prosper if there is to be progress and the victims or misfortunate must always be the remaining masses of people. Labor need only be paid "to subsist and perpetuate their race, without either increase or diminution," so stated Ricardo. In "An Essay on the Principles of Population," Malthus argued the natural population grows at exponential rate, but its increase in food production is linear. More people are born that can possibly survive.

Charles Darwin was influenced by Malthus' idea about the struggle for existence and made the leap *On the Origin of Species* in 1859—that while organisms vary from one another, even within a species, the weakest perish and the strongest survive and pass on their traits to their offspring. Over time the transmission of traits will lead to a new species that is more adaptable to the current environment than the previous species. Those that do not adapt will die off in the struggle for existence.

The law of nature inspired Herbert Spencer, another English scholar, to introduce the idea of "survival of the fittest" in 1852. Although the phrase was originally used by Darwin in a biological context, Spencer used it in a social context to make an argument against social welfare and a justification for free markets and the laws of social evolution. He claimed that unless nature was allowed to take its course, unfit people would survive and reproduce at the detriment to society. Survival of the fittest and the evolutionary idea of Darwin's notion of adaptability—why certain animals survive and others don't—became part of the rationale for *laissez-faire* ideology. Spencer held that free competition was a natural law of economics and was the great arbitrator at wealth and poverty, and how profits were distributed. Any concession to this natural law of competition would lead to socialism and stifle progress—causing unemployment and falling prices and profits.

Spencer had a social conscious that was ignored by the business and cultural elite. In *Social Statistics*, published in 1851, he commented that people never start out on equal footing when it came to competition. Inequality begins at birth and is governed by class bias and unequal holdings of wealth and assets. He maintained all people had the moral right to an equal share of the land and earth's resources; everyone should have a fair chance to become landlords and tenants, and everyone should be able to profit from their own labor. To implement this scheme, he called for the nationalization of land—at best impractical, at worst a Marxian idea that did not fit well with those in power. Spencer advocated a progressive death tax to help redistribute property and wealth that had been accumulated by a few families that he felt was traceable to ancient crimes, more or less a Hobbesian or bleak view of history. He took the notion of equal justice seriously and argued for a system of legal aid for the working masses. He was eventually forced to retreat from his moral position and notions of land ownership, taxes, and legal aid.

Many readers who are knowledgeable about Spencer read him in different ways, sought of the way Carnegie (below) is also read with divergent results. Spencer was considered by his peers as perhaps the most influential social thinker of the nineteenth century, but his influence—compared to Darwin, Huxley and Marx—waned because of his conflicting views on capitalism and socialism and the fact that he wrote in many fields of social science which made him a master of none and diluted his influence in each area.

William Graham Sumner, a Yale sociologist and disciple of Spencer, rejected any extension of state activity into social matters as compromising individualism and weakening the laws of economics. "The social order is fixed by laws of nature precisely analogous to those of the physical order. The most a man can do is by his ignorance and conceit to mar the operation of the social laws." Sumner argued that economic contests were struggles for larger shares of profits in which every man had the opportunity to exert his strength and intelligence; this contest was better left to the natural laws of economics, and the doctrine of *laissez faire*, than to allow government legislation.

Sumner strongly believed in the doctrines of economic individualism, competition and survival of the fittest. Those with superior ability and intelligence would win the race in the struggle for resources. Inequality was part of human nature and no one could modify or change it The more resources are limited, the more intense the struggle and the more important are the strengths and talents of the individual. The more competitive is the society, he argued, the greater the progress of the society. "It may shock you to hear me say, but when you get over the shock, it will do you good to think of it: A drunk in the gutter is just what he ought to be," he told a group of historians in 1883. "Nature is working away at him to get him out of the way." No one has the moral right to ask for help or expect special treatment. To lessen inequalities by social legislation or any other artificial method was to penalize the bright and hardworking people and to reward the slow and lazy.

"In no sense whatsoever does a man who accumulates a fortune by legitimate industry exploit his employees; or make his capital 'out of' anybody else," he declared. "The wealth he wins would not be but for him [and] it is a necessary condition of many forms of social advance." The wealthy did not owe anything to anyone, much less the common person, for the captains of industry had made their money supposedly on their own talents and hard work. For Sumner, the common people had only excuses and selfish reasons to hold back a superior person's force and drive of genius and productivity—all to the detriment of individual achievement and social progress.

Sumner was hypocritical behind the façade of criticizing his critics and the reformers of the era. In *War and Other Essays* in 1881, he stated: "The friends of humanity start out with certain benevolent feelings towards 'the poor,' 'the weak,' 'the laborers,' and others of whom they make pets . . . They appeal to sympathy and generosity and to all the other noble sentiments of human heart." Their remedy "consists in a transfer of capital from the better off to the worse off." For society to progress, however, capital must be used for investment and not "given to a shiftless and inefficient member of society who makes no return for it is diverted from a reproductive use; but, if it was put to reproductive use, it would [be for] wages to an efficient productive laborer." The same idea is apparent today among conservative pundits who put a premium on reducing taxes for the wealthy in order to stimulate the productive use of capital, investments and jobs. These are the same voices that want to reduce social programs for the poor and unemployed since it supposedly encourages lazy and unproductive behavior.

Sumner goes on to make a case against safety nets and welfare programs. "There is an almost invincible prejudice that a man who gives a dollar to a beggar is generous and kind-hearted, but that a man who refused the beggar and puts the dollar in a savings-bank is stingy and mean. The former is putting capital where it is very sure to be wasted, and where it will be a kind of seed for a long succession of future dollars," compared to turning the dollar "into capital and given to a laborer, while earning it, would have reproduced it" for the benefit of society. "The working man needs no improvement in his condition except to be freed from the parasites who are living on them." And, here we have the makings today of cultural warfare, and that all plans to provide safety nets for working people are at best patronizing and at worst antithetical to economic growth.

Now listen to what Andrew Carnegie had to say in 1889 in defending the theory of the elite, delighting in the self-made man and industrial giant. "While the law may be sometimes hard for the individual, it is best for the race, because it insures the survival of the fittest in every department." He bluntly continued, "We accept and welcome . . . great inequality of environment, the concentration of business [and wealth] in the hands of a few and the law of competition . . . as being not only beneficial, but essential for the future progress of the race." Based on "the law of competition . . . human society loses homogeneity and classes are formed." But the "socialist" who seeks to overturn present conditions is "attacking the foundation upon which civilization itself rests." In other words, any person or group trying to (1) regulate business practices, (2)limit huge conglomerates, (3) protect investors or shareholders, or (4) introduce progressive tax policies (to pay for human services such as health education or welfare) would be considered anti-capitalist and anti-American.

As for arrogance, hubris and big egos, Carnegie is considered the best of the robber barons because he cast the wealthy into the stewardship role of American opportunity by advocating the "millionaire [must become] a trustee for the poor." The person "who dies rich dies disgraced." It is the millionaire's duty to the poor to bring his "superior wisdom, experience, and ability to administer, doing for the better then they would or could for themselves."

Now consider one of the worst robber barons, a person who enjoyed the game of beating down his opponents and fleecing the public. Bragging he could break any strike, he said in 1886: "I can hire one half of the working class to kill the other half." As for the public, Gould would short the stock of his own railroad company, thus devaluing it, and wiping out a host of poor saps. Then, he would buy back the stock at half-price or even lower and in a few days stash away a small fortune.

A small percentage of the Gould types today are caught and forced to settle lawsuits brought by regulators and investors. Too often, however, federal regulators wink, and the members of the public shrug their shoulders not knowing what to do, even when they get ripped off and see their investments plunge and pensions sink. Gould is the forerunner of the modern-day Kenneth Lay (Enron), Bernard Ebbers (World Com), Michael Milken (junk bond broker) and Jack Grubman (stock analyst)—all who made fortunes cooking the books, promoting companies while the ship was sinking, and moving money around at a click of a mouse with little concerns about the fate of who they employed or the investors they advised. All of them were criminally accountable for destroying jobs and failing to act as stewards of investors' money (The first three were given jail sentences.)

Take a sixty-second breather and consider the Metropolitan Museum of Art in New York, the pre-eminent cultural institution of America, supported by donations of America's most famous "rogues" or robber barons. The list of benefactors and supporters is a mile long—from Andrew Carnegie to the Rockefeller family and Sandy Weil, the former CEO of Citigroup (who resembled Gould's strategy of raking in millions for himself while crushing his competitors). Here is Luigi Palma di Cresnola, the first Met director in 1879, illustrating the class divide in America. He refused to keep the place open on Sunday to accommodate working people, because he felt they were ill-bred and unfit to appreciate the museum's collections. He described them as "loafers" and "scum" and envisioned they would "peel bananas [and] even spit" in the museum.

Conceivably, the great figures in manufacturing, banking, railways, land development, mining, oil, steel, and other exploiters of natural resources were nothing more than manipulators of the marketplace who "seized the moment" or "got their first" and thus accumulated immense wealth, power, and fame. It might also be argued by the defenders of the faith that the great fortunes of the Rockefellers, Vanderbilts, Carnegies,

Mellons, etc, were based on their strength and natural intelligence, and that the rise of so many obscure, uneducated, and uncultivated men to wealth was evidence of the great opportunities of America—characterized by the American dream (rags to riches) and the cult of success.

The achievement of great fortunes might also have had something to do with the doctrine of Social Darwinism (the smartest and the strongest, certain in their own convictions, will shape the landscape and acquire its wealth). The application of Darwin's ideas were supported by *laissez-faire* economics, rooted in the ideas of Malthus and Ricardo; by *free competition* as a social and natural law, based on the thinking of Herbert Spencer; by what some preachers such as Henry Ward Beecher, considered part of the *divine order*, or that God had determined the success and failure of his children; or simply what the muckrakers later referred to as the *law of the jungle*.

IQ, Testing and Sorting

G. Stanley Hall and E.L. Thorndike, the two most influential psychologists at the turn of the twentieth century, also supported the cult of individual success and the notions that the inequality resulting from competition and differences in talent and abilities reflected heredity and that the outcomes and differences in human behavior were rooted in human nature or the gene pool. No one was responsible for this inequality, and there was no reason to penalize intelligent or superior people for their success. This type of relationship—superior and inferior, smart and dumb—is what some might innocently call a "sorting out process" or "tracking system" in school, whereas others would label it as discriminatory and as potential social dynamite. Nonetheless, this conflict becomes increasingly evident when the economic gap between the upper and lower echelons are continuously widened, and when the lower base comprises an overabundance of people who feel trapped or discriminated against.

For Hall and Thorndike, the main criterion for success or fortune was inherited intelligence. The captains of industry had forged their own success and accumulated fortunes because of their unique abilities. Their psychological theories not only fit into the business explanation of wealth, but also the religious explanation of stewardship and charity, including all those who used God and his infinite wisdom to support the business buccaneers and property interests of the wealthy class. Although no adequate tests existed at that period for determining the relationship between heredity and environment, and how they effected human traits or behaviors, their ideas led to the development of intelligence tests in 1908 by Alfred Binet, a French psychologist.

For the next thirty years, the IQ test would be used as in instrument to classify bright and slow students, to classify army recruits into designated assignments, to distinguish between officers and nonofficers, and to justify Anglo-Saxon superiority while stressing the shortcomings of immigrants from Southern and Eastern Europe and later an array of different minority groups. Melded with the idea of Darwinism (biological differences) and later Social Darwinism (social and cultural differences), the IQ test was also used to explain the innate mental superiority of the wealthy and the inferiority of the working class.

Similarly, it was argued that people of limited intelligence, who were suitable for farm and simple rural life, had moved to the cities. Along with the new immigrant arrivals from southern and eastern Europe who settled in urban areas, they were unable to deal with the complexities of city life and unsuitable for urban jobs except the lowest ones. The mass immigration melted the families and streets into an ethnic stew. The peasants and laborers arrived in the cities dazed and stunned, carrying their earthly belongings and bundles. Their fingers were callused and arms muscled by years of toil and drudgery, and their pockets lined with soil and fresh hope seeking a new life and a new identity, as working men and women of worth and dignity. But they were immediately marked by custom, language, and minimal skills and education. Living in dense areas, and often unemployed, these people of so-called low intelligence were considered responsible for committing crimes and pulling down the general level of American civilization. The difference in their abilities, coupled with their norms and behaviors, only validated the natural laws of economics, the rise of people with intelligence and drive and the leveling of the masses.

A Seventh Inning Stretch

Spencer, Sumner and their contemporaries failed to recognize that large amounts of wealth are created by the labor of others by the products or services rendered. As greater fortunes are made by a few people, and as the economy grows, the gap between the rich and poor widens. The outcome is a dominant-subordinate class relationship—a split within society that eventually tests the social and moral fiber of society. This may not be so evident in the United States, because of the "cult of success" and belief that the humble can rise to the top. Given the knowledge that the average person cannot easily rise (which Carnegie admitted to be a flaw in the social and economic system in his description of "the gospel of wealth"), even when talent and abilities are considered, this leads to a feeling of frustration and hostility bubbling within the system. It becomes compounded and more glaring when variables such as race, ethnicity, or gender are used to show differences in wealth and income. In a global economy, which includes more markets and people, the gap between entrepreneurial elites and average workers widens because information travels at an accelerated pace, markets expand, investors with money are more available—and the economic pie has ballooned.

A few people take "opportune risk" that others don't take and make huge sums of money. Were they smart or lucky—or both? Don't try to figure it out. It's a trick question, because all the upside goes to the "risk taker," the modern-day warlord (now called the "master of the universe" or "titans of industry"), and all the downside is absorbed by the public who invested their pensions and 401Ks in stocks and bonds. Whether we call them brokers, bankers, corporate executives or simply "orcs," the warlike creatures of Middle Earth in *The Lord of the Rings*, most have no intention to serve the common good, including small investors (the general public)—only to make vast amounts of money. They are modern-day plunders; their salaries, bonuses, and fees are highly lucrative and off the charts compared to ordinary people who are considered cost units by their employers and barely earn enough to pay their bills. Any attempt to impose strict regulations on the financial or corporate community, limit their economic pursuits or tax their profits is dismissed as class warfare, socialism, or liberal dogma. In a global economy, financial and entrepreneurial profits increase, but the distribution of gains remains unequal because morality and ethics have been drained from the system;

moreover, the playing field has always been uneven and the opportunities unequal.

The good society recognizes there are differences in talent and abilities and makes adjustments in a fair and just way; it also builds safeguards into the system to prevent the abuse of power and wealth. However, the conservative argument boils down to a belief in the "law of nature" and "law of competition," as well as the notion of individualism, evolution, and struggles of interests among people or groups for larger shares of wealth without any type of social legislation or government interference. The conservative defense views any concession or balancing act as a form of paternalism or socialism—even worse as corrupting the morality of the family, church, and country. It envisions any form of government regulation or increase in government powers over business as inefficient, disruptive, and even disastrous—as a boom to socialism.

One hundred years later, Steve Forbes, who is the chief editor of *Forbes* magazine, warned that "misguided government policies . . . dried up the flow of capital . . . and [caused] free-market failure" during the Great Depression of the 1930s and massive inflation of the late 1990s, and aggravated the economic meltdown of 2008-2009. "In the real world, therefore, free markets operate rationally and efficiently in a way that government regulators simply can't." Forbes also argues that the federal government is too powerful, "largely useless, even harmful." It cannot "eradicate the fallibility of human judgment," nor respond properly in a crisis. For example, the government saved Bear Sterns and then a few months later "allowed Lehman Brothers; a much larger institution, to go under." It permitted an easy money policy which distorted housing values and led to a housing bubble. It also permitted an interlocking and shadow banking and investment system to operate so that medium-sized investment banks like Lehman and Bears Stern could threaten the entire U.S. and global financial system.

What Forbes doesn't say, however, is that the bright idea to allow Lehman Brothers to collapse was a decision made by Hank Paulson, the "financial wizard" and free-market pundit from Wall Street and former CEO of Goldman Sachs (a competitor of Lehman.) Low interest rates were the wretched doings of Alan Greenspan, the chair of the Federal Reserve and mystical believer, like Forbes, that free markets are self-correcting. Moreover, low capital reserves of large banks that precipitated the market crash was a byproduct of the philosophy of Forbes, Paulson and

Greenspan. None of these Wall-Street pundits are willing to admit that nation's economy is hostage to lobbyists and bureaucrats whose interests are equally divided between serving the banking cartel and powerful politicians in Washington.

In his classic text *Free to Choose*, Milton Friedman argued that government intervention breeds conflict and inefficiency, and free markets breed cooperation and efficiency. At the end of the day, according to Friedman, political freedom and economic freedom go hand-in-hand; it is essential for political freedom to "recognize in the law each individual's natural right to property [and] that they have control over, and that they can dispose of." Elsewhere Friedman says, "Our first task: stop the growth of government. The second task is to shrink government spending and make government smaller." The idea is to make "people responsible for themselves and for their own care." Indeed, that makes sense if you believe in Social Darwinism, free and unrestricted markets, or if you are on top of the totem pole of success—so the hell with the less fortunate, the sickly, and the disenfranchised.

The idea of limiting government fails to consider the compact in America that everyone should do better, not just highly talented or privileged people by birth, not just those with entrepreneurial spirit or the temperament to win. By rejecting government intervention, both Forbes and Friedman evidence contempt for political and social reform and merely perpetuate the Hamiltonian view that the best government serves the moneyed class and those who own property. At the very least, a weak or unresponsive government permits almost limitless reward for those who have the right skills and connections, or get lucky, without having to share their gains with the rest of the community; it boils down to a few elites leaving everyone else behind.

Certainly one can argue that the conservative defense has not waivered, and that competition and survival of the fittest have been hallmarks of the Republican philosophy since the Reagan administration. The belief is that government should not meddle with the economy nor address social problems. Small government, free enterprise and rugged individualism are hallmarks of a vibrant economy and any imbalances or inequalities created by the system suggest that certain people are more competitive, smarter or talented. All other excuses are just excuses. People who fail are failures because they deserve to be, and they stand in marked contrast to people who succeed by means of ability, diligence and discipline. People who are poor are either lazy or dumb. People who are rich are hardworking and smart.

When the economy goes into free fall and working people become unemployed, sink further into debt or lose their homes, conservatives argue that's how the "cookie crumbles," "tough luck," "the market is not perfect; it needed a correction." Social Darwinism justifies the fact that the least fit will wind up at the bottom of the food chain, and social welfare programs restrict *individualism* and destroy *free enterprise*—the forces of economics, we are told, that made America great. Of course, those at the top of the food chain will not admit that it is nearly impossible for people to start out on equal footing in the struggle for limited resources and the race for profits and wealth. Those people with political and social contacts, powerful friends, and Ivy league and corporate connections have a huge advantage—starting out on third base while the rest are just trying to get up at bat.

Stuck in the Real World

Behavioral economics, which can be translated into "herd behavior," does not explain nor coincide with the natural laws of economics, but it can and often does lead to "bubbles." It's not only true with stock investments and pension funds, but it can also affect the housing market which many homeowners now understand. The instinct is to follow the "herd." In the short term, most people benefit because prices are forced upwards—and greed continues to stoke the engine. But eventually prices stumble and head south, due to one or more shocks in the economy. Then *fear* sets in and it replaces *greed* as the prevailing emotion.

Inherent in capitalism is the propensity to grow and prosper and then overreach because of arrogance or greed. When an institution or company is growing there needs to be some failure or slow down. Without stumbling and learning from mistakes, there is no discipline. Given most technical charts, when a particular sector of the economy grows too quickly, it is ripe for a correction or bubble. The need is for restraint, not to allow institutions and companies to grow too big to fail. Lack of restraint or discipline means the public is again at risk, and will likely pay the price tag again. The fact remains that government is held hostage by the financial and corporate sector of the economy.

We all know that big business is ripe with swindles, bribes and favors and Wall Street is emerced with greed, hubris and fraud. Bring up the issue in public, and conservative pundits yell foul. But unless there is legitimate government regulation, coupled with transparency, accountability, and punishment for the "bad guys,"—the latter will always exploit the little guy. In the real world, the big fish on Wall Street or in banking rarely give a hoot how much money they fleece from Main Street. This is the way it has worked since warlords plundered the countryside thousands of years ago—as they still do in nearly half the countries of the world.

The warlords in the U.S. now wear pin stripe suits, with crimson suspenders and power ties. Now they call themselves the "masters of the universe," running amok around the world and raking in millions, even billions. You might argue that the description is unfair hoopla, and you might consider that conservative television hosts like Larry Kudlow and Glenn Beck blame the mortgage and housing crisis (that precipitated the recent global meltdown) on government pressure (big government) to make undocumented loans to low-income homeowners (so they could realize the American dream). These people were mostly unqualified and unable to pay the monthly mortgage payments. The outcome: Medium home prices from a high of $230,000 in mid 2006 to $173,000 in mid 2009.

Conservative gurus refuse to admit that large fees (costing consumers an extra $20 billion between 2006 and 2010) were generated by the mortgage brokers, banks, and loan companies like former Countrywide Financial (the largest one whose chief executive Angel Mozilo was indicted for fraud and inside trading in 2009). Proponents refuse to admit that the subprime lenders created "liar loans," that is fraudulent stated-income loans. Countrywide and a host of other lending institutions, including many blue-blood banks, incorporated tricks and traps in the fine print of mortgage notes. There were "teaser" rates and changes in monthly payments. Then there was the bundling of these toxic mortgages into bonds and derivatives that were falsely rated triple A by credit agencies such as Moody's and Standard & Poor's and then sold worldwide to unsuspecting investors. There is no mention that the credit agencies, the so-called watchdog for investors, were paid by the financial companies they were monitoring, hardly an arm's length relationship. At the start of the 2007 bubble Moody's profits exceeded Exxon's. Ironically, the credit agencies still collect fees from the companies they evaluate. It's as if the baseball umpire was paid by the batter to call balls and strikes or if the judge's salary was paid by the prosecuting attorney's office.

To be sure, there is no admission that American capitalism became corrupted by quick profits and fraudulent transactions, by a financial industry that became too big to fail—representing 40 percent of corporate profits in 2007.[19] The system was built on sand: By financing inflated home prices (often with no money down), over extended credit cards, overleveraged banks, and phony ratings of bonds and derivatives (insurance policies) that were underfunded and could not be paid. Wall Street peddled to local and state governments all sorts of financial products (involving derivatives and interest rate swaps) many which were not understood by government authorities and turned into costly mistakes.

The dismantling of the Glass-Steagall Act during the Clinton years was the straw that broke the bank. It originally prevented banks from becoming investors and taking on massive risk and could have stopped Wall Street and banks—from holding the economy hostage and taxpayers (the common people) from footing the bailout bill. But it was pressure for free enterprise and small government by financial lobbyists paid by Wall Street and the banking industry. It was promoted by Secretary Treasurer Robert Rubin, the banking executive from Citigroup, along with the Federal Reserve Chair Alan Greenspan, a disciple of Ayn Rand's law of the jungle and free market doctrines. They castrated the need for financial regulation that led to the "liar loans," subprime frenzy and economic meltdown.

Not to anyone's surprise, conservative economists still argue that tax increases and a regulated economy leads to inertia and waste. In *The End of Prosperity*, Arthur Laffer and Steven Moore praise President Reagan for reducing taxes and business restrictions as well as for expanding trade. Entrepreneurship soared and the economy boomed. They now warn that increased taxes and regulations lead to fiscal insanity. More important, they refer to "fusion enterprise," the intermixing of government and business, that is when the government is the owner or major stock holder and it directs market decisions. Such a policy, they argue, will lead to economic disaster. Amid all this hysteria, conservative pundits are willing to tax ordinary citizens, take government bailouts, and accept pork-sponsored federal projects

MILLIONAIRES, BILLIONAIRES—AND WORKERS

Times haven't changed much as you might think or wish for most Americans. Let me start off gingerly, as if you were listening to a Johnie Cash jingle, and then work my way up to the pinnacle of wealth and power. For the last several generations, the bottom of the heap for all intensive purposes have remained at the bottom. This lack of mobility among the poor reflects what Oscar Lewis in *La Vida* called the "culture of poverty" and what Michael Harrington in *The Other America* referred to as "invisible Americans." Despite government reports in the early 1960s, Harrington concluded that as many as one third of Americans were living a desperate and invisible life of poverty—and no one with political muscle seemed to care.

Today the situation may be worse, despite increased social legislation and social programs which ballooned (partially as a result of Harrington's book) during President Johnson's "War on Poverty" and "Great Society." An increasing number of working-class and middle-class Americans, at least people who once thought they were part of the American dream, are teetering and trying to stay afloat. Increasingly, more people are left behind and forgotten, men and women with nothing more than a high-school diploma (about two thirds of the American populace) who once had descent blue-collar jobs, earning $20 to $30 per hour from World War II through the 1980s in manufacturing. They now earn half the amount as their jobs have vanished overseas where labor costs average $2 to $5 a day. Those were the days when a few giant firms like General Electric, Sears, U.S. Steel and General Motors dominated the market place in the U.S. and abroad. They made sufficient profits to make peace with the labor unions and pay descent wages to working people, thus allowing them to become middle class.

More threatening, in the battle between profits and wages, white-collar jobs requiring a college education and the cornerstone of our knowledge and high-tech society, have disappeared. Starting in the 1990s, these jobs have been outsourced by American companies to Asia and Eastern Europe. Many people who used to earn $75,000 to $150,000 have now been displaced by their counterparts in China, India, Singapore, and the former Soviet block in Eastern Europe for one third to one fourth the cost. Middle-class Americans have lost their jobs and have been forced to join the ranks of the unemployed and underemployed. The result is that for every job that pays $50,000 or more, there were twenty five to fifty five applicants in 2010.

Between 2000 and 2010, much of the growth of U.S. companies came from abroad; the revenues of multi-national companies from the rest of the world were up while sales at home were down. In 2005, the *Wall Street Journal* reported that 41 percent of the revenues for the S&P 500 companies came from overseas operations. By 2010, more than half the revenues of these companies are expected to came from outside the U.S. Similarly, American venture-capital firms are now raising more money to invest in foreign countries and emerging markets than in the U.S. The amount in the hundreds of billions earmarked overseas has increased from 25 percent of the total raised in 2001 to more than 50 percent in 2010. This trend translates into a loss of U.S. jobs, mostly the high-paying, high-tech types. The sad truth is that globalization equates to a massive loss of American jobs, much more than is generated from exports. There are many apt polemics (aphorisms) to describe the employment meltdown. One simple conclusion is the middle-class population is drowning, slowly going under and slowly disappearing—despite disbelief and counter claims among the "true believers" of free market capitalism.

Added to these ranks of people who once thought they were middle class are divorced women with children, college graduates burdened by massive debt, retirees (some 75 million) whose pensions have dwindled (and are now looking for work during their golden years), and people who have experienced huge medical bills. All these people are products of bad judgment or bad luck, wrong decisions and wrong choices, or being in the wrong place at the wrong time. Just a few curves or wrong turns on the so-called road to prosperity, or some burst of bad luck and the terrain becomes bumpy. A macro event that is uncontrollable such as a recessionary economy, a housing bubble or the fact that the world is now "flat" (meaning that people now compete for jobs on a global basis), and the world can shift abruptly from prosperity to hard times. Increasingly, more Americans are treading dangerous waters and hardly keeping afloat.

We are living in an "upside-down" economy where new inventions and technology have increased productivity on a national level and lowered the standard of living for most Americans, because the economic gains have been gobbled up by a few who have became part of the wealthy top one percent of the populace—the group of taxpayers earning $500,000 or more per year. The rich don't care, so long as the rest of us don't "storm the Bastille" or bang down their doors. The only time the rich and superrich ever cared about the plight of the common people was during the Great Depression in the 1930s, when unemployment reached 25 percent, millions of men were homeless, and soup kitchens were overwhelmed—and it looked that the social/economic structure was about to collapse. Then, for a short period, the economic elite concerned about their own life style and wealth, relinquished their grip on the people and the seats of power. They reluctantly permitted the Roosevelt administration to implement social and work programs for the victims of the Depression and allowed government meddling—in the formation of the Federal Reserve and the Securities and Exchange Commission. If you think there is another reason other than fear, why the business and financial sector helped the common man or permitted increased government tinkering of free markets, then you need a reality check. You might as well believe in the tooth fairy.

Amity Shales, a conservative stalwart and former writer for the *Wall Street Journal* presents the usual verbage by and for the political Right. In *The Forgotten Man*, she argues it was a "lack of faith . . . in the market place [and] government regulation . . . from 1929 to 1940 [that] helped to make the Depression Great." The book's title is an ironic twist. Roosevelt referred to the "forgotten man" as a victim, someone at the bottom of the economic heap. But William Graham Sumner first used the term in 1884 to describe the average working American who was being cajoled into believing the down-trodden people needed safety nets or relief programs—the very stuff and soul of Roosevelt's New Deal to combat the Depression.

Roosevelt's critics saw him as a traitor to the comfortable world of the patrician class and business class, but the American people knew better and elected him four times as president. When Bush II became president, he not only made great efforts to reshape and move Social Security into the private sector, but also he went to great pains to provide Wall Street a free hand by weakening government regulation and the controls imposed by the Federal Reserve and the SEC. We all know the outcome. Excessive financial fees, fraud and corruption, running madly off in all directions—almost like a headless horseman in one of Washington Irving's novels. But this news should be old news for anyone who knows history, because the warlords and kingmakers have always plundered the countryside: Vanquishing opponents, gobbling the riches of the land, and treating the workers as economic units who were considered fungible and disposable.

In 2010, the rich, the top 1% of the income bracket held the working-class and middle class "hostage" to ensure high-end tax cuts. The word "hostage" referred to the American people, ordinary Americans. The point is, the rich did not fear the collapse of the system nor that the unemployed would bring down the system. To be sure, those who earn over $500,000 a year should show their appreciation to the country that permitted their success and pay the extra tax to help out ordinary people who struggle daily to pay their bills. The government has allowed the top 1% to make millions over their lifetime because most legislators do not work for the people. Some may start out with good intentions, but they become puppets of Wall Street and big business—and the rich and powerful. Put in different terms, in 2010, some 44 percent of Congressmen were millionaires, and they make the laws. To be sure, there are all kinds of bailouts, handouts, tax loopholes and taxcuts for the politically connected and wealthy—and very little for working people and the middle class. And, that has been the way of the world—for the last 5,000 years of recorded history.

Fat Cats and Old Money

In the 1950s, Consuelo Vanderbilt, a symbol of American wealth, published the best-selling autobiography *The Glitter of Gold*, which described her miserable marriages, commonly arranged as a "link in the chain" among aristocratic families to cement her wealth through marriage. She was indoctrinated by her mother Alva to believe that happiness is reached through "practical arrangements of marriages" rather than romance, what Old Europe would refer to as "the protocol of marriage," in order to build an alliance or enhance wealth between ultrarich families. Fifty years later, in the biography *Consuelo and Alva Vanderbilt*, the mother in a moment of cynicism referred to wives as "paid legitimate prostitutes" who design their lives around finding "suitable" spouses, even if it means traveling across countries or oceans, to hold on to their elite statuses. The goal is to not dilute their wealth among "lower orders" of society, that is you and I. In modern corporate terms, marriage is like a hedge fund. If it works, great. If not there is always the daughter or son of the Duke of Marlborough of the King of Sardinia. Everyone is a rich man's world is fungible.

Although some of the titles and symbolic alliances of superwealthy families have disappeared over the last one hundred years, they still retain much of their privileges and continue to manipulate the corporate world and financial markets for their own benefit, as well as domestic and foreign policies of nations through private clubs and social and business relationships. (Given a worse-case scenario, the U.S. Supreme Court *appointment* of Bush to the presidency in 2000 is an example of this well-concealed web of favors and how "things" work behind the scenes, despite what the people say or how they *vote*.) Although not all of the elite families today are descendents of maligned monopolists or political scoundrels, they manage to live a life of splendor in places like Southampton, NY, Martha's Vineyard, MA, Kennebunkport, NH, Kenilworth, IL, or on some huge Texan ranch, with five hundred or more acres, in the style of the old Spanish hacienda from when El Zorro roamed the Mexican countryside and robbed form the rich and gave to the poor.

The ordinary person has no comprehension of the superrich lifestyle and the only contact they have with these kinds of families is that they serve as their workers or soldiers as these elites effect business mergers, make trade alliances, determine war, or make peace treaties To be sure, a few thousand families have much more to do than we realize with running the entire industrialized world, and indirectly through world economic organizations, international banks, and paramilitary and spy groups have a lot to say in determining the fate of third-world governments. This is a hard pill to swallow; it shakes the foundation of our faith, especially if we were brought up believing in the spirit of democracy and loyalty to the red, white and blue.

The White Anglo-Saxon Protestant (WASP),[20] a phrase coined by sociologist Digby Baltzell in his classic book *The Protestant Establishment*, is often the target of criticism: Considered as the forerunners of special privilege, unfettered individualism, land and railroad monopolists, and Wall Street speculators. Ironically, the WASP establishment has declined in power, influence, and wealth. This is largely due to their exclusion of Jews, Catholics, and minorities (reminiscent of the days when signs on hotels and clubs read "no dogs, Jews, or Catholics"), and its unwillingness to intermarry and/or allow into top echelons of business or their privileged world talented non-WASPS. A somewhat amusing idiosyncrasy is for the true-blue WASP to avoid any evidence of hard work or striving, as if this might suggest that you are not on top of the pyramid, nor a lord of wealth.

Economics 101

The process I am describing has nothing to do with democracy, progress, or economic growth. Although the players change over time, the cycle is endless. It dates back to the age of barbarism, an evolutionary step to from the warlords, then the dawn of nation-states and empires, to feudalism and the European nobility, to the Gilded Age in America and the rise of Wall Street and a few other financial centers such as London, Zurich, Hong Kong, Tokyo and now Shanghai. These people comprise a highly organized industrial and banking community, a small political elite and a handful of billionaires and chief executives from investment houses and banking who have a lot to say about global markets, finance and corporate capitalism.

This class of people shuttle from multiple homes, travel on private jets, and communicate with their Blackberrys. They work, but it's not the kind that characterizes how the multitude work, say from 9 to 5. At the top of this pyramid, business is as usual. These people devise self-serving rules, gamble on the market and put at risk the entire world economy, while managing to be sheltered from the dips and stresses of the economy—not because of genius but because of their interconnections and ability to engineer laws for their own benefit. For example, the person who is supposed to monitor Wall Street as Secretary Treasurer, Chief Economic Advisor to the President, or Chair of the New York Federal Reserve is often the main consultant or former executive of one of the banking giants like Citigroup or investment giants like Goldman Sachs.

It becomes more entangled, with greater need to scrutinize "back-room" deals, when we learn that Henry Paulson (the former CEO of Goldman Sachs), as Secretary Treasurer allowed Lehman Brothers (the former rival of Goldman Sachs) to go bankrupt during the financial crisis. He then directed AIG, the insurance giant, to pay Goldman Sachs $13 billion at par, instead of a discount they were more willing to accept. Then there is Stephen Friedman (a former Goldman Sachs director). When he was board member of the New York Federal Reserve, he purchased 37,000 shares of Goldman Sachs at the height of the meltdown. In simple terms, we have a conflict of interest: Owning shares in a company that the federal government is regulating. It's like the fox being paid to protect the hens. (In this case, the hens represent the people.) You can bet with near certainty when Tim Geithner and Larry Summer leave the inner financial circle of Washington, they will return to Wall Street as executives or consultants. In short, government is not of, by or for the people, as U.S. folklore depicts. Concentrated political power has always gone hand-in-hand with concentrated financial power—and such power has always been in the hands of a few. History confirms there is no other answer or explanation "blowing in the wind."

Americans accept the fact that communism is antidemocratic, but they fail to grasp the idea that capitalism can be also antidemocratic. If left unchecked and unrestrained, it leads to vast inequalities, survival of the fittest, and a host of get-rich schemes, as well as the perverted notion that "greed in good" as in fueling a free-market orthodoxy. These ideas are supported by a host of nineteenth-century theories and twentieth-century "scientific" models that few people comprehend but many have accepted with a faith bordering on religion. In simple terms, it means affluence accrues only to the top, just as cream rises to the top, and that big business needs no checks and controls. The rich are entitled to get richer, we are told, because they invest and create jobs—but what kind of jobs? At what pay scale? It took the Depression, followed then by the lowly Harvard instructor, John Kenneth Galbraith, to challenge these theories and remedy the economy by government interference and regulation. Thanks to Galbraith's longevity with many administrations, from Roosevelt to Kennedy and then Clinton, his advice and books (more than fifty) became the enemy of financers, bankers, and Wall Street manipulators—and the hope for the little guy.

If we need, still, another compass to direct our thinking, then we live in a divided world of unbridled materialism, consumerism, and excess on one end of the spectrum and a massive slosh of poverty, deprivation, and blight on the other end. More than 45 million Americans depend in food stamps. More than 1 billion people in the world are starving or malnourished. Adding to the agricultural woes of poor nations, the U.N. estimates that by 2050, when the world's population is expected to reach 9 billion people—global food production will need to increase 70 percent because of population growth and rising incomes. But a 70 percent increase in food production means increased rates of habitat destruction—including the acceleration or the extinction of annual species and deforestation for producing food and fuel. This in turn, has serious implications for climate change which was created by the industrialized nations (with the U.S. being number-one culprit) and whether there will be enough land and water to produce the food needed in the future.

Interest in international problems is often overshadowed by how the patricians prepare for life and see the world: Those who belong to a blue-blood, old boys club and those who do not; those who believe their ancestors amassed great fortunes from their brains and guts and those on the other side who are convinced the captains of industry, yesterday and today, made their money by trampling on the downtrodden and ripping off the consumer; those who get their first job with major investment firms and those who are regulated to small, local banks; people who are welcomed in the stateliness of the Episcopalian church and other people who listen to the sermons of the untutored clergy of the less prestigious dominations and sects; rich children who are connected by birth to Harvard or Yale and working-class kids who wind up at state colleges across the country.

Among western countries, however, the most blatant divide was in merry-old England at the turn of the twentieth century. The dukes and earls, the descendents of the old warlords, had an 800-year headstart on their American counterparts to accumulate wealth and pass it one from one generation to the next. According to Juliet Nicolson's *The Perfect Summer*, in 1911 700 families "owned a quarter of the country" while 16 percent of the labor force were servants. That may seem like a harsh pill to swallow, given that so many modern western ideas of freedom, liberty and equality first washed up on the shores of the English island. I guess, however, most influential leaders of western civilization would explicitly concede to the imperfections of their own causes and their own country—so why should the English be any different. But, the ticking clock has a way of changing even the fortunes of the most fortunate. Some of the superrich in England have seen their estates diluted by the misfortunes of war, divorce laws, and the dismantling of the empire. Now, the best guess is some 2,000 families own 25 percent of the English landscape. Some people on the political

Left who have an optimistic streak might call this progress. My response is a little more cynical: "Nuts."

The New Titans

In a nineteenth-century system based on survival of the fittest and a twentieth-century system based on free markets, and in both cases with little or no government intervention, the strong survive and the weak and poor are rendered "unfit"—destined to remain in the deep hollows, invisible and without a political or economic voice. In this business model, few, if any, safety nets are designed for slow runners and the uneducated and unlucky. The American economy—rooted in the ways of railroad magnates like Vanderbilt, trading tycoons like Gould, oil barons like Rockefeller, and mass manufactures like Ford—has been positioned by geography, resources and mass immigration of people seeking a better life. The idea has been to exploit the vast landscape and its workers. Safety nets for CEOs and other executives are plentiful; moreover, they know when to jump ship and sell their stock because they control the flow of information. They are provided with golden parachutes, amounting to tens of millions of dollars, sometimes hundreds of millions, while workers have watched their stocks and pensions tumble during an economic downslide.

Case in point, right before the 2008-2009 economic meltdown: Wallace Mallone received a $135 million parachute, after only fifteen months as Wachovia's vice chairman. James Kilts, who ran Gillette for four years, received $175 million when the company was sold to Proctor and Gamble. Phillip Parcell became eligible for a $113 million payout when he left Morgan Stanley. Company losses do not seem to matter. Pzifer's CEO Henry Mckinnell received a $200 million lump sum, in addition to his $6.5 million a year pension, despite the fact that the company lost $137 billion or 43 percent in value since he became the chief in 2001. EMC's chief executive received a 112 percent increase in compensation in 2005, but the company had a negative return of 8 percent. The Gap's CEO took home 125 percent more in 2005 than the previous year, but the company experienced a 17 percent loss. Home Depot's CEO Robert Nordelli was paid $245 million for his five years (2001-2005), during the same time when the company's stock declined 12 percent while the stock price of its principal competitor, Lowe's, soared 173 percent. After fourteen months of dismal company performance, Disney sent Michael Ovitz on his way with $140 million of stockholders' money, despite charges by Disney's CEO Michael Eisner that Ovitz had a "character problem" and was "too devious, too untrustworthy . . . and only out for himself."[21]

Franklin Raines, Fannie Mae's CEO, was allowed to keep $90 million in bonuses generated by accounting tricks that allowed him to meet bonus targets, while his company had to restate $10.6 billion in losses the same year. His company paid $400 million in fines, a slap on the wrist. Eventually the corporate ethos at Fannie Mae and its sister agency Freddie Mac led to the housing bubble in 2007. Their stock value dropped more than 95 percent of value by 2009. But Raines is not atypical. In 2008, when Merrill Lynch lost $15.3 billion and was forced to be taken over by the Bank of America, it paid billions in bonuses to executives that bank shareholders knew nothing about when they approved the deal. And, when the banks' CFO Kenneth Lewis retired in 2009, he stood to collect a $53 million pension, despite a 50 percent dip in the bank's stock at the year of his retirement. In 2009, a few weeks before Tribune Company (which publishes the *Los Angeles Times, Chicago Tribune, Baltimore Sun* and other newspapers and own television stations) filed bankruptcy, it paid millions in bonuses to the 700 top mangers under the guise of "incentivizing key mangers to battle all challenges." Forget that 2,000 people lost their jobs prior to bankruptcy; the system permitted the entitled to their gilded packages.[22]

Amidst proposed remedies by the federal government to limit executive pay, several corporations have recrafted pay policies for top executives. This includes "clawback" policies designated to penalize employees who cause companies to lose money. In 2009 approximately 70 percent of Fortune 500 companies introduced such policies, often allowing three to five years to force top executives to pay back a portion of their pay (usually in the form of stock) for their mistakes. Most critics are skeptical that such policies do any good at all; they merely see this as window dressing to keep regulators from emphasizing real reforms.

Given public dismay and frustration over executive pay in 2009, the median cash pay for 200 CEOs at the largest companies declined by 13 percent to $7.7 million; the average fell 15 percent to $9.5 million. The top 30 CEO salaries ranged from $15.1 million to $84 million, despite the fact that year revenues decreased in 15 of these 30 companies and net income decreased in 14.[23] In other words, CEO salaries had nothing to do with performance. Whatever deals are concocted behind closed doors in boardrooms, they are designed to buy time, gloss over the sins of capitalism, and keep the government from meddling in corporate America or curbing CEO salaries.

Bailouts and Bonuses

For Goldman Sachs, the symbol of American greed, speculation and money minting on Wall Street, their bonus rebounded in 2008 to nearly $20 billion in total for its 28,000 employees, or more than $750,000 a person, double the firm's $363,000 average the previous year. It also paid $5 million or more to its 78 top executives.[24] The 2009 bonuses were similar—some $16.2 billion, averaging about $600,000 a person. And it was its taxpayers that made it possible with bailout money that allowed the company to navigate the economic meltdown. Without apologizing for past mistakes that led to the economic meltdown, the six largest banks (Bank of America, Chase, Citigroup, Goldman Sachs, Morgan Stanley, and Wells Fargo) set aside more than $110 billion for salaries and bonuses in 2009, even though the majority of these companies did not meet analysts' expectations.[25] Of course, when you consider yourself the "masters of the universe" a bit of humility is out of the question; the hell with plebian society.

These are the same financial and corporate leaders, along with their conservative base, that have held a needed increase in the minimum wage hostage for more than a decade under the pretense that doing so is the best way for corporate America to compete in the global economy. They are the same people who were against extending unemployment benefits to the jobless whose benefits were running out in 2010, under the pretext that lazy behavior would be encouraged and the cost ($57 billion) was too high. Of course, it was not mentioned that the tax cut for millionaires in 2010 cost more than ten times the amount. This giveaway package to the super rich helps explain how power in the U.S. (both political and economic) is aligned, a web of political and economic interests condoned by law. Similarly, these are the same people who consistently ensure that Congressional bills and tax laws are written to support their life styles and corporate interests while keeping the minimum wage flat for the ten years, working wages flat for the last thirty years and forcing unions into pay cuts and reduced benefits when the economy faulted. In the meantime, the top 1% saw their income after inflation increase nearly 300 percent since 1980.

In all, 4,793 bankers and traders received a bonus of at least $1 million in 2008. The bonuses reflect one of the worst aspects of government-banking collusion, and the hazards of mixing the goals of capitalism with the public interest. Remember, Wall Street and the banks survived the 2008-09 economic crisis thanks to government hand outs. As much as $165 billion of public money were paid to the nine large investment houses and banks to ward off bankruptcy. The same money was then comingled with other accounts to pay bonuses. Of those nine institutions that received bailout money, the bonuses totaled $32.6 billion but their losses were $81 billion. [26] In short, the tax payer—who lost billions in the meltdown such as lost wages, reduced values in retirement funds and investments, and reduced home values and home foreclosures—paid the bonuses. To be sure, money does not trickle downward, as we are told by the free marketers. Money is scooped from the bottom to the top, from ordinary people to the rich and then super rich. This flow of money explains why financial reform can only be limited and whitewashed.

In this connection, compensation and bonuses are not necessarily related to profits or performance. For example, compensation in 2008 (at the height of the recession) at Morgan Stanley was seven times larger than profits. It's the robber baron attitude, rooted in the Gilded Age, among banking investors that is crucial! It's like a bunch of drunken pirates raiding ships and running off with the loot, with no concern about the consequences nor concern for investors or the public. If the enterprise fails or if it looks like they might go hungry, the government will bail them out.

According to Barry Ritholtz, the author of *Bailout Nation*, the government's total bailout package, including the rescue of Bear Stearns, Merrill Lynch, the nine big banks, AIG, Fannie Mae, Freddie Mac and General Motors, plus the stimulus package and mortgage assistance, cost taxpayers an estimated $14 trillion—equivalent to the U.S. Gross Domestic Product in 2007. The number sounds high, but Ritholtz is a Wall Street insider. For him, the rescue of Long-Term Capital Management in 1998, a hedge fund that was over leveraged and saddled by bad investments, was the forerunner for the 2008 meltdown. Had the hedge fund been allowed to go belly up and not saved by the Feds, those lenders such as Bear Stearns,

Merrill Lynch, and Lehman Brothers might have learned a good lesson and might not have gotten over their heads in 2008; hence, the economic crisis might have been averted. All this is hypothetical, sought of a stretch. But if the Feds are not allied with Wall Street, I submit as does Ritholtz, the government are enablers. It created the "too big to fail" atmosphere ten years prior to the economic meltdown.

Of course, if there were honest and systematic risk regulators to serve as an early warning system, lots of questionable mortgages, credit-default swaps (that is insurance policies which lacked sufficient funds against default), phony triple A investment ratings and over leveraged and high-risk concentration of investments might have been prevented. The issue is, when problems are uncovered, someone must have the guts and ethical fiber (not to be paid off to look the other way) to react.

The rating agencies have managed to slip under the radar screen and have been ignored by the media. Not only did they lack transparency, they were also bought off and corrupted by their clients—the big banks who packaged and sold their junk investments to other banks and pension funds. The agencies made hundreds of millions in fees as they rated thousands of deals in mortgage securities and collaterized debt obligations. By 2010, 91 percent of their Triple A assessments for 2007 were downgraded to junk status, along with 93 percent of those issued in 2006 and 53 percent in 2005.[27]

Had the banks and pension fund known they were paying good money for junk, it is unlikely these institutions would have purchased the investments and unlikely the world economy would have nose-dived in 2008 and 2009. As reform proposals are set in motion to fix these agencies, the executives of Moody and Standard & Poors remain off the hook—not even a slap on their wrists—as big government and Wall Street make their next deal behind closed doors. To be sure, rating agencies perform a public function; they need to be regulated and not paid by private clients that stand to profit by the ratings.

In short, mortgage companies, bank lenders and investors, hedge fund managers, insurance companies, and Wall Street traders and brokers all need to be restrained, supervised, and held accountable—basic Business I terms. However, if some people believe that government regulation is the big boogey-man—or that the problem is too much government involvement—then ideological blinders will undermine government remedies. It takes a great deal of faith, a huge *ism*, to blame the economic crisis on big government. The big lie is to say that unfettered capitalism is healthy and altruism and safety nets are destructive policies.

The Issue of Compensation

When it comes to retirement, the *average retirement package* for Fortune 500 company's chief executives exceeded $1 million per year from 2008 to 2010 in terms of pension pay and perks, with some companies such as Exxon, Pfizer, SBC Communications, United Airlines, and United Health dishing more than $5 million *per year* for retirement of executives. Compare the $1 million annual CEO figure to the private pension of the average American, amounting to less than $5,000 per year, and the multiplier is 200; the $5 million pay-out figure equates to 1,000 times. These outrageous figures are dismissed by consultants for big corporations: A retirement plan replaces income; it does not create wealth, so we are told. The fact is, if you take into consideration life expectancy of the various CEOs, these pensions amount to annuities worth approximately $100 million, and they are not linked to performance measures or company stock earnings.

The same kind of inequality exists with *average annual compensation* for the average chief executive of the Fortune 500 and that of the average worker in the company. From 2000 to 2010, the ratio has fluctuated from 275 times to 531 times, compared to the ratio in Japan which was 10 to 25 times. No question big financial rewards motivate people to excel, and thus helps the economy to grow. But when rewards are lopsided (someone earns a $10 million annual bonus) in a winner-take-all situation, while ordinary workers in the same company are told they must tighten their belts, it destroys morale and the desire to work hard among the majority of people. (This is what happened with Enron and WorldCom, and more recently with Merrill Lynch, AIG, and the *Tribune*.)

Often members of a compensation committee are former chief executives who identify with other executives and have a tough time saying no to salary increases of fellow executives. Furthermore, CEOs benefit from one another's pay increases because compensation packages are often compared or based on a survey of what their peers are earning.

It's like an "old boy" network, each person taking care of and benefitting from the salary demands of their fellow club members. What's new and strange is the degree to which CEOs (and other) high-paid sports and entertainment people) inhabit their own Manichean make-believe world; they actually believe their vivid fictions—they are worth the enormous compensation they receive.

Although outside consultant firms assure the public that CEO salaries and pensions are competitive and in line with what other CEOs earn, they fail to reveal the lucrative relationships with the same company executives they are evaluating to determine executive pay and other compensation matters such as bonuses, stock options, etc. One example among many firms is Hewitt Associates, which earned $2.8 billion in one year for consulting and investment advice and wore two hats with companies like Boeing, Morgan Stanley, Nortel, Procter & Gamble, Toro, and Verizon. They were hired by corporate boards to provide advice on paying corporate executives, the same people who hired them for other consulting services. This is the closest thing to corporate incest, although the consulting firms claim they are offering a broad range of services and can manage the potential conflict of interests. Their response might be great for public consumption, but it is hard for a stockholder to swallow who is counting on the company's performance and profit for his or her retirement and watching the stock go down while the CEO's compensation goes up and up each year. I would like to think that the day of reckoning is due, that pouring money into the pockets of CEOs without justification is coming to an end.

Despite whatever spin someone puts on CEO pensions and payout plans, it becomes tragic when we consider GMs announcements, that after losing sales for two decades to its Asian rivals, it had offered buyouts to 113,000 factory workers. This is on top of its previous announcement that it would eliminate 30,000 factory jobs and close down 12 plants in the Midwest through 2008. Once the pride of America's manufacturing might and largest private employer, it announced in 2009 that it would drop half its brands, close 5 more plants, and eliminate 47,000 additional jobs. And to ward off criticism of its bloated management, 400 of its 1300 top executives resigned or retired. To be sure the closing of the plants and loss of jobs is symbolic of a larger issue—the demise of 24,000 U.S. manufacturing plants and the loss of more than 5 million factory jobs between 2000 and 2010.[28]

Buyouts for GM ranged from $35,000 to $140,000 for those who had ten to twenty-six years on the job and were willing to surrender health-care coverage. Now compare it to someone who received $135 to $200 million for working fifteen months (Mallone) to five years (McKinnell) as a CEO. Do the math any way you want. Use any model you think is appropriate, and ask how do we respond to the issues of equity and fairness or the simple fact that no one, except perhaps McDonald's or Wal-Mart at $8 or $9 an hour, will hire a "washed-up" thirty-year veteran GM worker. I don't think we have to worry about people like Mallone, and McKinnell, but we do have to worry that CEO payout plans create huge inequality which in turn affects the standard of living of *all* Americans (because their purchasing power drives up prices for the rest of Americans).

The consuming patterns of the super wealthy affect all of us—our way of life, our attitudes and behaviors. Knowing that someone built a 10,000 square foot home, or bought a 50 foot yacht or spent a million dollars on a birthday party shapes norms and behaviors of the larger society: We can build a bigger house, buy a bigger boat, or make a more expensive wedding when we cannot afford it. This perception combines with the notion of relative deprivation, and it drives us to buy more and bigger and march deeper into debt. Thus, Robert Frank in *Falling Behind* notes that the medium sized new home between 1980 and 2001 increased from 1,600 to 2,100 square feet; and, if I may add, home prices increased more than 400 percent, even though the median household income increased about 2 ½ percent each year. The end result: Americans work 13 hours longer per week than their European counterparts, save less and borrow more. And it was this massive U.S. debt, coupled with undocumented loans for people who were able to obtain larger mortgages, that was a major factor behind the 2008-10 housing and economic collapse in the country.

In the midst of working Americans losing jobs, pensions, and health plans as corporations reorganize or declare bankruptcy, huge executive pay and pensions lead the average American to conclude that business funnels money from workers to the rich, and thus the rich get richer. If executives are making lots of money, it has to come from someone's pocket. To be sure, a recent Roper poll concluded that 72 percent of the public believes there is widespread wrongdoing in the business world. But the public feels helpless. In a Harris poll, 90 percent of respondents maintained that big business either highly influences or runs big government. The chief executive of Delphi, the auto parts company and former subsidiary of

GM, put it bluntly: "Society has come to believe that the term 'crooked CEO' is redundant."

Teddy Roosevelt was following public opinion when he broke up the monopolies at the turn of the twentieth century. One hundred years later, it's time to clamp down on business wrongdoing, better regulate big business, and require that shareholders approve executive pay and executive parachutes. We also need to put sufficient pressure on external auditors and public attorneys, who we expect to guarantee public trust and ethical corporate behavior, to do their job. The big banks need larger capital reserves to meet more prudent standards, and the web of interconnection among investment banks need to be splintered. The only institution that can enforce these ideas is government, but it is deemed by the public as inefficient and incapable. But government is unwilling to do anything because big business is often in bed with politicians. What also hurts the American workers is the silence of the victims and the bystanders who are capable of going to the ballot box and voting for reform, instead wink at betrayal or say "losing is a way of life."

CONCLUSION

Paul Krugman, the Princeton economist and *New York Times* columnist, is much more optimistic about the future of the U.S. than the author, despite the fact that in his book, *The Conscience of a Liberal*, he feels that the Bush administration set us so far back that it will take decades before people from around the world "regard the U.S. as a fully sane country." Not only did the administration promote the interests of the rich at the expense of everyone else, but it also turned the government into a huge spoils system based on cronism and ideology. It was the Bush administration that bankrupted the economy by allowing Wall Street to go unchecked and unregulated, while special interest groups, government contractors and business lobbyists stole billions of dollars, both on a national (Katrina) and international level (Iraq). Of course, a defense can be mounted. Wall Street and big businesses have run amok since the Gilded Age, and business and government officials have engaged in corruption and bribery since the dawn of civilization.

Krugman feels that several years from now we are going to look back and get the full story and it's going to be much worse than we realize now. Still, he feels we will pull out of the present mess like we did after the Great Depression. The period we are in now will be written off as if "it was a time of testing, but America came through." I'm not so sure. Discard the old dictionary and the old dream. His analysis assumes we will still be running the world's economy, our technological advances will keep us ahead of our competitors, and brain drain will continue to flow in our direction and not be siphoned off by other countries.

Our students cannot compete with other industrialized nations in math and science, and we have too many smart people looking to become financial engineers and not real engineers and trying to make money on Wall Street instead of making real things or new things. We have pushed out most talented students to the largely unproductive chase on Wall Street while nothing of substance is produced and the corporate mentality is focused on profits. The outcome is becoming clear. The U.S. and rich nations of the world, the so-called G-8, will no longer be running the world order. Moreover, the expectation is that the U.S. will no longer serve as the chief engine of the global economy. The good days are past; the sun is beginning to decline in the West. (At the turn of the twenty-first century, America represented 5 percent of the world's populace but consumed 25 percent of its resources). We need to get used to leaner times, including a dip in the standard of living among the bottom 99 percent of the American populace.

All great nations and empires rise and fall—or overreach and decline. Not only have good jobs been permanently lost over seas, but also there can be no substantial recovery when corporations at home are intent on minimizing payroll and labor costs by squeezing the the pay of those on the job and hiring part-timers and independent contractors without benefits instead of full-time workers with benefits.

All these trends, coupled with increased plastic debt, forclosures, bankruptcy filings, collapse of employment opportunities and refusal of taxpayers to pay for infrastructure repairs and education are all part of the new economy that is in store for the American populace. Our standard of living is in steady free fall. It's been in freefall for the last thirty years, evidenced by the median salary remaining flat during these years, but masked by plastic debt and increasing home prices and mortgage payments (more debt). Nor do these trends take into account that most middle—and upper middle-class families are dependent on two breadwinners. So to figure out the true impact on most American families, all these household numbers have to be halved to derive the effect of our economic decline.

Liberal Pundits feel that the Democrats are the party of and for the people, but putting too much faith in the Dems can be mistaken. The harsh fact is that many Democratic senators like Dodd, Kerry, and Schumer for years supported Wall Street and the banking industry, stifled government regulation, supported tax breaks for the rich, including hedge fund managers, and received large "donations" from the financial industry. It's nice to mention the hearings and proposals for reforming the financial industry (reducing risk-taking, cutting down the size of banks (so as not to become too big to fail) and providing more oversight of big banks). But we should not expect too many changes, given the historical linkage between politics and money and the army of lobbyists who regularly descend on Capitol Hill. John Bogle, the founder of the giant Vangard Fund, puts it bluntly. "We need to try, but all the lawyers and geniuses on Wall Street are going to figure out ways to get around everything."[29]

That said, continue to expect huge risks in pursuit of quick profits and huge bonuses at the expense of investors and taxpayers. Whether you consider it practical, or "the way the cookie crumbles," government believes that the underlining risks involved in the business of investing and lending should be borne by the public (or little person) and the profits awarded to investors and lending institutions. There is no patchy grass or bumpy road for Wall Street tycoons and investment bankers. Heads they win; tails we lose.

Now when people are paid by the amount of business or by short-term profits, then the risk factor is pushed aside and people get caught up in a frenzy, including the ordinary person who often invests his live savings in mutual funds or a spec house which he expects to flip. Prices go higher, as an increasing number of large and small investors participate in the frenzy to catch the train before it leaves the station. Economic resources get directed where they shouldn't, and a bear market follows and serves as a corrective mechanism and rule of reason. The little person who is unknowledgeable about day to day investment fluctuations is usually the last person to get off the train or see the coming bear market; the person either sinks or sells for a severe loss, while the big fish with inside information and/or knowledge of the industry manages to hedge or limit his risk—or even pull his money out before the crash. Large financial companies are often slower to react, but are then considered too big to fail, they are connected to advisors of big government and receive special treatment.

As the tax debate unfolds, and you find it difficult to comprehend the complexities of the numbers, there is a guiding principle to keep in mind that dates back to the time Moses carried down the tablets from the mountaintop. The rich are undertaxed because they have a voice and the ear of political leaders. Today, in the U.S. they pay the lobbyists and the experts to maintain favorable treatment. They pay 15 cents in federal taxes on their investments and profits, while the rest of us pay 25 to 35 percent on wages. The kings and queens of wealth call their income "capital gains" and present the argument that it deserves a lower tax rate than "wages," (as well as other "incentives") because their behavior stimulates growth and prosperity. But you can also make the same point about labor, that sweat and toil drives the economic engine, but you will not get anywhere with the argument because the ordinary person has a limited voice.

The tax law conforms to Internal Revenue standards, but you need to understand the law is not based on God's law or the dictums of Zeus—or any moral or classical doctrine. It's a law based on politics, and the influence of lobbyists and experts who testify before Congress and are paid by big business and Wall Street interests to represent free market ideology. It is also supported by political contributions and donations that annually amount to millions of dollars. It comes down to simple math. For every dollar "invested," spent or donated by business interests and rich folks, they make back thousands of dollars in tax savings and thus are able to accumulate more wealth at the expense of ordinary people who pay twice the tax rate on their wages. Under this policy, the working person is doomed to a second-class status while the wealthy solidify their aristocratic status.

Now things could be worse. One of the reasons for the French Revolution was that the peasants and workers were overtaxed while the nobility paid no taxes. In the U.S., the impetus behind the Shays rebellion, and later the Whiskey uprising, was that the agrarian class was being taxed while the property class had no taxes. The reason is simple. The latter group had the political power between the framing of the Constitution in 1787 and the election of Thomas Jefferson in 1800.

The French Revolution and American Revolution were based on equalitarian ideals which the economic elites and conservatives in both countries saw as disorder and an attack on their interpretation of human nature: Men by birth are unequal and these innate differences lead to inequality of property and wealth. The situation faced by President Obama is similar to the one faced by Jefferson more than 200 years ago. The passions and desires of men do not necessarily conform to reason, fairness or justice, especially when money and property are at stake. Hamilton opposed Jefferson and argued that government must be strong to protect the property class against the people he labeled as the "mob" or "herd." Obama's thinking is rooted in Jeffersonian logic—that government must serve the people and protect them from the money class. But a host of conservative pundits and lawmakers, steeped in Hamiltonian orthodoxy, argue today that Obama's policies are a grave peril to capitalism and will lead us down the path to socialism.

What we have in this country is disguised warfare between the rich and superrich and the rest of the people—or what Ben Stein, a liberal economist and *New York Times* columnist, called a continuation "down the road to the Bastille." I would add that we are still debating the ideas of the Enlightenment, and the words of the Declaration of Independence; that is, whether ordinary people are equal (or not equal) to the wealthy or noble class and whether ordinary people (Hamilton's "mob") are entitled to an even playing field for opportunity and success.

Finally allow me some vivid prose. You might say that I'm some ideologue, a liberal or worse—that I make your skin creep. But no matter how you slice the economy, it's a hard rain, a hard life for most of us. For those people who say I'm too rough-edged and visceral—simply unpatriotic or a pinko in disguise, for those people, I say that we are speaking a different language. I'm supported by of 5,000 years of history. You either haven't lived in the working trenches—or you still believe in sugar-coated stories and magical thinking: the Wizard of Oz, Mary Poppins and Horatio Algier. Given the structural changes in the American economy (massive debt, outsourced jobs, disposable workers, unemployment and underemployment), I hope you are still able to find your own rainbow.

Chapter 5

QUESTIONS TO CONSIDER

1. Why is formal education more important in the twenty-first century than the nineteenth or early twentieth century?

2. What is the role of the school in a democratic society? In providing economic opportunity? In socializing youth? In enhancing a national identity?

3. Who were the pioneers of free public schooling? Why did they spearhead the push for universal education?

4. How would you describe the relationship between schooling and equal opportunity?

5. Can schools overcome the effects of class? What other social conditions effect economic outcomes? How are less fortunate students supposed to overcome money, power, privilege, and political connections that more fortunate students posses?

6. Why might some people argue that schools are no longer the great social or economic equalizer?

7. How did William Harris and Charles Eliot influence American education? How would you describe their economic philosophy and principles of competition?

8. How is inequality related to the notion of survival of the fittest and unfettered competition?

9. Why were most social reformers unconcerned about extremely low percentages of students graduating from high school and entering college at the turn of the twentieth century?

10. Why did some early twentieth century critics link immigration to civil strife and the downfall of the country?

11. As society succeeds in equalizing opportunity, why do genetic factors become increasingly more important in determining economic outcomes? Why is it that the correlation between IQ and school achievement increases through successive grade levels?

12. What is the modern or current view of inequality of educational opportunity?

13. Why does the discussion of race, ethnicity, and religion in the U.S. lead to hotly contested debates compared to other societies such as Japan or Norway?

14. What is the relationship between excellence and education? Excellence and luck? Education credentials and performance?

15. How should we define excellence and equality? How should society balance excellence and equality?

Chapter 5

EXCELLENCE, EQUALITY, AND EDUCATION

No country has taken the idea of *equality* more seriously than the United States. Politically, the idea is rooted in the Declaration of Independence and the Constitution. We have fought two wars over the definition of equality: the American Revolution and the Civil War. Starting in the 1960s, first with the War on Poverty and then the civil rights movement, the language of progressive thought and protest became associated with inequality. The concern focused on poor and minority rights, including women.

Inequality in today's world deals with the growing gap in income and wealth between the rich and rest of us, the top 1 to 10 percent and the bottom 90 to 99 percent. The difference in percentages is a function of the authors, bias and what point they are trying to delineate. If the discussion is about a small zip code such as Greenich, Ct; Fisher Island, Fl; or the Hamptons in New York, the discussion can be limited to the top 1 percent. If the discussion focuses on a broader population, then the top 10 percent suffice.

The notion of *excellence* is a recent concept, first introduced by the British sociologist Michael Young in 1958 in his book, *The Rise of the Meritocracy*, in which the process of advancement by merit is outlined. The best and highest-paid positions in society are obtained on the basis of individual performance, rather than positions being allocated at random, by group characteristics such as race or gender, or by political and social networking, patronage or nepotism. Of course, such a society does not exist and the book is a utopian concept.

In the United States, John Gardner, the founder of Common Cause, wrote a small pocket-sized book in 1961 called *Excellence: Can We Be Equal Too?* In this book, he points out the need for a democratic society to balance excellence and equality. It must reward people for their abilities, but it also needs to make provisions for the less able person. In both books, the authors remind us that family origins should not count as an advantage or handicap in determining economic outcomes. The key to economic success should be attritable to the person's abilities and education (or training) that should make the person more valuable to society.

DEFINITIONS AND LABELS

Every modern society must deal with the relationship between excellence, equality, and education. When society considers *excellence*, it must deal with the division of labor and what it will pay for certain jobs. When 95 percent of the jobs in the U.S. pay less than $100,000 per year, we need to ask why certain other jobs pay a million dollars or more—and are the benefits and importance (or responsibilities) of the high-paying jobs worth the cost. If merit is defined in terms of performance, we need to distinguish between performance and credentials. (Having the appropriate education credentials does not necessary guarantee good performance.) We must also work out definitions or criteria for performance (good, average, poor etc.), tests and evaluation procedures in school and in the work place for determining merit and performance—and then what are appropriate rewards.

Society must consider *equality* in terms of power and wealth—which people or groups earn more or less (and how much more or less) than the average income—and why. The more egalitarian or progressive the society, the more safety nets it will provide to help ordinary, slow, unqualified and disabled workers to obtain and pay for essential human goods (such as food and shelter) and services (such as health, education and transportation). The exact benefits and standards for obtaining the benefits must be worked our politically. Hence, it depends on what political group (liberal or conservative) sets the agenda. The more benefits available—unemployment insurance, health insurance, pensions and

Social Security for the poor, disabled and aged—the more egalitarian the society.

From its birth in 1776 to the turn of the twentieth century, the United States moved from an agrarian to an industrial society. *Education* and training were important but not crucial factors for increasing opportunity. Farm and industrial societies are primarily based on muscle power and not brain power, so that a good deal of mobility could be achieved without a high school or college diploma. Apprenticeships, training, and learning on the job were more important than a formal education for the masses to live a descent life.

As society became more complex and bureaucratic, education became more important. With the coming of the information age and knowledge-based society at the mid-twentieth century, formal education took on even greater importance for opportunity and mobility. Brain power now substituted muscle power as the crucial factor for economic advancement. The female liberation movement, which started in the 1950s with its demand for more equality, coincides with the coming information/knowledge revolution. The movement provided a much easier vehicle for women to obtain middle-class jobs, economic independence, and greater equality in just a few decades.

Here it should be noted that the three E-factors—excellence, equality, and education—are impressionistic and idiosyncratic. Although these three labels serve as working definitions, education is the glue or lever that helps balance excellence and equality. And if I may add a touch of poetry, in the language of Dr. Suess, it's the "Cat in the Hat" that prevents the waste of talent and curbs the vestiges of stratification.

Education, today, is the link between excellence and equality. It is considered essential for promoting a person's opportunity and mobility and for improving the productivity of society. In a society dedicated to the pursuit of social justice, intensive efforts should be devoted to providing the best education for all its citizens and to close the education gaps that exist between the "haves" and "have nots," rich and poor students. It must not write off its disadvantaged populations as "uneducable" or slot them into poorly funded schools and second rate programs. Our Founding Fathers understood the notion of social justice, although they called it by different names such as "freedom," "liberty" and "natural rights" of man. They wanted the children of the common people to have a fair chance to grow up as equal as possible. Equal opportunity, regardless of parentage, combined with the need for civic responsibility, were the driving forces for schooling in America.

Starting with the spirit of 1776, allow the author to plow though 235 years of history to pin down the notion of equality and education. I promise not to inflict too much pain or expose you to the fossilizations of dead thought.

THE ROLE OF THE SCHOOLS

The origins of American public schools are demonstrated by the concept of equal opportunity and the notion of universal and free education. Thomas Jefferson understood that the full development of talent among all classes could and should be developed in the New World, and especially among the common class. "Geniuses will be raked from the rubbish," he wrote in his *Notes on the State of Virginia* in 1782. He added that the common people of America had the opportunity and ability for discussing social and political problems denied to them in the Old World.

Writing during the same Revolutionary period, Thomas Paine who was an unknown recent arrival from England began publishing several pamphlets including the best known *Common Sense* and *The Crisis*. As an anti-monarch, pro-democratic pamphleteer, Paine lashed out against the vestiges of the property and landholding class and argued that government had the power to abolish poverty and provide social and economic security by introducing policies and programs for the disabled and aged by imposing inheritance taxes and rents on government land. The idea that inequality could be reduced and social programs could be implemented by government was a revolutionary idea—and rooted in Rousseau's notion of a social contract between government and its citizens.

Paine also believed that the farmers, artisans and mechanics and other plain people had not taken part in the intellectual and artistic life of the colonies (and for that matter in any other previous society) and declared they should have the opportunity for education and culture. He rejected the common notion that education and culture, as well as philosophical and intellectual concepts, were limited to the province of the aristocracy and church.

Rush: Education for Progress

Benjamin Rush, a well-known Philadelphian physician and signer of the Declaration of Independence, asserted that the role of education was essential if democracy was to succeed. The youth must be trained in civil and patriotic duties and in practical skills in order to retain their political and economic independence as adults. Writing a short essay, "Of the Mode of Education in a Republic," he argued that the "form of government we have assumed has created a new class of duties for every American." Education was the key for preparing young Americans for public service and jobs. In order for the blessings of liberty and equality to spread in the New World, the education system had to "prepare the principles, morals and manners of [its] citizens" for a new form of government and new pattern of thought.

The American Revolution had opened up a new chapter in human affairs, one that elevated the dignity of the common man and the humbling of the aristocracy—and all the special privileges which tarnish the dignity and equality of humankind. On trying to elevate the national character, Rush warned about the rise of the banking and finance class and that "a nation debased by the love of money is a spectacle far more awful" than the evils of war.

Jefferson: Education for Citizenship

When Jefferson introduced "the pursuit of happiness" at the end of Locke's famous statement "life, liberty and property"—Jefferson (like Paine and Rush) was implying that the common man had the natural right for a descent life, for opportunity and success, and to participate in the social progress of the nation. Such an idea stemmed from the humanitarian spirit of the Enlightenment, although it defied 5,000 plus years of actual history: Ordinary people had no rights and no expectations to live beyond poverty or subsistence levels. In arguing for human rights (what he called "natural rights"), Jefferson was implying a legal and moral duty for equality among people, even between the patrician class and plain people. Education was the key to equality.

Faith in the agrarian society and distrust toward the proletariat of the cities were basic in Thomas Jefferson's idea of democracy. A man of wide-ranging interests that embraced politics, agriculture, architecture, science and education, Jefferson assumed the state had the responsibility to cultivate an educated and liberated citizenry to ensure a democratic society. In "A Bill for the More General Diffusion of Knowledge," Jefferson advocated a plan that provided educational opportunities for both common people and landed gentry "at the expense of all." To Jefferson, formal education was largely a state or civic concern, rather than a matter reserved to religious or upper-class groups. Schools should be financed through public taxes.

Webster: Education for Nationalism

Even though same leaders of the new country mistrusted the masses of the people and continued to favor the classical curriculum, with its emphasis on Greek, Latin, rhetoric and logic, the popular movement in government mobilized against the money class and the old school curriculum based on English traditions. Accompanying this growing political liberalism was an emerging cultural nationalism led by Noah Webster—a demand for an American language, an American culture, and an American educational system free of English ideas from the past. As a new nation, America sought its own political system and culture—and this thinking spilled over into the schools.

Often called the "American School Master," Webster realized that a national language and literature conveyed a sense of national identity, and thus he set out to reshape U.S. English through the schools. He believed that a unified American language would eliminate the remains of European usage, create a uniform means of communication free of localism and provincialism, and promote opportunity, citizenship and nationalism. Webster urged Americans to "unshackle [their] minds and act like independent beings. You have been children long enough, subject to the control and subservient to the interests of a haughty parent . . . You have an empire to save . . . and a natural character to establish and extend by your wisdom and judgment."

Because books read by students would shape their thoughts, Webster spent much of his time writing and publishing spelling and reading books. For his era, Webster wrote the most influential American grammar book in 1783, the most widely used *American Spelling Book* (which had sold an estimated 15 million copies by 1873) and the first *American Dictionary* which was completed in 1825 after 25 years of laborious work.

The Common School Movement

Both Rush and Jefferson were concerned with equal education opportunity and proposed universal education for all children and methods for identifying students of superior ability who were to receive free high school and college educations. Their plans for their respective states (Pennsylvania and Virginia) were never approved.

Horace Mann also understood the need for schooling, and argued that education was the chief avenue where "humble and ambitious youth" could expect to rise. The rise of "common school" was spearheaded by Mann in the 1820s. In the words of Columbia University's Lawrence Cremin, in *The Republic and the School*, Mann envisioned the schools as "the great equalizer of the condition of men—the balance wheel of the social machinery." Mann also saw the schools serving a social need, that is, to assimilate immigrants into the American culture. He skillfully rallied public support for the common school by appealing to various segments of the population. To enlist the business community, Mann sought to demonstrate that "education has a market value" with a yield similar to "common bullion." The "aim of industry . . . and wealth of the country" would be augmented "in proportion to the diffusion of knowledge." Workers would be more diligent and more productive.

Mann also established a stewardship theory, aimed at the upper class, that the public good would be enhanced by public education. Schools for all children would create a stable society in which people would obey the laws and add to the nation's political and economic well being. To the workers and farmers, Mann asserted that the common school would be a means of social mobility for their children. To the Protestant community, he argued that the common school would assimilate ethnic and religious groups, promote a common culture, and help immigrant children learn English and the customs and laws of the land. He was convinced that the common school was crucial for the American system of equality and opportunity, for a sense of community to be shared by all Americans, and for the promotion of a national identity.

Although the pattern for establishing common schools varied among the states, and the quality of education varied as well, the foundation of the American public school was being forged though this system. The schools were common in the sense that they housed youngsters of all socioeconomic and religious backgrounds, from age six to fourteen or fifteen, and were jointly owned, cared for, and used by the local community. Because a variety of subjects was taught to children of all ages, teachers had to plan as many as ten to fifteen different lessons a day. Teachers also had to try to keep their schoolrooms warm in the winter—a responsibility shared by the older boys, who cut and fetched wood—and cool in the summer. Schoolhouses were often in need of considerable repair, and teachers were paid miserably low salaries.

The immigrants and workers saw the schools as a social vehicle for upward mobility, to help their children realize the American dream. Equality of opportunity in this context would not lead to equality of outcomes; this concept did not attempt a classless society. As Stanford Professor David Tyack wrote in *Turning Points in American Educational History,* "For the most part, working men did not seek to pull down the rich"; rather they sought equality of "opportunity for their children, an equal chance at the main chance."

Equality of opportunity in the nineteenth and early twentieth centuries meant an equal start for all children, but the assumption was that some would go farther than others. Differences in backgrounds and abilities, a well as motivation and personality, would create differences in outcomes among individuals, but the school would assure that children born into any class would have the opportunity to achieve status as persons born into other classes. Implicit in the view was that the schools represented the means of achieving the goal of equal chances of success relative to all children in all strata.

The connection with schooling and society was symbolized by the "little red school house" on the prairie and idealized by the Horatio Alger`s themes in his sentimental books on the self-made man, vision of the American dream, and power of the individual to rise above his social class. The goal of schooling fit into the popular biographies of Andrew Johnson and Abe Lincoln, how they rose from their log cabins on the frontier to become president, and it fit with words of poet Russell Lowell, that the essence of the American promise was "to lift artificial weights from all shoulders [and] afford all an unfettered start, a fair chance, in the race of life."

OPPS, A DIFFERENT HISTORICAL PERSPECTIVE

In retrospect, the schools did not fully achieve the goal of equal opportunity, because school achievement and economic outcomes are highly related to social class and family background. Had the schools not existed, however, social mobility would have been further reduced. The failure of the common school to provide social mobility raises the question of the role of school in achieving equality—and the question of just what the school can and cannot do to affect cognitive and economic outcomes. Can schooling overcome the effects of class? Such factors as family conditions, peer groups, and community surroundings—all components of class—influence learning. Just what should the school be expected to accomplish in the few hours each day it has with students who spend more than three-fourths of their time with their family, friends, and community?

Class is a matter of culture—what educators now call "social capital," the kind of family and community resources available to children. The difference in capital leads to a system of inequality in terms of how students perform in schools and what kinds of jobs they eventually obtain. The question of fairness or equity is how we interpret this inequality. Do middle-class children simply "outcompete" their poor and working-class counterparts in school and therefore land better jobs (a conservative perspective) or is it discrimination and exploitation that ensures the latter group performs poorly in school and their parents, who clean up offices and hotels or work on assembly plants, earn significantly less than their bosses (a liberal perspective).

As middle and upper-class parents jockey for the best schools for their children and hire private tutors and worry about their children's SAT scores, how are less fortunate students supposed to overcome money, power and privilege. How is education expected to overcome a system of inequality that leads to the rich to pressure the government to reduce their taxes while it cuts services for the poor, and provides them with second-rate schools, second-rate healthcare, and second-rate jobs?

The notion of differences in class and the relationship to heredity have remained in the background in American thought, an idea rooted in the Old World to help explain the success of the noble class. The same notion was later used by conservative-thinking Americans to explain the rise of the plantation, merchant, and banking class in colonial America, and then the capitalist class in the late nineteenth century during the Gilded Age. By the 1880s, Herbert Spencer, the English philosopher, maintained that the poor were "unfit" and should be eliminated through competition and the "survival of the fittest." Because the evolutionary process involved long periods of time, according to laws independent of human behavior, education could never serve as an important factor in social and economic progress. The best the schools could do is to provide basic knowledge that enabled people to adapt and survive within their environment. What Spencer failed to grasp is that with an educated mind, the character and speed of evolution for humans change, moving from a traditional and static society to a dynamic and rapid changing society.

From 1873 (when the Kalamazoo, Michigan court decision provided for free public schools) to 1900, questions revolved around the school curriculum: What should be taught at the elementary and secondary school? What courses should comprise the curriculum? Who should attend high school? Should there be separate tracks or programs for smart and slow students? Should the same education be available for all students? Should the high school be considered prepatory for college? What curriculum provisions should be made for terminal students? Who should attend college?

The Conservative Slant

William Harris, the former St. Louis Commissioner of Education from 1861 to 1881 and U.S. Commissioner of Education from 1889 to 1906 and Charles Eliot, president of Harvard University from 1869 to 1909, dominated the reform movement during this period. Both educators were traditionalists and moralists. Harris had Mann's faith in free public schools.

Harris wrote in 1871, "If the rising generation does not grow up with democratic principles, the fault will lie in the system of popular education." He thought that the common schools should teach morality and citizenship, "lift all classes of people into a participation in civilized life [and] instill social order." Whereas Mann saw the common school as a great equalizer and force for social morality, Harris saw it as an instrument to preserve society's customs and norms. Mann saw schools as a key to a child's growth and development, whereas Harris saw schools as an extension of society, not as an agent of change.

At the high school level, Harris emphasized the classics, Greek and Latin and mathematics. His curriculum was rigorously academic, and it discouraged working-class and ordinary children from attending high school. Harris resisted the idea of a vocational or practical curriculum, arguing that all children should follow the same curriculum. Lawrence Cremin, the education historian summed it up in *The Transformation of the School*: Harris "consolidated the revolution Mann had wrought" but was patiently conservative. Harris's emphasis was "on order rather than freedom, on work rather than play, on effort rather than interest, on prescription rather than election or regularity [and] silence" and on preserving the civil order. Harris stressed rules, testing and grading, and failed to recognize that the poor and average student could not compete, simply because the academic track he delineated was too rigorous and there was no compensatory assistance for them.

Harris believed in the natural (Hegelian) laws of history and the (Darwinist) laws of nature, reinforced by the economic doctrines of Herbert Spencer—and that the free market was the great regulator of the economy. In this context, he argued that American prosperity was due to the principles of self-help, competition and the sanctity of private property. The U.S. represented the culmination of the world spirit which he linked to *laissez-faire* economics and the self-realization of the individual. Socialism was a primitive form of economics, rooted in the Old World and its feudal economy which hindered individual achievement and a nation-states development. Harris not only refuted all doctrines of social and progressive reform, but also maintained that such reform would destroy American civilization and throw it back to primitive stages.[30]

Charles Eliot was even more conservative. He saw "civilized society" as comprising four layers:(1) the upper one, "thin" in numbers and consisting of "the managing, leading and guiding class—the intellectuals, discovers, the inventors, the organizers, and the managers";(2) a "much more numerous class, namely, the highly trained hard-workers who functioned as "skilled manual labor", (3) a populous "commercial class" consisting of those who engage in "buying, selling, and distributing" and (4) a large class engaged in "household work, agriculture, mining, quarrying, and forestry." Schools, Eliot argued, must offer programs to all four classes, but the content and instruction would reflect the abilities, as what he referred to as the "capacity" of the child. The more progressive and democratic reformers of the era saw Eliot's class system as elitist and biased.

The resulting influence of Harris and Eliot was that the school reform committees of the 1890s and early 1900s emphasized that training of the mind, tough subject matter, and the evolutionary thesis of Darwinism and Spencerism. The development of mind and nature of academic work in the high school coincided with the so called "laws of nature," and that only very small percentage of students were expected to succeed in high school or go on to college. Most people accepted this argument and social and economic improvement for the masses, based on education opportunity, was exasperatingly slow. The outcome is that by 1900, only 11.5 percent of 14 to 17 year olds were enrolled in high school, 6.5 percent graduated and 4 percent of 18 to 21 year olds were enrolled in college.[31] Not too many people were concerned about these figures, since America was still a farm and factory-based society with plenty of "manly" jobs available for working people—who worked with their hands, not their minds.

Thus, at the turn of the century, in his book *The Future of America,* English author H.G. Wells linked peasant immigration to the country as the downfall of America. "I believe that if things go on as they are going, the great mass of them will remain a very low lower class" and the U.S. population "will remain largely illiterate industrial peasants." Today, the debate is couched in terms like "human capital," "brain-drain" and "illegal immigration." Many Americans contend we are attracting low-wage, low-educated tomato and cabbage pickers, hotel workers, and landscapers while discouraging the foreign-educated students, scientists, and engineers on which the American economy depends.

Ellwood Cubberly, a former school superintendent and professor of education at Stanford University, and one of the most influential education voices at the turn of the twentieth century, feared the arrival of immigrants from Southern and Eastern Europe. In *Changing Conceptions of Education*, he argued they were slow-witted and stupid compared to the Anglo-Teutonic stock of immigrants. The new immigrants were "illiterate, docile, lacking in self-reliance and initiative, and not possessing the Anglo-Teutonic conceptions of law, national stock, and government." Their numbers would "dilute tremendously our national stock and corrupt our civil life." The role of the school was not only to "amalgamate" them, but also to prepare them for vocational pursuits as "common wage concerns." The new immigrant and working-class children had little need for an academic curriculum, according to Cubberley, as they were lacking in mental ability and character; in fact, he insisted the common man demanded vocational training for their children. It was foolhardy to saturate these immigrant and working-class children "with a mass of knowledge that can have little application for their lives."

Although progressive educators were concerned about the education of poor, work-class, and immigrant children, the fact remains that the great change in school enrollment did not occur until just prior to and during the Great Depression. Adolescent students were encouraged to attend high school so as not to compete with adults for jobs. By 1930, as many as 50 percent of 14-to 17-year olds were attending high school, 51 percent of 17-year olds graduated, and 12 percent of 18-to 21 year olds were enrolled in college.[32] The concept of mass education was just beginning to take shape— as America moved from a farm to industrial-based country.

Sputnik and Post-Sputnik

Enrollment in high school continued to increase so that twenty years later as many as three quarters of eligible students were attending high school. During the Sputnik and Cold War era, James Conant, the Harvard University president wrote two books, *The American High School Today* in 1959 and *Slums and Suburbs* in 1961. In the first book, he argued that in order to stay competitive with the Soviets the schools had to pay special attention to the gifted and talented students as well as the above average or top 20 percent, and to encourage them to attend college and major in science, math and foreign languages. The curriculum had to be beefed up with more homework, more testing, and more honor and advanced study courses. The average and below average student was considered more or less as "a postscript" or "nonstudent," someone who could always get a job and contribute to society.

As for the second book, the civil rights movement was just at its infancy stage and Conant sensed the need for greater education and employment opportunities for minority youth. He warned that "social dynamite" was building in the cities because of massive unemployment among black youth and adults. He compared suburban and city schools in terms of resources and revenues, and advocated vocational curriculum for nonacademic students attending slum schools as a method for providing them with future jobs. Although his reform ideas were accepted by the Establishment, the minority and reform community in later years condemned his views as racist; it was argued that blacks would be slotted in a second rate curriculum and be limited to vocational and blue collar jobs. Conant never responded to his critics.

From the 1950s through the 1990s, conservative psychologists such as William Shockley, Arthur Jensen, and Richard Herrnstein, placed heavy emphasis on heredity as the main factor for intelligence—and the reason why the poor remained poor from one generation to the next. Although the arguments were written in educational terms, the implications were political and implied class warfare. Most disturbing, it resulted in a stereotype for explaining mental inferiority among the lower class, especially blacks, thereby explaining the need for vocational programs and putting blacks on the defensive.

According to Richard Herrnstein, in *IQ in the Meritocracy,* intelligence tests measure both heritable and socially significant factors. Although the exact percentages are unknown, the genetic factor is estimated between 45 to 80 percent, depending on the research cited. But as society succeeds in equalizing opportunity, "the genetic factors likely become relatively more important, simply because the nongenetic factors having been equalized, no longer contribute to the differences among people." To make matters worse, in western societies where there are no rearranged marriages and smart people tend to intermarry, genetic factors are more important and contribute to class differences among future generations. These outcomes, Herrnstein claimed, is "lethal to all forms of egalitarianism." However, he failed to understand that most Americans believe human nature is plastic and capable of improvement through improved social environment and opportunity.

The common purpose of intelligence testing is to predict success in school and suitability for various occupations. The correlation between IQ and school success increases though successive years because the skills called on by conventional intelligence tests (as well as aptitude tests such as the Scholastic Aptitude Test or Miller Analogy Test)—vocabulary, reading comprehension, logic, and abstract reasoning—coincide with advanced school work. So long as school and college stress verbal and mathematical skills, IQ tests (and various aptitude tests) are predictive of future academic performance. Children with low IQs usually do poorly in school and children with high IQs cover the range from excellent to poor performance. Here noncognitive factors such as motivation, emotional well-being, and work ethic play a role. High IQ offers merely the potential for academic success and preparation for professional jobs.

Depending on whether someone is for or against intelligence testing, IO partially explains class differences. In fact, Herrnstein contends that wherever equal opportunity exists, supposedly in Anglo-speaking countries, income distribution correlates with IQ distribution. Most thoughtful people rather not hear or accept this analysis because the policy implications reject the values of a democratic society and coincide with the out moded belief that lower-class people and blacks are intellectually inferior. Generally speaking, today, the progressive thought rejects the IQ thesis and schools rarely use IQ tests.

Herrnstein talked a great deal about the backlash and name calling he experienced as a result of his publication. To some extent he is right: Barring drastic egalitarian policies the gifted and talented will move to the top of totem pole and earn the most money. Most of us accept this type of mobility and it is the kind of society that leads to the most productivity. What Herrnstein failed to recognize is that capable people are often held back and prevented from realizing their potential because of discrimination or finances. In fact, throughout the ages societies have often wasted human talent by denying them social and education opportunities. In today`s scientific and technological world, this spells disaster for such a society—and is a factor why many nations remain undeveloped.

As mentioned earlier, in 1900 only about 4 percent of the college-age population enrolled in college, because viable jobs existed for men without a formal education and because of class barriers that prevented opportunities for lower-and working-class youth. Not until post-World War II, with the G.I. bill, were large numbers of capable students attending college. Even then, occupational choices and opportunities did not always reflect IQ potential—rather social circumstances and family and personal expectations. Nevertheless, by the year 2000, more than 15.3 million students were enrolled in degree granting institutions of higher education. Ten years later, the number totaled 19 million, more than a 20 percent increase—illustrating the growing need for a college education in order to economically succeed. The fact is, mass education is a major reason for why the U.S. is the leading economic engine of the world.

At the same time, however, the argument can be made that the American work force is over educated and there are too many college graduates and not enough plumbers and electricians. Given the recession from 2008 to 2010, with official unemployment figures hovering at 9 percent, the hiring of college graduates decreased 28 percent from 2008 to 2010. Only "20 percent of graduating seniors looking for jobs were lucky enough to land one."[33] Middle-class parents have invested hundreds of thousands of dollars and taken on enormous debt, and at the end their child was sitting at home surfing the internet. When the author graduated college in 1962, only 11 percent of the 21-25 year-olds had a college degree (compared to nearly 33 percent now). Less than 35 percent of high-school graduates went to college; now we send 70 percent. Moreover, there was no word called "outsourcing" of jobs. The economy was expanding (not constricting or melting down). The average four-year college graduate had 3 to 5 job offerings fifty years ago. Today, 50 to 100 or more college-educated applicants apply for the same job.

Not only has the gap in starting salaries for college graduates declined vis a vie high school graduates in the last twenty-five years, but college debt has increased twice the rate of inflation because tuition costs in both private and public college have dramatically increased. The situation gives up pause: Whether too many students are going to college or whether low-achieving students should go to college at public expense. Keep in mind more and more college graduates fill jobs for which they are academically overqualified, or cannot find jobs. If you look at college as an economic investment, then consider there is little relationship between the skills acquired in college and the skills required for many jobs.

But the private, high tuition policy has never been popular among working-class and middle-class parents who often cannot save enough money for their children's college education—and requires paying a part of the tuition in the form of student loans. Aid levels have not kept up with tuition costs and tuition hikes have outstripped working wages 300 to 400 percent in the last 20 years. A simple solution is to provide adequate public dollars for students who study in areas of national need such as health, math, science and engineering—fields that serve the public interest and common good. The subsidies should not go to the universities, but directly to students in the form of a voucher or to their parents in the form of tax credits.

However, one might also make the argument, which some conservative educators do, that half of all children are statistically below the average in IQ and basic achievement, and many just do not belong in college. According to Charles Murray, the co-author of *The Bell Curve,* "if you don't have a lot of g," that is general intelligence, "when you enter kindergarten, you are never going to have a lot of it. No change in the educational system will change that hard fact."[34] Now that is a tough pill to swallow, especially in a society that prides itself in being egalitarian or among school people who are reform oriented and believe in the power of education and the opportunities that go along with it.

For Murray, the top 25 percent of high school graduates have the abilities to make good use of a college education, and the remaining youth would do better in vocational training. Combine those who are unqualified and those who are qualified and unmotivated, and the majority of college students today are putting a false premium on attending college and looking for something that college was not designed to provide. Few working-and middle-class parents, who are spending tens of thousands of dollars a year on their child's college education, want to hear this analysis—or even worse that perhaps their children should become plumbers or electricians and get their hands dirty.

Now, it may also be too frightening for the rich and well-born to suppose that the reason for their fortunes has little to do with intelligence. In a longitudinal study of 7,400 Americans between 1979 and 2004, Ohio State's Professor Jay Zagorsky found no meaningful correlation between wealth and high IQ scores. "Those with low intelligence should not believe they are handicapped and those with high intelligence should not believe they have an advantage." There was a slight correlation with IQ sores and income; each point in IQ scores was associated with about $400 of income a year.[35] Assuming a 10-point spread in IQ and 40 years of work, the difference is only $160,000 which can evaporate in one or two bad financial decisions. The IQ link breaks down with wealth, that is the accumulation of assets, because smart people are just as likely as others to make bad financial choices over their lifetime. One very bad decision can wipe out a lifetime savings. (Investors of the Madoff ponzi scheme certainly learned this fact of life the hard way.) More important, wealth often takes generations to accumulate and to pass from one generation to the next.

What all this seems to mean is that the sorting out process between IQ, education, and economic outcomes are not easy to separate or pigeon-hole into neat predictions. Not only do Americans have multiple chances to succeed, but also you don't have to be an intellectual whiz-kid or a college graduate to succeed. Michael Dell, Bill Gates, Steve Jobs, Evan Williams (of Twitter) and Mark Zuckerberg (of Facebook) never finished college. We would like to think that the American education system is designed, at least in theory, to enable every youngster to fulfill his human potential, regardless of race, ethnicity, gender, or class and regardless of intelligence or creativity. But education, although important, is only one factor to consider in explaining economic mobility and social stratification.

Educational and Economic Opportunity

The modern view of educational equality, which emerged in the 1950s, goes much further than the old view that was concerned with equal opportunity. In light of this, James Coleman, when he was professor of education at John Hopkins University, outlined in the *Harvard Educational Review* five views of inequality of educational opportunity, paralleling liberal philosophy: (1) inequality defined by the same curriculum for all children, with the intent that school facilities be equal; (2) inequality defined in terms of social or racial composition of the schools; (3) inequality defined in terms of such intangible characteristics as teacher morale and teacher expectation of students;(4) inequality based on school consequences or outcomes for students with equal backgrounds and abilities; and (5) inequality based on school consequences for students with unequal backgrounds and abilities.

The first two definitions deal with race and social class; the next definition deals with concepts that are hard to define and hard to change; the fourth definition deals with school finances and expenditures. The fifth definition is a revisionist interpretation: Equality is reached only when the outcomes of schooling are similar for all students—those who are lower class and minority as well as middle class and majority.

All these definitions and nuances may be hard for the reader to follow, so let me sum up. The easiest and most explicit way is to rely on the *New York Times* Op writer David Brooks dittie: "Liberals emphasize inequality . . . . Conservatives believe inequality is acceptable so long as there is opportunity." Now let me advance on step further. Most communities in the U.S. are stratified by income, and public schooling cannot compensate for tremendous variations in wealth and status. But within the community, the people spend about the same amount of money on each student and are inclined to let the best student go to Harvard or Yale and the best person to win in economic matters.

When great economic divides exist, the solutions are unclear and open to more debate. New York City, for example, with 8 million people has roughly 700,000 residents worth a million dollars or more and another 1.5 million residents living in poverty. How can education, or that matter any policy short of redistribution of wealth, rectify this gap, the inequality between the rich and poor. The public generally accepts wide discrepancies in achievement and reward, partially because of the notion of the "self-made man" and American dream. Nonetheless, it should be opposed to excess or extremes at both ends of the scales—and without critics stifling debate by using labels such as "socialist", "class warfare" or "redistribution."

When inequality is defined in terms of unequal outcomes (both cognitive and economic), we start comparing racial, ethnic, and religious groups. In a heterogeneous society like ours, this results in some hotly debated issues, including how much to invest in human capital, how to determine the cost effectiveness of social and educational programs, who should be taxed and how much, to what extent we are to handicap our brightest and most talented minds (the swift racers) to enable those who are slow to catch up, and whether affirmative action policies lead to reverse discrimination. Indeed, we cannot treat these issues lightly, because they affect most of us in one way or another and lead to questions over which wars have been fought in the past.

In a more homogeneous society, such as Japan, South Korea, Norway or Germany, the discussion of race, ethnicity, or religion would not deserve special attention nor require judicial measures. Although it is unclear if increased spending in big-city schools (where poor and minority students are concentrated) would dramatically effect educational outcomes, poor and minority students still deserve equal education spending—better-paid teachers, small class sizes, high-tech resources, new textbooks, and clean bathrooms—as in affluent suburbs where expenditures often are twice or more the amount in adjacent cities.

Students deserve equality of expenditures simply on the basis that schools are public institutions, not private. In a democracy, citizens and their children are entitled to similar treatment, especially because intellectual capital is a national concern, not designed for the benefit of one class or group of students nor the exclusion of another group. It can also be argued that the poor are entitled to special treatment because in the long run the health and vitality of the nation are at stake. Sadly, in comparison to other industrialized nations, the U.S. enrolls the largest percentage of poor students, approximately 24 to 25 percent. Since school performance reflects the social and economic system, this high percentage of poverty explains why, among other factors, the U.S. students on international test scores consistently fall behind their industrialized counterparts.

There is no question other factors arise that prevent equal school spending that are not simply symptoms of racism or class prejudice. They deal with notion of values and the rights of people: the preservation of neighborhood schools, concern about big government and state-imposed policies directed at the local level, fear of increased taxation and why someone should have to pay for someone else's child's education, and the inability of politicians to curtail well-to-do parents form supporting their own neighborhood schools and property values. The question is how much education equality should we strive for? We can have greater equality by lowering standards or by pulling down bright students. We can have more equality by handicapping bright students (as in affirmative action) or by providing an enormous amount of additional resources for low-performing students (as in compensatory funding). But eventually we come to a slippery slope and ask: How much money? Who is to pay for it?

In his classic book on *Excellence,* John Gardner, who we have already mentioned, points out that in a democracy the differences among groups cannot be dwelled on and we go out of the way to ignore them. He describes the dilemma: "Extreme equalitarianism . . . . which ignores differences in native capacity and achievement, has not served democracy well. Carried far enough, it means . . . the end of that striving for excellence which has produced mankind's greatest achievement." Gardner contends that if a society cannot pursue excellence "the consequences will be felt in everything it undertakes. The resulting debility will be felt in all parts of the system." Gardner also asserts that "no democracy can give itself over to emphasize extreme individual performance and retain its democratic principles—or extreme equalitarianism and retain its vitality." Our society should seek to develop "all potentialities at all levels. It takes more than educated elite to run a complex, technological society." Every modern society, as well as every ancient society, has learned this hard lesson, some only after tremendous bloodshed and loss of life.

If we stop and meditate a little, how both sides of the political aisle embrace the vision of America and how the "meritocrats" and "egalitarians" of society phrase their words in the public arena, we can get a better feel how divided the American people are on the issue of mobility and opportunity. The Republicans during the Bush administration cut the tax rates of the rich at the same time when they were amassing huge fortunes and while the gap between wealthy and working people were widening. The Democrats seem married to a system of affirmative action that judges people on the basis of race—not merit—and are less inclined to embrace standardized tests for schools and colleges that results in decisions based on student performance. The assumption is that more people would be willing to accept some kind of affirmative action program based on income and thus widen the idea of equality for more Americans. Of course, self-help is crucial; the goal is not to bury test scores nor provide a free ride for incompetents.

Talent and Tests

Every efficient and innovative society has also learned to recognize and reward various abilities, talents, and creative endeavors. In school, and other aspects of American society, the chief instrument for identifying ability and talent is a standardized test. It is not surprising, according to Gardner, that such tests are the object of criticism and hostility, because they encourage the sorting and selecting of students into special tracks and programs. The fact is, "the tests are designed to do an unpopular job." They are designed to measure what a person knows or how well a person can perform particular tasks. The data can be used to compare people and make decisions—such as who gets into what college and who gets selected for various jobs. Tests are also used for applying standards to determine quality—and who gets ahead in schools and society. Although, in our society unlike most other societies, we are given multiple chances to succeed, Gardner is still concerned that the search for talent and the outcomes of education in our high-tech and knowledge-based society will lead to increasing inequality among educated and uneducated individuals.

While consideration for efficiency and objectivity are good reasons for relying on standardized tests, they should not be allowed to distort or limit our notion of talent. There are many different forms of talent—creative, artistic, athletic, etc.—that don't rely on academic emphasis nor are measured by standardized tests. The demand for talent is crucial in a bureaucratic and complex society, but the importance of formal education is not always paramount for exceptional and special kinds of talent.

There are not only talented physicians and engineers to nurture, but we need also to recognize talented plumbers and talented chefs. While we need to reward different forms and types of talent, society needs to be realistic and discourage negative talents like the ability to pick pockets or deemphasize esoteric talents such as the ability to stand on your head. A democratic society must recognize multiple talents, and not only talents based on academic or cognitive intelligence. That is the genius of a progressive and democratic society.

Allow me to throw another factor into the mix. The question of talent and rewards go hand-in-hand and lead to results related to inequality—and the values of society. What rewards should highly talented individuals earn? In 2008, the mean salary for American wage earners was approximately $36,000 and more than 95 percent of workers annually earned less than $ 100,000.[36] When someone is paid tens of millions of dollars because of a special talent related to entrepreneurial risk, acting or sports, we need to consider how these earnings contribute to inequality, as well as the emotional consequences felt by middle-income and professional people who have college degrees, play by the book and can barely keep up with payment of their bills. We need to consider whether the rewards, especially if excessive, contribute to the common good and needs of society, to what extent these extraordinary earnings lead to inequality, and how they affect the standard of living of ordinary working people that comprise the foundation of American democracy. Since services and goods are limited, people with vast amounts of income drive up the prices of homes, autos, college tuition, and even baseball tickets.

The average cost for attending a baseball game in Chicago or Denver for a family of four, including sandwiches and cokes, parking and tickets in the second tier between third base and left field now cost between $500 and $600. This amount is more than the take weekly home pay of the average worker in America. Of course, Yankee Stadium has history and is located in the "Big Apple," where prices are often sky-high. A box seat at the stadium runs $2,500—available only for Wall Street buccaneers and global high-flying capitalists—considered now the majority populace as the *bastards* and *plunders* of the world, but for blue bloods and aspiring MBA's *heroes* and *superstars* to emulate.

Consider that the average salary of the top twenty-five fund managers was $365 million in 2005, sometimes only with single digit returns. The total $9.1 billion, was equal to what two thirds (1.8 million) of the nation's 2.8 million teachers earned for the same year. [37] Here is a pop Quiz! Should 25 people who move money around and produce nothing, and played some role in the economic meltdown of 2008 and 2009, earn the same amount as 1.8 million teachers who perform an essential service for the nation.

Now let me knock your socks off your feet and reinforce the reflective populism of our time: That the capitalist lives for money and makes money from of the expense of others. While global markets were crashing and amid fears that banks would collapse, millions of Americans lost their jobs and/or homes and trillions of dollars lost by bankers were repaid in higher taxes by all the people (and their children) who had no responsibility for its disappearance. During the same period, the top 25 hedge fund managers averaged $1 billion each in 2009. The top ten earned $19 billion, with Dave Tepper earning $4 billion and George Soros earning $3.3 billion. [38] To be sure, it's hard work counting all the zeroes (the reason for spelling out the amount).

Put into the mix the public outrage over pay packages of Wall Street and banking executives, the economic pain and lost hopes they inflicted on the masses and the growing gaps between the rich and the rest of us. It's fair to conclude that the system is going to come apart if nothing is done to curb this new super money class. Anyone who has a sense of justice or fairness or anyone who can barely make ends meet (the poor, working class and most middle class people), knows intuitively the system has been impacted by greed and arrogance, and in some cases, even fraud. It needs to be over hauled. Most people in the U.S. seem reluctant to push this idea too hard because it is truly a radical idea that flies in the face of capitalism and the American dream.

In the novel, *A Week in December*, the author Sebastian Faulks raises a tantalizing question. Who is the worst villain: the jihadist who wants to blow us up or the super capitalist who sits by the computer screen, analyzes stock charts and figures out ways for making money from the behavior and fears of others. Who causes more damage and suffering? What is worse—terrorism or financial panic, blowing up a building and killing 1,000 people or ruining the lives of tens of millions of working and middle-class Americans. Who should be in prison? Someone obsessed with religion and willing to murder or someone obsessed with money and willing to ruin the financial lives of people.

Of course if you adopt the notion that greed is good or necessary to drive the economic engine, as Alan Greenspan (the former Federal Reserve Chair) or Steve Forbes (the CEO of *Forbes* magazine) and a host of Wall Street pundits believe, then it comes down to "the hell with ordinary people"—the same people who fight our wars, protect our streets, build our bridges and teach our children. Here is where Hobbes's gloomy and wretched world, and Darwin's jungle and notion of supremacy, intersect with the raw capitalism of the Gilded Age I and II.

EQUALITY AND EQUITY

The emphasis on individual achievement is highly regarded in the United States. No feature of our society is more prized than the opportunity for each person to reach his maximum potential. Most of us would like to believe that the humblest and poorest who are smart and gifted can lift up their head and achieve new heights. The sky is the limit in our folklore, not only in terms of becoming a super athlete like Tiger Woods or Alex Rodriguez, a captain of industry like Andrew Carnegie or Bill Gates, but also in becoming the president of U.S.—as with Andrew Jackson and Abe Lincoln who grew up in log cabins or in the case of Barack Obama who grew up in a broken home and is black.

But how intelligent were the hedge fund managers who earned hundreds of millions of dollars in one year? How much smarter are they compared to our teachers who earned a pittance in terms of what these managers made? Was the deciding factor brains? Or was it dad's connections that got them the job, and their cunning and competitive nature that gave them an edge over anybody who got in their way. Is that not the same personaity that put the global financial system at risk and have caused abuses from Enron to subprime markets?

In our society does the individual's future income really depend on his own gifts or talent? What about heredity privilege and nepotism? What other factors play into the mix—and result in class differences? To what extent is there an alliance between the old rich and new dollars? Why do business people, with power and privilege, so often abuse the system, lie and cheat, and engage in fraudulent practices—at the expense of the masses or average American?

Maybe it has something to do with our historical DNA? Maybe Walt Whitman, more than 125 years ago got in right in describing the economic turmoil of his era in *Democratic Vistas*. He recognized the nation's "almost maniacal appetite for wealth." He also noted the vulgarity of the success gene and the immoral underpinnings of the prowealth and capitalist class. How does society correct the gross corruptible practices on Wall Street and in banking which lead to gross inequalities? What kind of restraints need to be imposed on the powerful and privileged in order to prevent the likes of "Enronism," Madoff, and AIG-—and to ensure "life, liberty, and pursuit of happiness" for working Americans? What kind of restraints are needed so that the materialism drive is curbed and doesn't lead to excesses which usually piles up against plain people who are just trying to make ends meet.

The issues that have been raised will not go away, at least not in our democratic and competitive society; they directly affect the social fabric of the country and the notions of social mobility, education opportunity, and economic outcomes of life. While we need to examine differences between excellence and equality, and the need to achieve some balance in a democratic society, we should also distinguish between equality and equity. The powerful and troubling analysis of equality and equity persist, best analyzed today by Nathan Glazer and Christopher Jencks—Harvard professors and sociologists who have spent a lifetime studying inequality as it relates to race and class.

Forget the academic "mumbo jumbo." There is no equality or equity when the drive for power or money, under the guise of achievement or success, run amok. What we need to do is to curb the unabashed and zealous ambitions of wealth and success; then, the issues of equality and equity will fall into place. Although this may seem too nuanced for some readers, the simple truth is that great inequality of wealth hinders equality and equity and leads to concentrated power and a financial oligarchy which corrupts government and society.

Equality has to do with similarity in opportunity or results, but equity (or fairness) deals with a person's or group's effort and the reward (or outcomes) for that effort. Inequality occurs when a person or group works hard but achieves little reward or, reverse, when a person or group works less and receives most of the rewards. Someone who is unqualified or unable to perform at prescribed levels cannot expect to achieve the same results given the same effort as a highly qualified person. Of course, the race card or the notion of victimization has been used in the past to neutralize the lack of qualifications. With rising expectations of groups who define themselves as a political minority (previously discriminated against and now entitled to certain benefits or preferential treatment), the expectations become politicized and society is forced to compromise, negotiate or litigate.

The economic crisis of 2008-09 was also a moral crisis. The elite institutions that caused the problems, and the same top executives on Wall Street and in banking who cheated the public out of their pensions and savings, were still in their positions after the government bailouts. None of the culprits were jailed. Thus, these executives were able to cover up their malpractices. Had new CEOs been hired and tougher regulations implemented, the American people would have found out what happened. We need to understand that Treasury Secretary Tim Geithner and Larry Summers, the former chief economist for the Obama administration, came out of the same banking mold; in fact, both are protégés of Robert Rubin from Citibank. More ironical, two years prior to his government position, Summers was a consultant for a major hedge fund and paid more than $5 million for his part-time advice. Sadly, big business and big government work side-by-side and take good care of each other. When Geithner and Summers retire, they will go back to Wall Street or banking, like Robert Rubin did when he left the Clinton Administration for Citi. Until we change this type of arrangement between government and business, all our discussions on a brighter economic future for average Americans—and our standards related to equality—are for naught.

Equal Opportunity—For Whom?

Inequity involves lack of opportunity, whereby the laws and/or social institutions discriminate against certain people or groups based on a perceived characteristic; henceforth, those people will be disadvantaged in society. To be sure, the design of society—equal opportunity or unequal opportunity—determines what happens to people in education, jobs, healthcare, housing, etc. and how income and wealth will be distributed among people.

By considering equal opportunity, the question ultimately arises who gets what jobs and what rewards. If a discriminatory pattern exists, based on race, religion, ethnicity, or gender then conflict is going to eventually arise. The more evident the inequality, the greater the chances for disruption in a democratic society. The more egalitarian the society, the more evenly distributed are earnings among its citizens and the more likely pay differences can be settled through compromise.

In a highly diverse society like ours, any group that defines itself as a political minority will become sensitive to group differences in test scores, educational achievement levels, economic outcomes—and demand modifications that move society toward equalization. The larger society may have to water down standards, but the other alternative is continuous dispute and conflict. Questions arise whether the new standards will influence striving for excellence and whether the change in standards is justified in terms of penalizing high-performing members of society or helping those who have experienced past discrimination. The first part of the question has long-term economic implications and the second part has moral implications.

Here we are not attempting to achieve equal results, which ignores the concept of effort or ability and assumes that everyone is entitled to equal rewards, regardless of effort or ability. Such an assumption has more to do with affirmative action and quotas. With equity, we are seeking some sort of fairness. We want to avoid a stacked deck, the existence of inequality and inequity—that is no matter what effort or ability some people will always be discriminated against. The potential effects are more than just economic or moral; the outcomes have social, political, and emotional consequences, resulting in feelings of inferiority, anger, self-hatred and hatred of others, producing pathological and delinquent behavior (in terms of crime, delinquency, and drugs), and detrimentally affects the productivity and vitality of the nation. If a qualified person cannot find viable work, if the deck is always stacked against a person, the argument can be made That system is unfair and it is easier to drop out.

When we talk about equal opportunity, eventually the question arises as to whether everyone should have the right to go to college. If everyone has the right to go to a high school education, why not college? But the pool of abilities and talent varies, and there are many children whose academic limitations cannot be traced to poverty or deprivation. Children who come from upper-class homes have the advantage of social capital, and have parents who can hire private tutors, if necessary. They also have the ability to move to a successful school district—where schools are cleaner and more modern, where teachers are better paid and generally have more education and experience, and the school climate is more conducive to learning.

Others who are less fortunate start out on a less than equal footing and continue to experience family, school, peer group, and community handicaps that only increase their disadvantages—and thus are often doomed to disappointment. A culture of poverty exists in the United States, that is where poverty is passed on from one generation to the next—as if these people weve living in an underdeveloped country. They become maligned as modern-day primitives, allowed to live on welfare or near poverty levels, and journey through a parallel Hobbesian world.

College and Class

Children from advantaged homes have parents with political and social connections as well as alumni and business-related connections by birth that help get them into Ivy League colleges and high-paying jobs. Competition for good jobs requires that you get into the right university, not just a university. According to former Harvard President Lawrence Summers, "Just 3 percent of students at the nation's top 146 colleges come from families in the bottom socioeconomic quartile," that is the bottom 25 percent. These figures are echoed in a 2006 higher education report that less than ten percent of the students in the most selective colleges come from the bottom half of the income scale, whereas 74 percent come from the top quarter, evidencing marked disparities based on income. The inference here is either the bottom half of the income scale of student population is stupid, a rehash of Spencerism (as well as Charles Eliot and Ellwood Cubberely) and the genetic school of thought that dominated late nineteenth and early twentieth century thinking, or that prestigious institutions of higher learning discriminate against students on the basis of tuition and price out the majority of applications because of financial need.

Brian Berry of Colombia University spins the same point in *Why Social Justice Matters.* Some 35 percent of undergraduates at Princeton are from "non-sectarian private school: over 20 times their 1.7 percent in school population." These figures may be slightly higher than the average for other elite universities, "but not a lot out of line with the others." You don't have to be a rocket scientist to get into Yale or Harvard or to work on Wall Street, and many people who accumulate the usual clutch of mansions, fancy cars, and millionaire baubles possess fewer abilities and are "C" students. Ironically, the business world is depressingly full of millionaires who ignore their head start in life and equate their net worth with brains, that is wealthy boys and girls born on third base who think they hold the major league record for triples.

The fact is rich children with average SAT scores, and whose parents are well connected, manage to get into an Ivy League school while those with above average test scores are content with being accepted to a good state university. Colleges often say they are not backing away to attract low-or moderate-income students. In fact, some institutions espouse a twisted logic by saying they take more students who can afford to pay full or nearly full tuition in order to recruit and better serve those who cannot. But the reality is that there is a limit on how many needy students can be admitted and they are often wait listed and dropped to less prestigious and less expensive colleges. Wealthy students have a distinct advantage of being admitted, and only very wealthy institutions with endowments in the billions can afford, today, to be need-blind. But let's be clear about class and connections. Attending Harvard or Yale is part of the "old-boy network" and "blue-blood club" that permits "C" students the opportunity to rise above their potential—and possibly wreck a company or country—not only in the United States but also in any place in the world.

We would like to believe that those who attend Harvard or Yale might consider their education is not designed to make them rich, and that the majority of Ivy League graduates do not want to work in some super-duper law firm in Boston or New York or on Wall Street and earn hundreds of thousands or millions of dollars a year. We would like to think that a sizeable number think about public service and other careers (in health, education, and science) beyond the legal and financial world and the high-priced consulting, lobbyist and guest-speaking world. The number of Ivy League students wanting to work on Wall Street (approximately 50 percent) reached its all-time high just before the bubble burst in 2008.

During the "meltdown," some hot careers were venture capital, overseas companies, and energy. For the good of the nation, talent might shift from pinstripes to lab coats, from moving money to building bridges and investing in green technology—and that there would be a revival of the Sputnik era, when the talented chose science and engineering. But our values get in the way. When the market rebounds, high-achieving ("type A" students) will most likely enter a new race to Wall Street, banking and white-shoe law firms.

Somehow, I do believe that many Ivy League students start out idealistic, wanting to change the world for the better or to make a mark in some creative endeavor. Yet, the lure of "big bucks" and a big house, that is the trappings of "success," and the conversations of classmates and friends about money and more money take their toll on idealism and service-oriented careers. We live in a highly materialistic society, driven by greed (softened by the word "ambition"), conspicuous consumption (softened by "consumer spending"), and corruption (softened by the words "reality" or "politics").

It is hard to say no to the world of unfettered capitalism, as opposed to egalitarianism or social justice, when you are being recruited with fancy dinners and starting six-figure salaries. At Wall Street, top tier-talent with MBAs start at $300,000, plus bonuses, according to the *2007 Private Equity Compensation Report.* It`s real easy to sit behind a computer and apply for 25 or 30 jobs, put down your Harvard or Yale credentials, and wait for E-mail messages to bounce on your screen. It`s much easier, or at least more practical, to use your talent and abilities to gain financial security than to serve your community or country—and that has something to do with the values of our society. To be sure, the rich are better off then the poor or working man—not because they are made of better stuff, but because they are spared the indignity of always needing a handout or always asking for a 50-cent raise.

We would like to believe in the image of a person who rose from nothing and who owed nothing to parentage. This is part of the American dream and the notion of the self-made person; and there is just enough possibility and truth in these stories, a testimony to American democracy. But the humblest and poorest rarely rise to the top. Statistically the odds do not coincide with popular literature or folklore. We would also like to believe that an under achiever in school, someone with average or even less then average abilities could rise to fame and fortune through hard work and luck. It`s the perfect antidote for a country reeling from an underachiever, who got into Yale because of daddy`s alumni status, and who rose to fame and fortune because of political connections, powerful friends, and patronage.

Most underachievers sleep walk through life, engage in muddled thinking and have trouble completing whole sentences in the public arena; in short, the majority of "C" students have difficulty adjusting to a complex society, where extensive information must be understood and complex judgments and decisions must be made (The answer is not to brag that you speak to God or make decisions by gut feeling.) While democracy releases the energy and talents of every human being, heredity privilege rewards ignorance and puts a lid on aspirations and the pursuit of excellence. No question in our society, "hidden gifts" and special talent can be discovered—and the popular literature is full of such images.

For every "C" student that becomes a governor or president, a captain of industry or a super athlete, hundreds of thousands are doomed to live out their life in the same quintile they started, or slightly move an inch or two higher. (During a twenty-five year period, ending in 2004, 61 percent of families in the lowest income quintile remained at the same level. In reverse, 59 percent in the highest income quintile remained at the same level.) Given a highly competitive society, life is not a bowl of cherries or a rose garden and sometimes there is more rain than sunshine. All you have to do is listen to the songs of Muddy Waters, A.P. Carter, and Johnny Cash—and you hear a prickle or sad story about the human condition and vissitudes of life.

Knowledge/ Information Society

The phrase "postindustrial society" coined in 1973 by Harvard's Daniel Bell, in *The Coming of Post-Industrial Society*, describes the scientific-technological societies evolving in developed countries in the second half of the twentieth century. The singular feature of this society is the importance of scientific, mathematical and technical knowledge as the source of production, innovation, and policy formulation. Emerging from the older economic systems in both advanced capitalistic and socialistic countries is a *knowledge* and *information* society based on preeminence of professionals and managers. In the United States during the 1950s and 1960s, Bell notes, "this group outpaced . . . all others in rate of growth, which was . . . seven times more than the overall rate for workers".

Reflecting the paradigm shift of the times, University of Chicago President Robert Hutchins wrote an overstuffed and stiff book, *The Learning Society*, geared for the academic mind—and not for mass consumption. In the book, he predicted that the knowledge industry was producing a host of professionals and technocrats such as scientists, engineers, researchers and financial analysts who would take economic advantage of this new paradigm or shift impacting on society. Moreover, the effect of the knowledge revolution was "to accelerate technical change without thought of its social consequences." Today, the technological revolution has created economic opportunities for entrepreneurial and gifted people—way beyond their imagination, intellectual capabilities, and levels of education might suggest.

In the 1990s computer and high-tech sectors outpaced the entire economy, reflected by a soaring NASDAQ market whose bubble burst in 2000. The stratification structure of this new society has produced a highly trained, knowledge-based elite, which is supported by a large scientific, mathematical and technical staff and which has become the economic engine for the new century. Moreover, it is only the part of society that has successfully competed with the patrician (super-rich) society, at least up to the point where the "blue bloods" have taken notice of who is being admitted into Harvard and working on Wall Street, as well as what are the latest tech trends in Silicon Valley or North Carolina's "Golden Triangle".

Bostered by free markets and an unregulated system of capitalism, a wing of the knowledge industry became affiliated with Wall Street and the banking industry. They created a global financial system that few people understood and subsequently depended on "knowledgeable" and ethical people to manage and protect their pensions and savings. This led to a new cottage industry including TV programs like "Squak Box," "Fast Money" and "Nightly Business Report" and pundits from the likes of Larry Kudlow and Jim Cramer to the "spin master" Alan Greenspan. They were supposed to provide Americans with an informed analysis of financial and economic trends.

The new financial programs and pundits, armed and sophisticated financial formulas and statistical models, helped create an interconnected global economy and a new mindset on Wall Street and in banking based on greed, corruption and fraud. It was riddled with toxic mortgages to disguise their limited value, short selling and the hollowing out of healthy companies, bogus accounting statements, outrageous bonuses to executives who often crippled their own companies because of excess risk, selling and buying of derivatives or insurance guarantees that could not be paid and falsified ratings of companies which were on the verge of bankruptcy.[39]

Instead of carrying out their traditional role as the stewards of money, many bankers and brokers risked the money of clients and stockholders. The outcome was massive losses of public and private pensions and personal savings of ordinary Americans, nearly $7 trillion in stocks and $8 trillion in housing value—a total of $15 trillion. In short, the new mindset unleashed and magnified America's rise of inequality, the decline of labor, and the waning of the middle class. And, just to insert a small needle into the mix: What went unnoticed was U.S. consumer addiction to plastic debt, totaling a record $950 billion in 2008, with defaults in 2009 reaching nearly $100 billion.[40]

With the benefits of hindsight, the reverberations from the downturn in the global markets has led to an overall weakened American economy and a dispirited nation. Moreover, the American collapse has led to strife throughout the world as emerging and developing nations who were dependent on American consumers felt the ripple effects that has undermined American prosperity. To be sure, the driving force behind this financial collapse has been the old desire for money and quick profits. But part of the blame must be shouldered by the knowledge industry—the so called professionals, with their advanced degrees and expectations to earn a lot of money, who ignored risk and was sucked into the casino-like atmosphere.

A CHANGE IN MERITOCRACY

The basis of achievement in the postindustrial society is education and high academic expectations. Merit and differentials in status, power, and income are awarded to highly educated and trained experts with credentials; they are seen as the decision makers who will inherit the power structure in business, finance and government. Achievement and mobility are also related to entrepreneurship and risk taking: What Ben Franklin would call hard work and *Forbes* magazine might call "making money the old-fashioned way."

In a book called *Class: A Guide Through the American Status System*, Paul Fussell, a University of Pennsylvania sociologist, labeled these postindustrial "knowledge workers" as the "X class." C. Wright Mills, the author of *The Organization Man*, one of the most significant nonfiction books of the 1950s, said the middle-class person was "always somebody's man" whereas the X person is nobody's. X people are highly independent, educated, and achievement oriented: "Retirement being a concept meaningful only to hired personnel or wage slaves who despise their hard work." It might also be said that X people can negotiate the color line that has run smack through American history—adding to the notion of the American dream; or, to borrow from the words of Lorraine Hansberry, "Look what the new world hath wrought."

This trend toward a meritocracy of the intellectual elite has aggravated inequalities. The majority of people in a democratic society accept this form of inequality, because it is based on individual talent and achievement—not inherited privilege or rank—and because this form of meritocracy is designed to benefit the common good. Because of socioeconomic deprivation and limited education, poor and working-class groups are unable to compete successfully in a society based on educational credentials and educational achievement. Without the appropriate certificates, they are not needed by the economy; not necessarily exploited, but underpaid for their services; not necessarily discriminated against, but not in demand; not necessarily misfits or misfortunates, but not able to easily climb the mobility ladder of American society.

The knowledge and information industry has raised education requirements for jobs. Those that were formerly filled by elementary training now demand high school graduates, and those that were formerly filled by secondary training now require a college degree. To be sure, there is a casual connection between education and jobs, which encourage parents to save and send their children to college. However, many social scientists argue that bright students and well-to-do students stay in school longer, inferring that the *cause-effect* relationship to jobs is not schooling, rather IQ and income. Likewise, if employers have a choice between having an uneducated and educated person, the latter will be chosen not necessarily because he or she will perform better rather education levels are an easy way to sort out candidates for jobs. The assumption is the schools have performed the sorting out process for the employer.

The knowledge and information society also created the need for jobs filled by workers who had verbal and quantitative skills, as opposed to workers who had muscle skills during the industrial age and growth of factories. We live in a highly technological-based economy that values an educated workforce and permits most college graduates opportunity to live and maintain a middle-class life style.

Today, however, we need individuals who can create innovations. Our standardized tests and science and math courses need to go beyond basic quantitative problems and emphasize increased spatial skills that prove critical to technology and robotics. We have many high school students that excel in traditional math and science course work and related tests. We also need students with a harder-to-define skills related to innovation and invention, that is who are creative and intuitive and can successfully deal with hunches and multiple relationships in math, science and engineering. Since the 1960s, coinciding with the War on Poverty and civil rights movement, the schools have put emphasis on educating low-achieving students at the expense of high-achieving and talented students. Given the global and knowledge-based economy we live in, our needs and goals have changed and so must our education focus. We cannot let politically correct ideas stifle or blur the need to nurture and support talented and gifted students.

Merit and Achievement

In a society that prizes merit and achievement, the reward structure is linked to a person's natural ability. In *The Rise of Meritocracy*, Young warned that such a society would put most of its resources in effective programs and schools that favored the academic elite, thus pushing the gifted and talented to the top and the less gifted and talented behind. Even worse, the process would continue over generations because of the assertive and class-based mating and the component of heredity, which people in a democracy prefer not to discuss because of its uncomfortable implications. Both bright and slow students and adults will continue to compete in school and society, partially fortified by class distinctions (environment) and heredity. Barring drastic government policies, the search for merit and achievement will move capable people to the top and less capable people to the bottom. Although some say this is the most ideal-type society, as it gives everyone the chance to rise to the top, it has serious implications for average and dull people, and with people who have fewer opportunities because of class. If left unchecked or unregulated, it leads to increasing inequality, and ultimately where one group feels they belong to another species—very high or very low.

If there is a stranger word than whoops, it applies here: When smart people come to believe that their success is based on skill, achievement and hard work, and the absence of patronage, nepotism, or discrimination. Even worse is when they fail to recognize that luck, both good or bad, is a major factor in determining economic outcomes. Eventually they justify their income and wealth, and any degree of inequality that comes about due to meritocracy. Here is Young again, writing a 2001 *Guardian* news article called *"Down With Meritocracy."*

If people come to believe their advancement is based on their merits, "they can feel they deserve whatever they can get. They can be insufferably smug," more so than someone who knows their advancement is based on politics or discrimination. "The newcomers can actually believe they have morality on their side. So assured have the [new] elite become that there is almost no block on the rewards they arrogate to themselves." Thus inequality becomes more grievous as the years pass, and no one seems to raise questions. In this light, meritocracy based on achievement cannot fully justify large rewards which create significant inequality.

A new form of arrogance can develop by the creation of meritocracy, by the same people who once believed in and exemplified the political theories of Jeffersonian democracy and the stories of Horatio Alger. If true merit becomes associated with heredity or innate ability, as it often is construed, as opposed to the notion of opportunity, than meritocracy becomes less of a virtue and more of a propaganda tool for patricians and conservatives to wave and use against the populace who have fewer opportunities (and less luck) because of their social and economic status. An achievement-oriented society based on academic credentials and standardized tests (which compare individuals in relation to a group score, say in IQ, achievement, or aptitude) condemns many people who cannot compete on an intellectual or cognitive level to the low end of stratification structure. It is the classic problem: the rich (who have more resources for better education) get richer and the poor get poorer—and gaps between the "haves" and "have nots" have dramatically increased in the last decade.

Put in more precise terms, for the last twenty-five years, one-fifth of the population (on the income pyramid) has been improving its prospects while the remaining 80 percent has lagged behind. During the Bush administration, it is the top 10 percent that glommed almost all of the economic growth because of an expanding world economy, Wall Street get-rich schemes, and free-market policies. A few economists such as Robert Reich and Paul Krugman would argue, as I would, that the top 1 percent were the real beneficiaries of the Bush tax cuts. It was their greed and corruption that characterized Wall Street and many parts of the banking and home mortgage industry, in turn, which led to the bubble bursting in 2008. The bubble turned into a world-wide recession because of an interconnected global banking system and global trade system that was falsely propted up by American consumerism and American debt.

Surprisingly, no one has rebelled, although discontent is mounting. The majority of the populace have not imposed higher taxes on the wealthy; in fact, the opposite has occurred, partially because conservative forces since the Nixon administration have dominated the White House or Congress. During the Obama administration, however, society seriously contemplated methods for reducing inequality (in income and wealth) between the rich and the rest of us.

In education terms, however, what counts today is how the government spends money on intellectual capital—federal support of schools, college scholarships, retraining of labor, etc. Human capital (educated and credentialed professionals and innovators) is the key for creating economic capital. Should Alexander Hamilton's mob be educated (his view of the common people), and to what extent? In the final analysis, human capital (Thomas Jefferson's position) is more important than economic capital (Hamilton's position) if democracy is to survive and if the country is going to continue to prosper. The irony is, however, inequality is exacerbated by the rise of human capital, that is, by an increase of knowledge workers. Inequality is greater in cities such as New York, Boston, and Los Angles because knowledge workers easily find work in these cities and earn considerably more than people who engage in routine tasks, or low-tech and low-end jobs. But the other side of the coin is that knowledge workers contribute more to society and therefore deserve to be paid more.

But there is another consideration, what some economists and sociologists might call a "hidden" or "invisible" tax: Paying nonproductive workers more than their actual worth because they are a protected class (by government legislation or by labor unions), and paying productive people less than their value. The employee who is twice as productive as another co-worker performing the same job rarely receives twice the salary. Even the most innovative companies rarely make those kinds of distinctions because of morale factors, resources or legal issues involved in pay differentials. But productive workers have an advantage during an economic downturn; they are the last to be fired. In good times, they are the first to be promoted, subject to affirmative action. Measured over time, productive workers tend to be promoted faster and earn more than least productive workers. This ideal is rooted in the notion of merit and helps foster an innovative and productive society.

Of course, it is not easy to objectively evaluate workers in a company because there are many political and social considerations. Government agencies try to avoid some of these problems by paying and promoting people based on education and experience. That said, the workers' output is not always easy to quantify and separate from other co-workers. The number of bricks cemented per hour is easy to quantify, but a teacher's influence on a student's reading test is not easy to separate from the impact of the previous teacher much less the teacher from two years ago.

In today's knowledge society, there are several "intangibles" that cannot be measured in terms of value or predict how they may be used in the future. Patients, trademarks, copyrights and brand names are intangibles that have real value in an information and innovative society, but they cannot be judged on a balance sheet. The same holds true in trying to assess a company's research and development, managerial expertise, marketing and advertising ability—that is the intellectual property it owns. These intangibles do not coincide with accounting procedures in terms of income or expenses, credits or debits, assets or liabilities.

Although these intangibles have no agreed market value today, they can make or break a company (or person), given the nature of competition, free markets, and the new economy based on information and technology. Reformers and leading business schools talk about a new "triple bottom line" in terms of "people, planet and profit." But that doesn't really help in determining the potential worth of a company's or person's intangible assets. We are at the early stages of defining or redefining innovation in a knowledge society as well as specific fields of knowledge. Given the complexity of our society, we are dependent on many kinds of talents, many kinds of achievement, and many kinds of knowledge and complex judgments. In the new economy, all this know-how and intellectual property boils down to future jobs—mostly middle-class, white-collar jobs—and wealth.

Americans now produce fewer and fewer products; however, we produce intellectual property (i.e. pharmaceutical research, computer chips, software, etc.) which has dramatically increased the nation's innovative, information and high-tech economy. This type of intellect has led to millions of new jobs and opportunities, the reason for focusing on human capital. In some respects, human capital is more important than economic capital because the latter is limited to a fixed amount. Developing human capital, on the other hand, permits us to address society's present and future problems, its potential for creating wealth is limitless.

Bill Gates, who blends Jefferson's politics with Hamilton's economics, is critical of the nation for rationing education on wealthy and suburban children at the expense of low-income and urban children. He has personally committed $1.2 billion for high school reform that would ensure that all students receive a college prep curriculum. The fact is, however, the human capital agenda starts at the prekindergarten level, the developmental age when cognitive development is rapid and considered a foundation for future growth and development. In fact, according to Benjamin Bloom, in *Stability and Change in Human Characteristics*, 50 percent of potential for learning has been developed by age 4, another 25 percent by age nine, and the remaining 25 percent by age 17. This suggests that infant education, kindergarten and the primary grades (1-3) are essential in terms of nurturing student achievement—and where education dollars should be allocated.

Will the efforts of Bill Gates and other reformers help achieve a more meritorious society? People are human, complicated by a host of flaws including greed and arrogance. If those who advance come to believe they have achieved economic success on their own merits, they may come to believe they are entitled to what they get—and the hell with stupid, slow or average people. Many newcomers of wealth, the academic elite and knowledge-based people, actually come to believe they have morality, justice and the common good of society on their side. But all their propositions are nothing more than old-fashion Spencerism—the notion of "survival of the fittest" and the evolutionary process that favors the stronger and smarter animal or person, and the law of nature that reinforces the doctrines of classical economists.

The idea is that success is tied to some innate ability or heritable gene is the modern version of the preaching of success which has become an honored profession since the vogue of Horatio Alger who wrote 119 books idealizing success, the sentiment you can't keep a good man down, "and every man has a goose that lays golden eggs, if he only knew it." Alger wrote his stories in simple, easy-to-read style, with little imagination or substance. His heroes were obscure boys whose start in life was unknown and unprivileged, but who were willing to take risks, act bold, and grasp the golden ring; eventually, his sentimental stories merged into the American dream.

Of course, historically, the masses are still dragged down by inherent political, social and monetary advantage of the rich: People born on the more fortunate side of the economic divide who use their parent`s economic resources and social connections to rise up the ladder of success. The old rich do not need to rely on education or effort, intelligence or talent, to pass their wealth on to their offspring. They do not need a theory of natural abilities or gene for success that extends from one generation to the next. They have relied on cunning, drive and risk, coupled with many other factors (including fraud and theft which is often camouflaged as commercial drive and success and) that have little to do with problem solving or abstract thinking. They have taken advantage of geography, timing and luck. They have the natural advantage of wealth on their side, and have coopted the political process to preserve their wealth, which supersedes talent or merit. Education cannot match or stand up to this extreme wealth. The catch up process involves several generations and tax policies that favor assets already in place and discriminate against salaries and wages which are taxed at higher rates than earnings from wealth. Only if inequalities of income and wealth are kept within narrow ranges can education help in equalizing differences between the rich and rest of us.

Bridging Excellence and Equality

Unquestionably, the past is a foreign land. The people think differently and do things differently. Like most good clichés, these words have the disadvantage of being useful, and they seem especially so in thinking about the people described in this book. What we have is some sort of a balancing act that goes back to the debates of Jefferson's liberalism and Hamilton's conservatism—to what extent the ordinary American will be given the chance to succeed in school and society. Then there is the distinctive differences in the view of world order: at the two extremes, there is Marx (promoting collectivism, world struggle against privilege, and the expression of equality) and Darwin and Spencer (advocating the acceptance of individual strength, privilege, and inequality). In modern times perhaps it all boils down to whether you see capitalists as robber barons or philanthropists, whether you accept or reject a free-market economy or whether you accept human nature and desires as good or bad. It also boils down to whether you believe that capitalism must be restrained or regulated or whether you accept Ayn Rand's philosophy that "greed is good" and is the driving force for a healthy economy.

These philosophical differences reflect to what extent modern-day Brahmins and patricians in our country fear the multitude (Hamilton's sentiments), and thus put restraints on and check their mobility and opportunities—and what kind of economic system they devise. To be sure, power and money go hand–in–hand since the beginning of civilization. Working people (defined by Hamilton as the "herd") are merely pawns or working units that keep the system operating. We must recognize that, since the colonial period, Latin schools and private tutoring—the gateway to Harvard and Yale—were for rich children, whereas common schools, meager in outlook, were for children of common stock. We must also recognize that the rich make the laws in America and elsewhere; therefore, the tax system, banking laws, and financial markets as well as the school systems, will favor the rich. (For example, investment, profits and dividends are taxed at a much lower rate than labor; trusts are devised for rich children at birth so they have a financial advantage at the starting gate.)

The poor live without a social contract—at least a contract that Locke, Rousseau, or Jefferson would have written or welcomed. The poor have no government that represents them; they are constrained, checked, and choked by policymakers, the arm of law, and their own miseducation and misfortunes. It is the same system that led to the philosopher-kings of Athens. the caesars of Rome and the aristocratic tenants of the ancient world—all bolstered by a slave system and peasant farm system. It also gave birth to the nobility class and feudal system of Old Europe which our Founding Fathers feared and tried to prevent from spreading in the New World.

CONCLUSION

We need to find a balance, some entitlement or safety net, that protects working people or ordinary people while identifying and rewarding performance. Part of the search for balance (or fairness) is to adopt an uncompromising commitment to produce a society which permits the great masses to rise under conditions of social and economic mobility. Motivating the masses to achieve, and allowing them some opportunity to do so, is the driving force that has resulted in the rise of America as a super power. To reduce inequality, however, we need to increase opportunity among working and middle-class people and tax luck—not achievement or talent. We need only to clarify what percentage of a person's economic outcome is related to luck.

It should be clear that we do not want a society that leads to quotas or equality of results based on reverse discrimination. Similarly, we do not want a society that encourages unbridled competition where most of the rewards go to a few. Statistically, overtime, we will wind up with the same "winners" and "losers" in schools and on the job, and many losers will eventually drop out of school and society. There is no magic formula, no agreed set of recommendations for balancing or achieving both excellence and equality. The nuances are too complex. Perhaps someone in a little cabaret in South Texas (a Johnny Cash jingo) or a coffee shop in Hoboken, New Jersey (a Philip Roth location) or a church in Yoknapatawpha County (William Faulkner's fictional but real place) can figure out a solution, since our leaders and statesmen cannot come to a consensus and regularly engage in negative nabobs. All we can hope for is some balance—some sense of fairness in the search for talent and in a reward system that drives society and provides some sense of fairness in the distribution of wealth.

We don't have to bash Bush and Cheney—now seemingly nothing more than "tweedledum and tweedledee," two peas in the pod. We don't have to lionize FDR, LBJ or Obama as champions of the little people. All we have to do is abolish social and economic hierarchies that stratify society and create differences in income and wealth. We need to create a floor and ceiling on income and wealth, one that is linked to the common good and not the whims of "Enronism." We need to curb greedy business executives who cook their company books (to create the illusion of profits) and fleece the public.

A free market system, without checks and balances, allows hereditary status, social privilege, and politics to determine the economic outcomes. Without restraints or regulation, abuses and extremes will characterize society under the guise of competition and merit. The outcome is, a society fueled by the ideas of Darwin, Spencer and Ayn Rand that can be traced to the wretched world of plunder and rape depicted by Hobbes.

Chapter 6

QUESTIONS TO CONSIDER

1. How does the Hobbesian philosophy compare to the notion of survival of fittest?

2. How would you compare the GM model with the Wal-Mart model?

3. How does geography influence culture? Thinking? Adoption of new ideas?

4. To what extent has western culture influenced the arts and sciences?

5. What factors have contributed to the rise of the West? Has the West peaked? Why? Why not?

6. In what way (and why) will China and India most likely clash in the near future?

7. How does "brain drain" influence American innovation?

8. Which immigrant groups seem the most entrepreneurial? Have accounted for the most patent filings?

9. How would you describe the U.S. visa policy?

10. Why do our best and brightest students often wind up on Wall Street? How can we change or reverse this trend?

11. Where are American centers of creativity? Why do diverse geographical areas promote new ides as compared to homogenous places?

12. What do you contribute the achievement gap in education of U.S. students to their industrialized counterparts?

13. Why do critics link America's decline in human capital to the international tests in science and math?

14. What do the terms "forgotten" and "disposal" Americans mean to you? How do these terms square with the American dream?

15. How has outsourcing of jobs enhanced short-term and long-term employment trends? Which sectors of the economy are most directly affected by outsourcing?

16. How do you link human invention and innovation to national wealth?

Chapter 6

INNOVATION AND HUMAN CAPITAL

We Americans are a "nation on the make." Our democracy has unleashed the energies of all its people, and with this new energy comes the dissolution of a stratified society. According to Walter McDougall, the American historian, we are "con artists" and "cowboys" and "dreamers" and "inventors," not because we are a different breed of species or better or worse than other nations, but because Americans have enjoyed immense opportunity to pursue their ambitions and dreams. On the positive side, these distinctions have helped Americans to have faith in themselves—to win the West, to innovate, to expand and make it big. We are not fixed by Old World church or state hierarchies and social or class distinctions that hold people in place and constrain their innovative spirit and energies, as in most parts of the world.

A CHANGING SOCIETY—PUSHING AHEAD

As a new culture and society, the humblest and poorest have been able to lift up their heads and face the future with confidence; we have increasingly relied on education as an integral part of this process of becoming. On the negative side, this forceful, driving and imaginative American characteristic has led to political excesses and abuses—nearly wiping out whole civilizations and extracting land from other people and places in order to further and/or protect our "interests." It has also produced some ghastly business practices—based on greed and creative corruption—highlighted by the Gilded Age I (125 years ago), and Gilded Age II (the world we now live in).

The new culture that evolved during Gilded Age I was sanctioned by Darwin's theories of natural selection and perpetual mutability. It fit well into the American faith in the doctrine of progress and where people could shape themselves. Little was considered fixed or static. Here people could rise from their low station in life and lift themselves from an unprivileged class to a privileged class. The American style of capitalism that emerged permitted the bold, adventurous and more adaptable person to realize profits from the labor and sweat of the working class. It is this unrestrained form of capitalism that continued to enjoy some vogue in the post Civil-War decades of the nineteenth century and early twentieth century, creating the bubble that led to the Great Depression. It is the same free market system, the false belief that the market can correct itself, which led to the bubble bursting again, 75 years later—and the deepest recession most living Americans have ever experienced.

Power and Privilege vs. Opportunity

The emphasis of survival of the fittest, rooted in the Hobbesian world of plunder and rape, suited the new business titans of the Gilded Age I who crushed ordinary workers when they vainly tried to stand up to them by organizing or striking for better working conditions or more pay. The barons and lords of wealth—the financial and industrial class—continued to beat down and exploit the debtor class—farmers, workers, small business people and even professionals (such as teachers, nurses, and engineers) in the name of free enterprise. One must understand that statistically for every immigrant or laborer that managed to rise to middle—class stature vast numbers were left to endure lives of quiet despair—a life of hardship and toil which over years deadens the spirit and numbs the mind—and turns potentially creative people into concrete thinkers and autons called factory workers, miners, and hamburger helpers.

Here in the modern world, amidst Gilded Age II (which started with the Reagan administration), survival of the fittest blends well with the unrestrained and raw capitalism of Ayn Rand and Alan Greenspan—keenly depicted by Gordon Greco in the movie *Wall Street*. Without checks and balances, and with minimal safety nets for workers, the American economy has produced a false sense of prosperity. The money class (top 1 percent) have become richer while real wages (considering inflation) for the bottom 99 percent have remained flat.

As of 2010, the richest 400 people in the U.S. owned more wealth than the bottom 150 million people. Some say we don't live in a democracy anymore; we live in a free-market society, more accurately an oligarchy. The rich and super rich have the better part of everything and it is difficult for them not to feel somewhat secretly and sometimes publically they are better than the rest of us.

Post World War II was an era of manufacturing when America was on top of the world, spearheaded by the auto industry, which transformed working people into the middle class.[41] It was an era when corporations and unions worked together to form safety nets for working people, including health benefits and pensions. As the country grew richer so did the American working and middle class, thus reinforcing the virtuous concept that democracy, capitalism, and unionism went hand-in-hand—and what was good for Ford and GM was good for the nation. During this period, the executive branch of government was pro-union or neutral, that is the era from Franklin Roosevelt to Jimmy Carter. But the good times came to an end under the Reagan administration, supported by the free market and small government theories of Milton Friedman.

It was Reagan`s stand against unions, starting with the air traffic controllers, coupled with increased global trade and less protection for American workers, that eventually crippled labor and then the American auto industry (which employs directly and indirectly ten percent of the U.S. workforce). Reagan's unprecedented dismissal of 13,000 skilled striking workers led to private companies to do the same to their striking employees. It's been downhill for the last three decades. The outcome has led to the replacement of the GM model (with good benefits and good pay for workers) with the Wal-Mart model (few benefits and low wages).

The Wal-Mart model is based on unfettered capitalism: Driving down prices, squeezing the competition, and flouting the rights of labor. Most of the workers have been women (trying to supplement their hubands' income) who are willing to work part-time, for cheap wages and few benefits and adopt a submissive role. Instead of encouraging leadership roles for their workers, according to Bethany Moreton's *To Serve God and*

Wal-Mart, the company encourages a "servant" role, based on a small-town rural ethos and a fundamentalist Christian outlook.

Rule-driven jobs, long hours and low wages, and union-busting tactics may have helped Wal-Mart's "retail revolution," but Wal-Mart has undermined labor practices and squashed the standard of living among its workforce (which is the largest among private companies in the U.S.). Their widespread employment, although fused with technological advances, has been one step above sweatshop status, largely because they have hired vast numbers of part-time workers who enjoy few employment rights and are unable to unionize. Why so many people would consider a job at Wal-Mart, and why it has so many boosters cheering on, shows the desperation and low expectations of the average American worker, given decades of living on the downside of the American income divide.

In the last 30 years, coinciding with the rise of unfettered capitalism (symbolized to some extent by Wal-Mart), the super-rich (top 1 percent) have gotten richer, not always by their wits or brains but often by a constant stream of fraud, corruption and the abuse of power. The prevailing attitude has been that government should not regulate or restrain big business or Wall Street without causing injustice and without stifling private enterprise and innovation. This doctrine is nothing more than a reaffirmation of the "good old days" that go back to the Gilded Age I—the doctrine of unfettered individualism, special privilege and lawlessness. It was a period that permitted a small number of people to seize the wealth of the nation, and to monopolize opportunities by a web of well-connected political, business and financial elites.

This type of economic inequality has been the rule of the day since the dawn of civilization—only that in America the ordinary person was supposed to have a fair chance in the contest for life, liberty and a livelihood. The dream is vanishing for the majority of Americans because the system is rigged, like at the casinos in Las Vegas, in favor of those who gain political power and get bought off by those who move money around—a historical link to the nobility class and merchant and banking class of old Europe. To be sure, labor in the U.S. is taxed at a higher rate than income derived from profits and investment; white collar crime, which can affect thousands or millions of people and destroy their lives, involves minimal prison time compared to violent crimes which usually involve only a few people. One reason is, the people who write the laws are potentially the same people who commit white collar crime or are paid in terms of donations or bribes by those who commit the crimes.

Following in the footsteps of Franklin Roosevelt and Lyndon Johnson, the Obama administration attempted to create a new economic paradigm: making America kinder and more responsive to working people, (traditionally beaten down by toil and deprivation), and requiring the industrial and financial class, (often governed by greed and corruption) to be more transparent and accountable for their actions. For the last three decades, working people in the U.S. knew something was wrong with the economic system and knew the wrong was not theirs. In the midst of huge increases in economic growth and corporate profits, their real wages (considering inflation) remained flat.

The plain people must understand they have the vote. The day-to-day struggle among the working classes—including the vast majority of people who think they are middle class but are also struggling—found a spokesman in the name of Obama as he tried to formulate protest and reform thought which was rooted in the muckraker philosophy and socialist thinking of the early twentieth century. It is doubtful if Mr. Obama read the old muckrakers such as Peter Cooper, Henry George, and Lincoln Steffens—who felt corporate wealth and Wall Street had came to control the government and threaten the whole scheme of American values.

Obama sought to finish the job that Robert La Follete, William Jennings Bryan, and Teddy Roosevelt started and who championed these scholars. Obama attempted to reign in some of the wealth amassed by big business and big banking who have framed plausible theories based on free enterprise and small government. But the system becomes nearly impossible to check or regulate when the regulators (such as those working in the Security Exchange Commission) are using their current position as a springboard to get a job in Wall Street or banking. It becomes a farce when the politicians on the banking committees (Senators Dodd, Frank, Kerry and Schumer, for example) are accepting large donations from Wall Street and the banking industry. Congress has pledged to reform the financial system, but too often over past years lawmakers have protected Wall Street and the big banks. The reason is, the financial industry is not only big campaign contributors, but also the politicians have strong professional ties and partisan history with the banks; they cannot be counted on shielding the public or putting public interest above political loyalties. About 25 to 30 percent of former Congress people are lobbyists for the corporations and/or financial industry.

All of us in one way or another have felt the effects of the last recession, global in nature and much deeper and larger than Alan Greenspan predicted when he spoke to Congress in his role of past Federal Reserve Chair. Faith in the capitalist system has suffered a severe blow, changing from one of optimism to one of cynicism, from belief in big business and Wall Street people as the "masters of the universe" to the despised corporate and Wall Street executive. A resentful and defiant world views American style capitalism as the root cause to the decline of the world economy, whereby emerging nations such as China, India, and Brazil and industrialized nations such as Japan and Russia are willing to challenge American economic policies. As Kenneth Rogoff, a Harvard economist asserts: "The U.S. brand name has clearly suffered from this [economic] crises, and the rest of the world is now no longer willing to sit quietly and be lectured by the United States on how they should conduct economic policy." In the past, American business leaders used to lecture government officials in emerging countries about free enterprise, open markets, and deregulation. Now these are the policies that are considered the culprit for the global economic meltdown.

And so, as we define our national legacy, we have the Enlightenment on one side with its faith in progress, opportunity, and education, as well as democracy with its cherished values of freedom, liberty and equality. On the other side, we have materialism, consumerism, and excess—and education that has been "softened" into entertainment, hustle that has turned into hucksterism and opportunity that is currently being diverted into financial oligarchism. We have liberals and conservatives, each with their own interpretation of what is right and wrong with society. Somehow it seems to go back to the isms of the past and present—between the philosophy and differences of Hamilton and Jefferson, Social Darwinism and Social Democracy, and patrician and egalitarian thought. Perhaps it goes back to how we distinguish ourselves from the Old World. Maybe it goes back to how we perceive truth and how we perceive the world around us, or whether the legacy and ideas of Hobbes are still alive or dead.

Geography and "Smart" Thinking

On a global, much more theoretical level, growth and prosperity among cultures and civilizations can be explained by environment, or by the limits of geographical isolation. Given a make-believe world in which every individual has identical genetic potential, there would still be large differences in education, skills, and related occupations and productivity among people because of demographic differences that over centuries shape human behavior and attitudes.

For Thomas Sowell, the conservative economist, nothing so much conflicts with desire for equality as geography; it is the physical setting—reflected by large bodies of water, deserts, mountains, forests, etc.—in which civilizations, nations and races have evolved and in turn produced different cultures. Put simply in *Conquest a Culture,* the people of the Himalayas have not had equal opportunity to acquire seafaring skills, and the Eskimos did not have equal opportunity to learn how to farm or grow oranges. Too often the influence of geography is assessed in terms of natural resources that directly influence national wealth. But geography also influences cultural differences and cognitive thinking, by either expanding or limiting the universe of ideas and inventions available to different people. The accidents of geography (and history), where you were born and when you were born, immensely influence opportunity and human capital. To be sure, had Warrant Buffet been born 500 years ago he most likely would have died on the battle field as a grunt or soldier. Had there been no civil war, Abraham Lincoln would have probably gone down as a mediocre president.

When geography isolates people, say by mountains, a desert, or a small island, the people have limited contact with the outside world and, subsequently, their technological and innovative advancement is limited. While the rest of the world trades skills, ideas, and values from a larger cultural pool, isolated people are limited by their own resources and what knowledge they have developed by themselves. Very few advances come from isolated cultures, and those that do are usually modified and improved by people that have learned to assimilate and adopt new ideas from other cultures. Until 9/11, we have had the advantage of geographical isolation and protection. This isolation did not hinder our progress because of the large influx of immigrants from around the world who not only brought their meager possessions to our shores but also their ideas, values, and aspirations.

For two thousand years, before the invention of railroads, trucks and airplanes, water was the key for traveling and exploring. Up to the 1850s, it was faster and cheaper to travel by water from San Francisco to China than overland to Chicago. The Europeans, since the Viking era, understood that geographical isolation could be overcome by the sea or ocean. Given their capitalistic and conquering zeal and attitudes of superiority, they went out and traded with, and also colonized, other peoples and other cultures. Subsequently, they made industrial and technological advances by adopting and modifying the ideas of other civilizations.

England, France, Portugal, Spain, and the Netherlands were tiny countries, compared to China and India, but the Europeans traveled the navigable waterways of their continent as well as the Atlantic. They came in contact with many countries and civilizations, including those in South America, Africa and Asia, and thus gained from their knowledge. But the older civilizations did not draw knowledge or ideas from the Europeans or from each other and eventually those great civilizations (which were once more advanced, but isolated) were overtaken and conquered by the smaller countries of Europe that had expanded their knowledge base.

Once Japan broke from its isolation, it became one of today's economic powers, and a comparable process is now shaping China and India. Similarly, the rise of the United States—in particular our skills, technology, innovations, and economic advances—is based on the history of immigration. Here we are referring to the people coming from all parts of the world, melting together, and exchanging knowledge and ideas. It is this constant flow of different people from different parts of the globe that helped create an American entrepreneurial spirit and sense of innovation and creativity not enjoyed in more static, less dynamic countries.

The first generation of immigrants may not score high on standardized reading tests, because of language differences, but their intellectual resources, hard work, and sweat have spearheaded much of our industrial machinery and muscle in the twentieth century and much of our high-tech/information in the twenty-first century. They represent a constant stream of innovation and invention—the keystone to the American economic engine. To be sure, the founders of Google, Yahoo, the U-Tube and Sun micro systems were immigrants, born in foreign countries. Of the 300 Americans who won noble prizes since 1901, about 70 were foreign born.

[42]Immigrants continue to make up a high percentage of contributions to the American economy and inventive spirit.

Reaffirming the Best and Brightest

We live in a society where few educated people in the Western world would dare admit at a cocktail party they never read Dante's *Inferno,* Cervantes's *Don Quiote* or at least one or two plays by Shakespeare. We also live in an age where many of us are unable to explain the difference between an atom or molecule and a galaxy or solar system. Most distressing, we live in a "dumbed down" society, illustrated by the NEA report in 2007 that "the proportion of 17-year olds who read nothing (unless required to do for school) more than doubled between 1984 and 2004."

C.P. Snow coined the term "two cultures," some 50 years ago, to illustrate the two worlds within Western society—consisting of humanities and literary scholars as one group and scientists as the second group. Both worlds were characterized by a "gulf of mutual incomprehension," each with their own data bases and research methods. His analysis of both groups were not subtle or vague. Like his English predecessor Herbert Spencer, Snow put his faith in science and believed scientists represented the future while the former group of intellectuals (from the humanities) "wished the future did not exist."

Although literary scholars had produced great works, they were morally flawed. Frederick Nietsche and Richard Wagner believed in the superman race. Ezra Pound and William Butler Yeats were closet facists. All of them, in their own way, contributed to the rise of Hitler and brought us that much closer to the Holocaust. Snow believed that science could improve society and shape the thoughts of future generations. Only the scientist would save the world through invention and innovation—and by doing so could reduce the wealth gap between rich and poor nations and subsequently reduce instability around the world.

He recommended that the Western world send scientists and technicians to the undeveloped parts of the world to help industrialize those nations and improve the standard of living of their people. Only by erasing the gap between rich and poor nations, between the scientific and unscientific world, could the West be assured of international stability and their way of life. Otherwise, the world of guns, drugs and lawlessness, if I may update Snow, would eventually bring down the West. When people live in absolute poverty, as do half the world, grievances fester and violence is close at hand. Indeed, we have first-hand knowledge with the drug violence spilling over from Columbia, Peru and Mexico into the United States. The worse case scenario is that more than half the world resents our arrogance, hubris and role as global cop—and would like to bring us down one or two notches. And who the hell are we to continuously intervene in foreign countries and tell people how to live and how to conduct their domestic affairs. Who gave us the right to insist that people in other parts of the world adapt our beliefs and way of life.

Of course, Snow never imagined that the West, especially the United States, would become more dependent on Asian-rim scientists and engineers, and other foreign-born talented students, to prop up our economy and maintain our technological edge—and the subsequent flow of wealth and jobs. How could Snow imagine this tilt of the earth, from the West to the East, given the fact he grew up in an era when whites were considered superior to darker people and English speaking and Teutonic people were still considered masters of the world with a mission to establish order where chaos reigned.

Charles Murray's *Human Accomplishment*, introduces a different twist to the record of human history and why Western nations have advanced more rapidly than other civilizations. Murray was coauthor of *The Bell Curve* in 1994, which relied on statistical data to make a case for innate and inherited intelligences as the crucial factor for success in society and the reason why different racial and ethnic groups think differently (some are more verbal, mathematical, or abstract). In his new book ten years later, he ranks geniuses throughout the ages (the last three thousand years). He identifies 4,002 influential scientists and artists, using a method which he claims allows him to rank individuals from numerous fields and different cultures.

Murray concludes that Western culture has contributed most to the arts and sciences. What the human condition is today and what human species have accomplished is largely due to people who hail from Western Europe in a half-dozen centuries. Sure to fire up the critics, as he did with his earlier book, he makes it clear that white males have been more creative and innovative than minorities and women. Whereas many people consider science and religion to be in opposition, he argues that cultures girded by Christianity have been more productive than cultures bolstered by other religions.

Among the top-ranked, most creative, innovative and influential people, according to Murray, are Galileo, Darwin, and Einstein in science and Aristotle, Plato, and Confucius in philosophy. Michelangelo is the greatest artist and Shakespeare is the greatest writer. Murray marvels that his conclusions coincide with current opinion. Bombast and pompous thinking come easy to Murray. He asserts the people must be right because his research gives them (not him) *face validity*. Murray cares little about opinion, or whether history or philosophy agrees with his conclusions, because his analysis is based on *quantifiable* methods and the opinions of others are based on *qualitative* thought. By the thunderous force of his ego, he dismisses his critics in advance as reflecting political correctness, trendy relativism, and postmodernist or antiestablishment beliefs. On the other hand, Murray claims he has science and research procedures on his side, and any other position is bogus.

Allow me a short aside. If one was a betting man and had been asked to choose in the medieval period which part of the world would dominate the others in knowledge and the arts for much of the coming millenniums, one would most likely have put their money on the Islam world—not Western Europe. The leading scientists, mathematicians, and intellectuals came from this part of the world, and it was the Islamic world that created the first global market, linking Europe with Asia through trade. How Europe and America rose to preeminence after the Middle Ages is for many historians and philosophers a puzzle. Some say it had something to do with the birth of the Renaissance; others refer to the Enlightenment and Age of Reason. In *The Rise of the West,* William McNeill, professor of history at the University of Chicago, credits Europe`s ascent to its warlike prowess, navigational skills, and resistance to disease.

Rodney Stark, a Catholic historian, argues in *The Victory of Reason* that the rise of the West is linked to the spread of Christianity, with its emphasis on preserving manuscripts and embracing the intellect and reason in advancing the faith. Whereas other religions looked to the past for spiritual guidance, Christianity looked to the future in the coming of the Messiah and thus was more progressive. In Thomistic Roman Catholic theology, faith and reason are complimentary and support each other.

The suggestion that Christianity is built on reason and is based on a progressive interpretation of the scriptures and/ or open to competing views is considered a fairy tale by secularists. But Murray also associates the West's rise to global dominance with Christianity, as well as its people having a respect for science, technology, and invention. For the last five or six centuries, the West has cornered the market in knowledge and the arts because of its intellect and open mind and because its thoughts have had a relation to reality—not faith or Zen—and rejected a rigid ideologue. He also argued (as others have) that Christian doctrine allied itself to Greek and Roman art and philosophy. But it is hard not to sense Murray's patrician and elitist background, as his interpretation of the world order is linked to Social Darwinism: Certain people are smarter than others and thus will rise to the top of the ladder and certain societies are more adaptive than others and thus will grow and prosper more than others, while their counterparts falter or decline.

Now for the bad news! Murray warns that the West has peaked. It has lost its vitality and benchmark for history's highest achievers. A champion of excellence, he asserts: "In another few hundred years," we will be explaining why "some completely different part of the world became the locus of great human accomplishment." Sadly, I don't think we will have to wait that long—not if the international test scores in science and math achievement that compare U.S. students to their industrialized counterparts in Europe and Asia are any barometer of the future, and not if the fact that China and India together graduate ten times more scientists and thirteen times more engineers than United States is an indicator of tomorrow's innovation and invention.

China and India

The next book on the "best and brightest" is bound to profile an increasing number of scientists, engineers, and knowledge producers from the non-Western world, with hundreds of hard to pronounce names from China and India, and even from Japan, South Korea, and Indonesia. Unless some idiosyncratic quirk occurs, America and its European cousins will lose inventive and innovative ground to the East, based on the world's increased production of scientists and engineers now coming from Asia and becoming assimilated into the state-capitalist run enterprise. Once Chinese students were organizing demonstrations for democracy. Now they are seeking economic opportunities and a chance to get rich. Chinese scientists and engineers are becoming assimilated into state-capitalist run enterprises. Mao is no longer the main chant; it's money, money, money.

And now for more bad news—which few Americans want to hear but intuitively sense, and that U.S. politicians refuse to admit publically because it contradicts our historical, economic and military view of infallibility and superiority. Three recent books, published in 2009, all point to the same theme as their titles suggest: Will Hutton's *Writing on the Wall*, Martin Jacque's *When China Rules the World*, and James Kynge's *China Shakes the World*. The writing is clear: The rise of China as a super power and the decline of the U.S. and the West. As countries become more powerful, they seek to shape the world according to their own needs, interests, and values. The U.S. has engaged in this practice for the last 100 years, and the West has engaged in it for the last 300 years. We should expect China to do the same as they rise to super economic and global status; it is futile to expect that China will continue to play by our rules.

In the early stages of economic growth, China needed us more than the U.S. needed China. The U.S. possessed (and still does) the largest consumer market (which China needed for exporting its goods) and was the gate keeper of the international economic system and served as the global cop. China avoided unnecessary conflict with the U.S. and West. But as power shifts to China (and the East), it will first become the most influential power of south and east Asia, displacing the U.S., and then seek to regain its historical status as the center of the world and its superiority to all civilizations. This is a view it had for thousands of years until the eighteenth century (when the Industrial Revolution left it weak, humiliated, and subject to foreign powers). We should expect China to act out its grievances and sense of inferiority which it suffered for the last 300 years at the hands of Western countries and Japan. China is expected to become the world's leading economic power sometime in the next 25 years. That said, Beijing will likely replace Washington D.C. as the global capital and Shanghai will likely replace New York as the financial capital.

As the two fastest growing economies (China and India) continue to expand, they are bound to clash both on an economic and military basis in their sphere of regional influence and possibly over the Himalayan borders. Although China recently became India's largest trading partner, as they both seek inroads in south Asia (with nations such as Bangladesh, Indonesia, Nepal, Malaysia, Pakistan and Sri Lanka) shifts in trade and conflict over resources and geopolitics are bound to foster tensions between both countries. However, if for some reason you are a contrarian, or engage in shrewd risk taking, you might *short* China. A tiny percentage of skeptics are concerned about the eye-popping growth rates of China and see a potential bubble or bearish economy for several years. Given the fact that in 2010 China became the second largest economy (bypassing Japan) and number-one export nation (bypassing Germany), most economists are still betting on China's surging and bullish economy.

Like it or not, the U.S. (and the West) will have to get used to the new world order; the U.S. will no longer have overwhelming power and prestige that it enjoyed during the last century. By the second half of the twenty-first century, the new world order will not be overwhelmingly Chinese and Asian in the way the pervious century was U.S. (and Western). We are going to have to learn to be less arrogant and more humble, in short, we will share power with emerging nations, such as the likes of China, India, Indonesia and Brazil (currently representing 40 percent of the world's population), with China increasingly being in the ascendant. The G-20 will replace the G-7 (or G-8) as the dominant economic voice. China and the U.S. will likely have an equal voice in the U.N.'s security council and International Monetary Fund, and Mandarin may rival or possibly supersede English as the primary internet language and business language.[43] On the positive side, The U.S. will not go into free fall as previous ruling empires—from Rome to Charlemagne, or as with the Spanish to Soviets before us.

Brain Drain Counts

The new wave of scientific and technological knowledge will come from Asia, given existing education and economic trends. There is a shift in brain power from the East to the West, commonly called "brain drain," as foreign students leave the U.S. or decline to attend first-rate U.S. institutions of higher learning. Bright foreign students are following the lure of economic opportunity, slowing down in the West and routed back to the East.

Not only has the number of foreign student's enrollments in U.S. colleges and universities dropped since 9/11, down from 583,000 to 565,000, fewer students are opting to come to the United States, even after being accepted. In the meantime, between 2003 and 2008, the number of students from China and India enrolled in Australian and Canadian universities increased four—to five-fold because of an immigration "point system" that puts a premium on education. Similarly, the European Union is in the process of issuing "blue cards" that will give talented people in science and technology a "fast track" to EU citizenship. And, here is the latest brain-drain score. As many as 10 percent of Australia's employed population are highly qualified foreigners. For Canada, it is 7 percent; for the U.S. it is 3 percent; and for the EU it's 1.7 percent.[44]

As for the U.S., the number of Chinese and Indian students, totaling 25 percent of all foreign students in 2008, has declined because of improved economies and opportunities in these two countries. The booming economies of emerging nations around the world are welcoming the return of their own talent that was once was taken for granted would leave, get educated and then remain in the U.S. The world is opening up to ambitious and educated foreigners at precisely the same time the U.S. is closing down. The outcome is, we are beginning to lose our competitive edge, since most of these students were enrolled in science, math, and technological fields and then remained in the United States.

The more graduate students in science and engineering we attract from Asia, the larger our pool of human capital that may wind up in Silicon Valley, North Carolina's Golden Triangle, and other high-tech and innovative centers. "Brain workers" migrate to "brain working" centers. Given the rapid increase in globalization and the internet, brain-based jobs are highly mobile. U.S. immigration policies must attract innovative and technological talent, not repel it by making it difficult to obtain student visas or science/engineering job visas. But Congress has not revised the visa rules for the last twenty years, and have added more restrictions since 9-11. Hence, there are many brilliant minds who try to get into the U.S. and go elsewhere. Most disturbing, the nation's competitiveness and wealth is tied to brain drain, which is now being reversed. In making immigration laws, the U.S. Congress tends to cater to big business' demand for cheap labor to fill the ranks of agribusiness, hotel and restaurant industries, and sweatshop manufacturing, while short-changing high-tech, high-wage industries and ignoring the economic advantages of human capital. For example, an estimated 75 percent of the agricultural work force is here illegally.

The fact is, foreign student graduates earn a significant percentage of the nation's degrees in science and engineering. For example, in 2007 the

U.S Department of Education reported that 27 percent of the science/
technology and 39 percent of the engineering masters degrees and 44
percent of the science/technology and 63 percent of the engineering
doctorate degrees were granted to foreign students. Immigrants make
up two thirds of the nation's supply of such workers (science, technology
and engineers), and it is estimated to be 75 percent by 2015. Their role
in innovative and economic growth is obvious, and the more we attract
talented immigrants the more likely new ideas will flourish and turn into
future jobs and national wealth. Congress is supposed to revise the student
visa rules currently caped at 85,000 per year and requiring foreigners to
wait six years or more for a green card. In the meantime, many of these
students are being lost to the United States—the nation that educated
them. What the U.S. needs to do is to maintain the flow of "brain drain"
from other countries by creating an immigration policy that slashes
the influx of unskilled immigrants and rewards human capital with a
point-system modeled after Canada and Australia.

Not only do our Asian American students prop up our international
test scores in science and math, they also bolster the virtues of legal
immigration. Just count the percentage of Intel finalists, which recognize
the top science and math high-school students in the nation. Out of 40
finalists in 2009, the parents of 25 came from Asia, with last names like
Anand, Jakpor, Ye, and Ying. They are "the key to keeping us ahead of
China," according to *New York Times* writer Tom Friedman.[45] They are
America's first-round science/math draft choices.

Duke University researchers conclude that approximately 25 percent
of science, engineering, and technology companies started from 1995
to 2005 had at least one senior executive or founder born outside the
United States. Immigrant entrepreneurial companies employed nearly
500,000 workers and generated more than $50 billion in sales in 2005.
[46] The Duke study also found that foreign-born inventors living in the
U.S. without citizenship accounted for 24 percent of the patient filings in
2005, compared to 7 percent in 1998. An estimated 7,300 U.S. research
and tech start-ups were founded by immigrants, and 26 percent have
Indian surnames. Another estimate is that the information and technology
sector, founded by foreigners living in the U.S., has accounted for half
of the nation's economic growth since 2000. Other studies reported by
the*Economist* show of all the firms in Silicon Valley, about 25 percent were

founded by Chinese and Indians. For every foreigner given an H1B visa, five new jobs are created for Americans. [47]

Instead of trying to lift H1B visa caps, to allow more foreign and talented students into the country, there are politicians seeking to reduce the number of these visas in order to ensure jobs for Americans. This kind of thinking is counter-productive to our economic health and vitality. It also fails to consider that job openings in science, engineering and technology are increasing and we lack American-born graduates with degrees in these subjects. Not only is American human capital slipping in these fields, we are taking mulligans on international tests in these areas of knowledge. In terms of the future, we are in high-tech decline. Given the U.S. cold shoulder toward immigrants since 9-11 and the status of U.S. education—compounded by under funding in math and science education and almost nothing for gifted and talented students (the top 3-4 percent) because they lack minority status and organized advocates—they create the perfect "gathering storm." In fact, the rise of Asia's human capital and potential for innovation can be analyzed in cold war terms—a "silent Sputnik."

Economists think of knowledge professionals, unlike physical goods, as nonrival. Ideas and innovation by one person do not preclude use by others. The knowledge industry is not a zero sum game, in fact, the common argument is one good innovation leads to another innovation; knowledge builds on knowledge. All well and good. But directing a talented mathematician into engineering or Wall Street is a zero sum game, since the number of skilled mathematicians are limited in the U.S. For every mathematician or potential engineer that chooses a career in finance, the nation loses about five other knowledge and technological jobs. We need to rethink paying "rookie" Wall Street players $ 250,000 to $350,000 (including bonuses) and "freshman" scientists and engineers $50,000 to $60,000. Eventually, this kind of thinking—where a company considers a Wall Street person a "profit" item or money maker and scientist or engineer as a "cost" item—is going to lead us into an economic hole and hobble us into decline.

We often hear concerns that U.S. schools and colleges are not keeping pace with foreign competition in math, science and engineering. A seminal report, *Steady as She Goes*, published in 2009 by Harold Salzman of Rutgers and B. Lindsay Lowell of Georgetown, suggests that is only part of the story. Among 1977 college graduates in these three areas of study only 35 percent were working in related fields ten years later. Although the percentage climbed to 44 percent among 1993 graduates, as categorized by their 2003 occupations, private companies were not doing enough to attract and keep these college graduates. They were simply not rewarding our best scientists, engineers, mathematicians—and many wind up following the money in other areas where the marketplace for talent pays higher. Even worse, with recent outsourcing of jobs, many of these talented graduates were excessed out of their careers.

The short and simple solution is to pay our best graduates in math, science and technology more money, to attract graduates into career paths needed for the U.S. to stay competitive. On the bright side, the U.S. is in a fortunate position. Its universities are highly regarded, its national character welcomes immigrants and its economy is dynamic, inventive and tech-driven. Hence, it does not have to advertise or make special efforts to attract talented foreigners. To keep competitive, all it needs to do is to expand the supply of visas and make it easier for talented foreigners to obtain citizenship. What we need to understand is that migration today is not only about poor people moving to rich countries for opportunities.

People from rich countries are now moving all over the world, chasing jobs that are being outsourced from rich to emerging countries. More important, skilled and educated immigrants have come to the realization that emerging countries are growing faster than the U.S. and the European Union; they are following jobs where there are opportunities. As a result, "brain drain" is being reversed—away from the U.S. These new shifts in world population need to be recognized if we are to retain American knowledge, innovation and wealth. The U.S. is still considered the top country in generating new ideas and adopting them quickly, according to a major European business school, INSEAD, based near Paris. But other studies by the World Bank rated the U.S. third in terms of innovation, behind Singapore and New Zealand.

Centers of Creativity

New knowledge in the United States doubles about every fifteen or twenty years. In many third-world countries the mule and horse is the main mode of transportation, and the local economy is mainly picking berries, dragging banana tress to market, or having children clean out goat intestines that can be turned into leather. This is the real China, India, Myanmar (formerly Burma), Bangladesh and the African continent—the rural hinterland which is possibly representative of 40 to 50 percent of the world. This is not to deny these countries don't have a corporate mentality and a class of people that remind us of both old-fashioned industrialists and a new brand of technocrats who are versed in computer software, media, and other high-tech and electronic ventures.

What is less clear is the extent to which this new economic growth and human capital trickles down to the masses who live in poverty, both in the countryside, far away from the "new economy" which deals with the exchange of knowledge and ideas, and in urban squalor, where old and new knowledge, ideas and values collide: East meets West and low-tech meets high-tech, causing a great cultural rift and the makings of revolution. Here we envision old catchphrases that divide people into new "winners" and "losers," societies of widening disparities, much worse than the United States because of government corruption and a lack of fair laws. We call it the gap between "rich" and "poor." Asians and Africans call it "light" and "darkness." Call it what you want. Extreme disparities and huge inequities hinder mobility around the world.

Anyone familiar with New York City, Chicago, or Los Angeles understands these cities, as well as smaller cities like Austin, Boston, and Seattle. They house people from a vast assortment of countries with different knowledge, ideas, and values. The old patrician class has always disrespected and discriminated against these people, but the quest for economic opportunity and the dynamic factors that drove great numbers of these people to migrate to America have managed to overcome some of the patrician forces, customs and laws that have tried to stifle newcomers landing in these cities.

Far from "celebrating" their particular ethnic or religious identities, most urban dwellers have contact with different people and become more "hip," "sophisticated," or "cosmopolitan" than their nonurban counterparts. Even kids who come from the backwaters of the world, say from rice paddies of Vietnam or the mountains of Montenegro, quickly become enculturated into American society, especially if they settle in large cities and they step out of their parents' culture and historical isolation. The computer and cell phone may increase our ability to communicate with people from around the world, but there is still a limitation on exposure to new thoughts without actual contact with different people.

Our thinking in America is shaped not only by our home environment and community but also by diverse people we come in contact with, who reshape and expand our thinking and imagination. Those of us who come in contact with people from around the world assimilate more information than those who remain trapped in urban ghettos, rural villages, or on mountains and islands. To be sure, you can live in most parts of Nebraska and Wyoming, safe from people who have funny-sounding names, different customs, and strange folklore, but you are not going to have the same opportunity to expand your thinking and creative juices. If, on the other hand, you live your life in a melting pot area, you will more likely be tolerant, pursue novel ideas, and resist large-scale bureaucracy, production lines, and routine jobs. The point is that human creativity is the ultimate economic resource and link to national wealth. The chances are, also, that the creative mind will raise productivity, earn more money, and enjoy his or her job compared to a close-minded individual who is insulated from different people with different ideas and different ways of thinking—or works on an assembly line and performs routine tasks.

ACHIEVEMENT GAPS IN EDUCATION

While we all seem to recognize the rise of Asia in the "knowledge" age, and that a country's human capital and potential for innovation is tied to their systems of higher education, we cannot overlook that the foundation for this talent is rooted in the K-12 education system. The key question is whether a nation's teaching and learning is "dumbed down" or promotes it's "best and brightest." The answer is clear. For nearly 50 years, since the early 1960s, despite hundreds of task force reports and attempts for school reform, and despite thousands of compensatory programs and tens of billions of dollars spent annually on low-income and low-achieving students, our education system is in a state of depression. Although we can point to individual schools and school districts that are successful, our system as a whole has not improved.

Achievement gaps between Asian and white students compared to Hispanic and black students remain alarmingly high, and by 2015 the later group of students will represent the majority enrollments. Comparatively U.S. students consistently score on achievement tests below students in other industrialized nations, despite the fact we spend more money per student on education than all the countries except Switzerland. The number of U.S. college students majoring in science, math and engineering are flat, and the percentage of graduates in these three essential areas in Western European and especially Asian countries have increasingly outpaced our nation.

The state of American education can be summed up by the report, *A Nation at Risk* published nearly 30 years ago, which indicated that a "rising tide of mediocrity" is eroding the well-being of the nation. This mediocrity is linked to the foundations of our educational institutions and is spilling over into the workplace and other sectors of society. The report listed several aspects of educational decline that were evident to educators and citizens alike: lower achievement scores, lower testing requirements, lower graduation requirements, lower teacher expectations, fewer academic courses, minimal homework, more remedial courses, and higher illiteracy rates. It noted that the schools have attempted to tackle too many social problems that the home and other agencies of society either will not or cannot resolve. The report called for tougher standards for graduation, more courses in science, mathematics and foreign language, a longer school day and school year, far more homework, improved and updated textbooks, more rigorous testing and higher expectations for student achievement, teacher accountability, higher salaries for teachers, and more rigorous certification standards for teachers.

The report was hailed by school administrators, policy makers, and business people as the most important government document published for and about educators and as the prescription for reform. The report could have been written today because almost nothing has changed; in fact, disappointingly it can be argued that conditions have worsened. H.G. Wells summed it up best: "History is a race between education and catastrophe." We are losing that race, and the odds of winning seem to worsen each year.

Although we can present a cascading number of facts and figures about our failure to achieve significant education progress, the idea in this book is to focus on the big picture and avoid scores of data. That said, after spending nearly half a trillion dollars on compensatory programs for low-income and low-achieving students, educators are still unable to agree on which programs work and whether more spending affects educational outcomes. Obviously, other variables need to be considered, some which may be considered unpleasant or politically incorrect.

The International Report Card

Moving on to the demands of knowledge and technology, the data are not impressive when comparisons are made between U.S. students in math and science and students in advanced technological countries. European and Asian students consistently outperform American students on international tests in science and mathematics, and the gaps consistently increase in the higher grades.

The international comparisons started in the 1960s, with the International Association for the Evaluation of Educational Achievement (IEA), in areas of mathematics, involving 133,000 elementary and secondary students and 5,450 schools in twelve technologically advanced countries.[48] Especially noticeable were the overall good showings of Japan and Israel and the poor showings of the United States. The range of difference between high and low performing countries decreased when the most able students were compared, indicating that the "cream of mathematics talent" is distributed equally over various countries. Student characteristics highly correlated with achievement, and the child's social class accounted for the greatest share of variation in learning. The study also showed that at every age level, and in most countries, boys outperformed girls.

In the next group of studies, the researchers embarked on a six subject survey, including science. In this study, 258,000 elementary and secondary students and 9,700 schools in nineteen countries (four of them undeveloped) were involved. U.S. students never finished first or second in any of the six subject areas and were last seven times; in science, they scored below the international average. Although the impact of the home was considerably greater than the direct effect of school variables the impact of schooling was shown to be generally more important for science and foreign language than for other areas. The suggestion that certain subjects might be more amenable to school influences is encouraging to those who feel that schools should have a significant effect on learning.

As a matter of common knowledge among text experts, there are unique limitations with large-scale international studies, including common content across countries, translation of content and selection or representation of students to be tested. Nevertheless, international test comparisons have continued for the last 45 years. For this policy agenda, the international report card for U.S. students would be around a "D."

Fast forwarding to the most recent and famous international tests in mathematics and science are the Trends in International Mathematics and Science Study (TIMSS), administered three times in grades 4, 8, and 12 in 1995, 1999, and 2003. In the first two studies, published between 1998 and 2001, U.S. fourth grade students in math ranked eighth out of eighteen among industrialized countries that participated, and in science tied for third place. In eighth grade, U.S. students ranked slightly below average in math (twenty-three out of thirty-eight industrialized countries) and slightly above average in science (below fourteen countries). By the twelfth grade, American students scored last in math among twenty industrialized countries, and in science they scored below sixteen countries. While the international average math/science scores were 500, the U.S. average in math was 461 and in science 480.[42]

International test comparisons were so bleak that for the third study, the U.S. government decided to compare U.S. scores and relative ranking with all countries, including those from the third world and poorest parts of the world. Not surprisingly, U.S. math and science scores were reported average or above average by *Newsweek, Time* and the *Wall Street Journal.* The U.S. public was mislead, pure and simple. For example, in 2003 science scores of fourth graders were seventh highest among 25 countries and eighth graders were twelfth highest among 44 other participating countries such as Armenia, Cyprus, Iran, Moldova, and Tunisia. What this proves is nothing of substance, since a high-tech nation is being compared with low-tech nations. In mathematics the results were similar. Fourth graders ranked twelfh among 25 countries and eighth graders outperformed their peers in twenty five out of 45 countries, including Bahrain, Botswana, Bulgaria, Egypt, and Jordon. Given the nature of the competition, the rankings for the U.S. don't hold much water and to some extent are meant to deceive U.S. tax payers who support the schools.

America's decline in human capital continues beyond the TIMSS studies. The Program for International Student Assessment (PISA) reported in 2003 the mathematical literacy and scientific literacy skills of 15-year olds among 28 other industrialized countries and 10 nonindustrialized countries. U.S. students scored lower than twenty of the industrialized countries and three of the nonindustrialized countries in math and lower than nineteen of the industrialized countries and three of its nonindustrialized countries in science. The average U.S. math score was lower (483) than the average student performance of the 28 others industrialized countries (500). For science the average U.S. score was 491 compared to the average score (500). Further analysis of the data revealed that a greater percentage of U.S. students than the industrialized average scored at the lowest levels of performance in mathematics literacy and all four broad areas of problem solving. (No information on specific science topics was available in PISA 2003.)

In the most recent PISA test, administered in 2006, the U.S. 15-year olds ranked 25 lowest out of 30 in math and 24 lowest out of 30 in science among other industrialized countries. That put our average on the same level with Portugal and Slovakia, rather than with other industrialized countries such as Australia, Canada or South Korea. Of all the industrialized countries, the U.S. had the greatest percentages of students at or below the lowest level of proficiency in math and science, called level 1, "limited knowledge."

Remember Sputnik!—When we had a wake up call. Not only were our skies vunerable, but we also found out that Ivan could read and solve calculus problems and Johnnie could not. The 2009 PISA test scores released in 2010, made it clear that Chinese are out to beat us! It was the first time they participated (represented by Shanghai, a city of 20 million people) in the international tests. China came out number-one in all three areas—reading, science and math. Where did the U.S fall? Our scores were "flat" compared to the previous international tests. In reading, we were 17th, in science 23rd, and in math 31st among 65 countries.[50]

Until now we were able to convince ourselves that Hong Kong (which was always in the top of the rankings on international tests) was special, reflecting British education and economic prosperity. (Hong Kong placed 3rd in science and math in the 2009 PISA tests.) We were also able to convince ourselves that China only wanted to lend us money and buy our bonds as well as undersell us and copycat our ideas.[51] Today, we must face the fact that China no longer produces toxic toys or teaches by rote learning. The wind has changed. China wants more than respect; it is out to surpass the rest of the world, including out-producing and out-educating the U.S. Think about how many more scientists and engineers they are now producing than we are (8:1 ratio), then project its new capacity for innovation and its expanding economy in 2025.

Then there is International Adult Literacy and Lifeskills Survey (All). It analyzed the degree to which the adult population could perform mathematical tasks in daily life and the work place. Specific areas of measurement included the ability to apply math skills to number sense, estimation, measurement and statistics. Six countries participated, including Switzerland, Norway, Canada, and Bermuda—all which scored higher than the U.S.—and Italy. Moreover, the Educational Testing Service has concluded that better educated people are leaving the workforce and being replaced by people with less education and skill. This trend reflects U.S. demographic changes—an increase in the minority population and a shift in the immigration policy.

For example, Hispanics scored 75 percent lower than whites and blacks scored 63 percent lower. Native-born whites and Asian Americans were tied for second place in the international ranking in literacy. Recent immigrants account for 40 percent of the U.S. labor force, but they rank 74 points behind native-born immigrants. In short, American productivity is partially based on the G.I. Bill and pre-1960 immigrants who were largely from Europe and were more skilled than today's immigrants who hail from non-European and non-industrialized nations. Soon the more skilled workers will be retiring and replaced by a less literate workforce. The effect on productivity and global competition, and the subsequent economic decline of the country, can be predicted by referring to the logic of our demographic outcomes.

The Economics of Schooling

As the U.S. falls further behind in achievement, the McKinsey consulting firm released a report, *The Economic Impact of the Achievement Gap in America's Schools* in 2009. The implications of the report revealed our national decline in productivity and jobs. Had America been able to close the gap in science and math achievement between 1983 and 1998 and raised its performance to the level of such nations as Canada, Finland and South Korea, the U.S. Gross Domestic Product in 1998 would have been approximately $2 trillion higher. If its achievement gap had been closed between black and Hispanic students and white and Asian students by 1998 the Gross Domestic Product in 2008 would have been about $400 to $500 billion higher. If the gap between America's low-income students and the remaining students had been similarly narrowed, GDP in 2008 would have been $400 to $670 billion higher. In terms of PISA math and science output and the amount of money we spend on each student, which is among the highest in the world, the report concluded that "we get 60 percent less for our education dollars in terms of average test score results than do other wealthy [industrialized] nations."

Classroom size or teacher-student ratios contribute to student learning and ultimately to test outcomes. Obviously, one-to-one learning (a coach and student) is ideal and more effective than a ten-to-one ratio of students to teacher, and this small group is more beneficial than a classroom size of twenty-five students. But the fact is social-class difference and racial difference (even when class is controlled) contribute to attitudes and behaviors related to learning. The U.S. average classroom size is 16 to 1 compared to Japan, South Korea, and Hong Kong where ratios are 19:1 to 28:1, yet the latter countries always outscore U.S. students in math and science tests.

The picture worsens when education spending is compared on an international level. Among industrialized countries reporting education spending, the United States spends only 3.5 percent of its GDP on education, ranking eighth among twenty industrialized countries. But our expenditures per student is higher—second only to Switzerland. In other words, other countries do not have same resources as we do, yet they make a greater effort by spending more of their GDP on education. The inference is that we do not get our money's worth in education spending—and money alone is not going to solve our education problems. To be sure, education is big business—and about $650 billion (in 2010) is annually spent on K-12 education. However, there is little indication that spending more on schools will improve student achievement. The issue involves human capital—the values, motivation and work and study ethic of the nation and its youth.

There is a wealth of data over a 50-year period, starting with the 1966 Coleman report entitled *Equal Educational Opportunity* to the 2008 National Mathematics Advisory Panel report, *Foundations for Success*, showing that the most important variable related to student achievement is the child's family background and the second most important factor is the peer group. Other variables, including, what the schools or teachers do, "are secondary or irrelevant" in the words of Harvard's Christopher Jencks. In fact, there is data from Rand Corporation suggesting that no more than 17 to 20 percent of the variance related to student learning is associated with schooling and teaching. People with political motives would prefer to bury this data and hold teachers and school accountable.

The point is, no person alive can say what education and social programs in schools have been consistently successful. Chapter by chapter, we have learned about the failure of one government program after another, including compensatory education, job training, urban renewal, and welfare—each of which cost tax payers billions of dollars a year. The analysis has suggested that with respect to school financing, we are already spending too much in terms of what we are getting in return. In the early stages of school and related compensatory programs, input increments have a high marginal return, but they gradually diminish as they are extended to large numbers of low-achieving children. Early gains fade out and there is virtually no increase in output; infact in many areas of education we reach a "flat area," less output in relation to input, or worse, no return.

Sadly, nearly half its nation's students who graduate high school test at the seventh grade level in math and eighth grade in science and one third below ninth grade in reading. Today's high school students are tomorrow's workforce. The effects of school achievement is seen in the erosion of America's global competitiveness—and future jobs which require skills that build on math and science literacy and reading. Business and military leaders complain that they are required to spend billions of dollars annually on costly remedial education and training programs in the basic skills, or the three Rs. Between 1980 and 2000, remedial mathematics courses in four-year colleges increased by 75 percent, and, by 2000, constituted one-fourth of all mathematic courses taught in these institutions. By 2010, more than 2 million, or 20 percent of college students in two-and four-year colleges were enrolled in "learning strategies" courses—a euphemism for "remedial courses"—another 1.2 million or 12 percent, were being tutored individually or in groups. As many as 25 percent of the recruits in the armed forces cannot read at the ninth-grade level. Teaching "learning strategies" and "study skills" has become a cottage industry at the high school, college, and armed service levels—what was once called "remedial education" before political correction entered the education arena.

Excuses and More Excuses

So what excuses can U.S. educators muster to explain the consistently low scores of American students, despite concerted federal, state, and local efforts since the post-Sputnik era to increase math and science achievement scores. I promised in the beginning pages of the book to be brief. So here is the short list—enough to give you a buzz or a feeling of lightness or weightlessness, like the second before you are about to pass out or the instant you are above the diving board and gravity hasn't yet grabbed you.

1. About 20 to 33 percent of American middle school and high school science and math teachers are teaching out of license; furthermore, nearly half of those certified to teach science and math teach subjects they are not qualified to teach. (For example, a biology teacher may not be qualified to teach chemistry or physics and a math teacher may not be qualified to teach calculus (only algebra and geometry).

2. Since the mid 1950s there has been a slight average increase in science and math coursework among graduating U.S. high school students, leveling at 2.5 and 2.9 years respectively. But the data are not impressive when comparisons are made with high school seniors in other advanced countries. Japanese, South Korean, and Hong Kong high school students, for example, average 1¼ science courses per year and 1 ½ math courses per year, including calculus and statistics. The result is that Japanese, South Korean and Hong Kong students consistently outperform American students on international tests.

3. Measuring the cumulative achievement on one short test may not sufficiently cover what students have learned. About 25 percent of the test items in math and science reflect topics not studied by American test takers.

4. American science and math textbooks are numerous—some above average, some average, some below average in quality—whereas textbooks in other counties are approved by the ministry of education so there is consistency of coverage. Our textbooks emphasize breadth of topics, to please a wide audience (14,000 different school districts) at the expense of depth of topics.

As a result, American textbooks (and teachers who rely on these textbooks) foster superficial learning of a large body of information, while teachers of countries with a ministry have more time to teach students to think about procedures, to help students form hypotheses, make procedures, and acquire skills to conduct experiments and contrast ideas and findings.

5.   American high school students have less homework (23 percent of eleventh graders report no assigned homework, 14 percent do not do their homework, and 26 percent do less than one hour per day of homework), and engage in more social activities, out-of-school activities, and part-time jobs than their international counterparts who often have four to five hours of homework daily.

6.   American students average 3.5 hours per day of TV viewing, not to mention Internet surfing and socializing, and we know there is an inverse relationship between TV viewing and student achievement, especially after the second or third grade. (The positive effects of watching Sesame Street and other language-skill programs become increasingly irrelevant after age seven or eight.)

7.   European and Asian students have a longer school day and school year, with European countries averaging 200 days and Asian countries averaging 220 days, compared to the United States which has about a 180-day school calendar.

8.   Student poverty among American students is the highest, about 21 to 25 percent. It is nearly 50 percent higher than in any other industrialized country; next is Australia with 14 percent and Canada with 13.5 percent. Moreover, we know poverty clearly correlates in an inverse relationship with student achievement. In addition, the United States has among the highest or highest student drug addiction, student violence, gang activity and teenage pregnancy among industrialized nations.

9.   The breakdown of the American family is well documented. More than 50 percent of American students live with a single head of household; it approaches 75 percent in our big cities, where student achievement is the lowest compared in other parts of the country.

10.   Finally, it should be assumed that the students taking the test in all countries are drawn from a normal bell curve or ability

distribution. Some countries—such as China, Japan, and Russia—may have certain political agendas, or sensitivity about "saving face," and are more selective in determining which students will take the test. Moreover, if you eliminate black and Hispanic students from the test pool, American white students compare favorably with European nations and Asian American students compare favorably with Asian nations which score the highest in math and science tests.[52]

Although all of these reasons help explain the low scores in math and science achievement among American students on international tests, part of the problem lies in the limited amount of course work in these twin subject areas. By way of example, if you want to learn how to drive, play tennis or chess, or read, you need to devote time to the endeavor. The more *instructional time*, the more proficient you should become. Thus, if Americans are concerned about math and science (and we should because of the information-technology age we live in), then we need to increase instructional time to allow for proficiency in these subjects. This consideration must be weighed against a belief among many educators that schools need to emphasize the whole child and the liberal arts, and that teachers should be paid on the basis of qualifications and experience with no differential for specific subjects such as math or science. Based on supply and demand, as well as the needs for the nation, free marketers would support higher pay for math and science teachers. In fact, in an era of high-stake testing, with most school districts focusing on reading and math achievement, there is concern among policy makers that science is getting shortchanged in the elementary and junior high schools.

While most of us recognize that spending money on education is an investment in the nation's future, pouring more money in schools scratches the surface of the larger problem of family structure and culture—which in turn deal with stratification and inequality. Society prepares the achievement gap before the students enter school; the poor and minority populations are the victims and test results are the evidence that society is unfair and unjust.

Trying to break the cycle of poverty or target education reform is hopeless on a larger scale. A few people will succeed in school, but the majority are doomed to failure because the so-called solution is isolated from larger social and economic issues—basically inequality. According to Richard Wilkinson and Kate Pickett, British social scientists, in rich countries where incomes are more evenly distributed, the citizens have higher education achievement, live longer and have fewer rates of obesity and delinquency. In their book *The Spirit Level*, higher taxes on the rich and smaller difference in pay lead to a better quality of life for all the citizens of that country. Where inequality is greatest, the lower classes and those who feel discriminated perform worse on cognitive tests than in countries where there are fewer differences in socio-economic states. In a society that rewards individual achievement and innovation, it is argued that lower taxes cause people to work harder and the argument for more equality breaks down. But given the recent global economic meltdown, and the fact that a goodly percentage of the rich got their money by arrogance, theft and fraud, the idea of equality may sound less socialistic and more sympathetic to Americans. We all know what economic growth can do for us, but we also know that most people in the United States do not share in the nation's prosperity on an equal basis. It is impossible to create incentives for Americans to move up the food chain, while we provide tax bonuses for millionaires and billionaires.

So where does all this leave us? What is saving America are not all the smart and rich people who graduated from Ivy League schools and wound up making millions on Wall Street. Actually, many of them helped cripple the American economy. What is saving us is "brain drain." What we need to do is encourage more talented immigrants to our shores to compensate for the over-all international failure of American students in science and math. The sad fact is that we have failed as a nation to achieve significant progress in science and math—and in remaking our schools. After 50 years of education failure, maybe it is time to think less about school-based solutions and more about the larger issues of inequality. Maybe its time to rethink the free market, and what Warren Buffet once said that "only when the tide goes out do you find who is not wearing a bathing suit." Well, you don't have to be a star gazer nor believe in the oracle to understand that the tide of technology and economic competition is turning—and not in our favor.

THE COLLAPSE OF THE INDUSTRIAL MODEL

The decline of U.S. manufacturing, highlighted by the recent near collapse of the auto industry, highlights a paradigm shift in society from manufacturing to knowledge and technology, from muscle power to brain power. It changes the fortunes of workers from the factory and assembly line, where convergent and concrete thinking is expected, to the office and computer where divergent and abstract thinking is rewarded. In our post-industrial society, no one with a college education seems to care nor understand the persistent prejudice against labor. Those who work with their hands are chastised as stupid, dull or irrelevant. It's a major problem given the large number of blue collar workers. The fall of industrial production in the U.S. revives an age-old quarrel about IQ, education and class: Certain people are good at working with their hands and machines while others are better working with their minds and processing information on wireless networks.

Few people are that resilient to work just as well with their hands and minds. How does government know which manufacturing companies to save? What is the "appropriate" size of any industry? Demand is supposed to decide, but then there is the issue of retraining workers and providing safety nets such as unemployment insurance, health insurance, and retirement benefits. Giving money to the loudest voices or the politically connected or the group that can deliver the most votes is often the case. But this does not necessarily solve the long-term dilemma and economic upheaval associated with the demise of workers and their families—subsequent unemployment or underemployment and the payment of bills.

Forgotten Americans

News reporter and author Louis Uchitelle, in *The Disposable American*, alerts a complacent nation to the millions of "forgotten" and "disposable" Americans—caught in the cycle of unemployment and underemployment—unable to share in the wealth of nation. As casualties of manufacturing decline, more than 50 percent of the 2.6 million displaced workers in the Midwest were forced to take jobs at an average of $13.25 an hour or less, amounting to no more than $27,000 a year. These figures do not consider the sad fact that nationwide one-third of all laid off workers, after two years of looking, were still not working. According to the Labor Department, 73 percent of laid-off workers earn less or have no job at all. Education and retraining are considered the great panacea for these people, but their wage loss is real and, multiplied by the millions of those laid off, it is staggering. Nearly every politician and education is sold on retraining and retooling of displaced workers, but few are willing to admit that the labor market has changed and retraining is not going to help much.

The outcome is that lay-offs have become an acceptable trend, part of the new economy. Displaced workers, along with those close to retirement who were forced to retire, as well as retired people whose pensions have been sliced up because of company losses, form a new category of older "invisible" and left-behind Americans. They are nothing more than a new statistic for sociologists and economics to analyze for the purpose of some report. This new social-economic category makes up part of the struggling American populace, those who may be labeled the "new poor," or just above the threshold of poverty. They are people in the fall and winter years who will have "no fun in the sun."

Simply put, there is nothing romantic or exotic about being 50 years or older, poor or near poor, relegated in small rooms and tired surroundings, when most of your life has passed you by. Living under the spell of poverty, or inches above it, in your declining years has the same flavor whether you are living in a northwestern fishing or ski village, some small rural town in Texas or Tennessee, or renting a hole-in-the-wall in the southern Keys of Florida. You might get used to it, but it's not the life most people bargained for, nor what I would wish for you or any American; it is certainly not a memory to celebrate or toast at your son's or daughter's wedding day or your dad's or mom's silver anniversary. There is nothing good about being poor and middle-aged or old, or living near the edge of poverty, unless perhaps you are some artist or gypsy living in the south of France or some far-off community or mountaintop wary of outsiders and in centuries of isolation.

It is not supposed to happen this way, but this is how life in America is shaping up. If the money spent for one month fighting in Iraq or Afghanistan could have been used for people to simply improve their lives, say for Social Security retirement benefits, the future I'm painting would have a much happier resolution. Considering the last five years of fighting, if the money ($450 to $500 billion per year) had been used for social and health benefits for those born between 1946 and 1964, then the baby boom generation would experience boom, golden years and not gloom, tarnished years as I'm predicting for tens of millions or at least half of the 70 million Americans sixty-five and older within the next three decades.

The Rise and Fall of Labor

Roosevelt was the first pro-labor president, largely due to the leadership of Frances Perkins, his Secretary of labor and first female U.S. cabinet secretary. As pointed out by Kristin Downey's *The Women Behind the New Deal*, Perkins developed and introduced Social Security (pensions for working people), unemployment insurance (for working people), and mortgage loans (to homeowners facing foreclosure). It was also the period when a minimum wage and forty-hour work week became policy. Roosevelt was a member of the upper crust and Brahmin class and did not necessarily favor politicians who came to the rescue of ordinary people or the labor class, but it was Perkins and her twelve-year tenure that served as his moral conscience. Under her leadership, the largest public working program (WPA) was financed in 1935, earmarking some $11 billion (equivalent to $200 billion in 2010 dollars) and putting to work some 8 million people. It was largely due to Perkins' influence that workers achieved the right to collective bargaining, sweat shops were eliminated, child labor laws were introduced, and union membership dramatically expanded.

The great majority of the working force had no thought of marching or demonstrating during the Great Depression; they did not favor socialistic principles of reform. But enough people organized, spoke out, and marched—and faith in the capitalistic system suffered a major blow. Images of the earlier robber barons at the turn of the century and the successful businessman of the 1920s was no longer a hero but often seen as a villain. Politicians who were allied closely with big business were discredited and tossed out of office. The Depression undermined the essential feeling of security, and there was concern of a complete collapse of the system—all which accelerated the rise of labor.

Post World War II was an era which catapulted many working people into the middle class—largely because the unions and corporations worked together to provide decent salaries and safety nets for ordinary working people. It was the largest movement in mobility among American people who were able to realize their dream—a house and a good job with health benefits and pensions. Almost all the strides made by unions in the 1950s through the 1970s have been wiped out, superseded by the service and retail industry model: low wages, few benefits and high turnover.

Actually, the union's decline began with the steel strike of 1959, when the U.S. steel industry began to flounder because of foreign competition and was forced to take back many of the previous gains given to steel workers. A once proud industry began its decline. Small towns that were robust and prosperous went bust as steel mills around the country closed in the late 1960s, somewhat similar to what happened to the U.S. auto industry and what previously happened to lumber, paper and printing industries, furniture, clothing and textile industries. Hence, union membership as a percent of U.S. employment peaked from 33 percent in 1955 to 22 percent in 1980 to 12 percent in 2008. Women accounted for 45 percent of the unionized workforce, up from 34 percent in 1983, [53] reflecting the shift from manufacturing to service and public-sector jobs.

There is no villain or mystery attached to what happened. Corporate profits rose after World War II largely because there was no global competition; all the major industrial countries were in rubble after the War. Wages in the U.S. steadily increased year after year, and there was the belief among workers that their children would be better off than they were. (Similarly, the dollar was "king" in Europe and Asia, and it sold for a premium because it was considered to be the only stable currency.

When wages leveled off in the early 1980s, coinciding with the free market ideology of President Reagan, fathers worked longer hours and mothers were forced to enter the workforce to help pay family bills. At the same time, the feminist movement sparked the new wave of female employment. As the deal between corporations and unions slowly disintegrated, families began to go into debt and refinance their homes, as if they were "piggy banks," to maintain their standard of living. Moreover, as Yale Professor Jacob Hacker states in *The Great Risk Shift*, companies transferred the payments of benefits and safety nets to individual workers. The fall of GM, once the mightiest company in the world, which had the best benefits for workers (a cost of $1,500 per car by the turn of the 21st century) is symbolic of today's global market and the decline of the

U.S. workforce. It is also symbolized by the endless rot and squalor, block after block and mile after mile, of Detroit. Here is a major American city, still home to nearly 1 million people, in complete ruin—a cross between ancient sacked Rome and postwar bombed-out Berlin.

The American workforce has lost its place in the sun, along with its industrial model. It was good while it lasted, and we were the envy of the rest of the world. They were good days for workers and allowed them to move up the mobility ladder into the middle class. To be sure, the twentieth century was dominated by the U.S. but now it is coming to an end. We need to understand that America as a nation is moving into the slow lane. Our last cutting-edge industries—semiconductors, telecommunications, computer software, nanotechnology, and internet services—are slowly being moved to the Asian rim where talented technical specialists are cheaper and in abundance. Similarly, U.S. science and technology companies are being challenged by the technological, industrial, and entrepreneurial growth of Asian countries and even parts of Eastern Europe. It's happening all around us.

The best advice: If your job can be digitized, it is only time before it becomes moveable to the other side of the world. Technology permits companies to rapidly grow and become larger. China, India, and a few other Asian countries such as Japan, South Korea, and Singapore in short time will be the center of action; this is where new products and new ideas will derive from, the center of the future global workplace. If you think I'm talking about some far-off place or a fantasy world, then you need to read Thomas Friedman's best-selling book *The World is Flat*. He warns that the economic playing field had been leveled by computers, broadband and cellular networks, and the Internet. Global trends indicate continuous growth in investments and jobs in China, India and other Asian countries and the slow demise of American workers who are unable to compete in a global economy and if I may add, the slow transfer of trillions of dollars of wealth from the Unites States to the Asian rim countries.

But Americans have never been ones to lay back and let history take its course. Since coming to the Promised Land in 1624, Americans have ventured into the wilderness to seek their fortunes and have navigated through storms to protect their freedoms. Since the turn of the twentieth century, we have come to the aid of our allies to ward off despots and totalitarianism. Although the "good guys" won the twentieth century, it is doubtful who will win the twenty-first century. (If I was force to bet on the U.S., I would expect 2:1 or 3:1 odds.)

Not long ago, Japan was the "economic miracle," and for the last 40 years its manufacturing powers was rivaling the U.S. Now China's booming export economy and Japan's crushing debt is accelerating the inevitable. China has become the world's second largest economy—with game changing ramifications in trade, diplomacy, and military power.[54] In the meantime, the dollar has sunk to its lowest value in the last 100 years, and gold has reached new heights—reflecting the dollar devaluation.

Here are a few eye-popping statistics to show China's gradually moving into first place, increasing its wealth, ambitions and power.

1) Initial public offerings—In the year 2000, the U.S. $63 billion and China $19.4 billion. In 2009, the U.S. $13.7 billion (-78%) and China $34.8 billion (+79%).

2) Trade balance—The year 2000, the U.S.—$422 billion and China +$28 billion. By 2009, the U.S.—$853 billion (102% deficit increase) and China +$267 billion (841% surplus increase).

3) Gross Domestic Product—In 2000, the U.S. $9.8 trillion and China $1.2 trillion. The year 2009, the U.S. $14.2 trillion (45% increase) and China $4.3 trillion (261% increase).

4) Fortune 500 Global Companies—In 1960, the U.S. (180) and China (8). By 2009, the U.S., 140 (-22%) and China, 37 (+45%). [55]

China doesn't just dominate global trade; it roams the world for resources, has the fastest growing number of billionaires and most initial public offerings (IPOS), supplanting the U.S. in 2009 and 2010.

Most pessimists are betting that the new century we are entering will most likely be dominated by China—given its manufacturing prowess, reserve currency and favorable trade position. America is experiencing the opposite—producing very little, plagued by a weak dollar, and running huge budget and trade deficits.[56] Personally, I think China has a huge underbelly of impoverished people. As one economist, Fred Bergstein, says, "It's a very bipolar society." Per capita income is small, about $3,200, which is less than 10 percent of the U.S.A. As I point out later in this chapter, India is the dark horse that should not be pooh-poohed. The decline of America will take more than a couple of decades, but it could happen sooner if we do not get our financial house in order. The U.S. must rein in spending and borrowing, pursue growth that is based on real assets and avoid financial bubbles by regulating Wall Street and banking which have nearly wrecked the American dollar.

The economic crisis we now face could become a generational journey and part of history, one we might face for the remaining century, as we try to transform ourselves and cope with the coming storms. This crisis will not be solved by rallies in the streets (a liberal response) or by paying executives more money (a conservative response). The real revolution that must take place is one of attitudes, values and ideas. It will be resolved by painful changes involving a shared moral foundation and a sense of justice, adopting new policies that protect American workers from corporate American and foreign competition, rewarding scientists, engineers, and math/science teachers, providing progressive taxes and regulating markets, and marching to the ballot boxes in record numbers in order to elect people willing to make these kinds of changes.

Visions of Reform

The naysayers and critics have to admit there were some "good old days," when Ford and GM were models of corporate responsibility and there seemed to be a social contract between employers and employees. I guess that period coincides with the production of the Model T in the 1920s up to the post-Sputnik years, except for the years of the Great Depression. Do you remember your mom or dad, or maybe your grandma or granddad, telling you about growing up in some small town in America? Do you remember those old days—the moss-laden landscape of yesterday, with the white picket fence, the Sunday mass and church choir, the Boy Scouts or Girl Scouts, the school hop, and a family of four with a mom and a dad?

Those old days lasted right up to when "Mr. Rogers" taught us about charming neighborhoods in small, simple rural and suburban towns, further reinforced by *Dick and Jane* readers, the *Reader's Digest* and *Saturday Evening Post*. No one seemed to challenge the social and economic order, except perhaps a few angry populists from places that no one had ever heard of or could locate on a state map, and a few radical anarchists who spoke about human misery and workers' rights. However, all these ideas were foreign to those who supported or belonged to the church choir and Boy (Girl) Scouts of America. And yet, today, any policy or campaign to achieve economic well-being for average Americans must rest on strong moral and religious foundations, consistent with compassion for common people and concern for the common good, a social ethos you would expect to find in small communities. People have a choice, to act as one nation indivisible, as a community of people who are willing to help one another and share in the wealth of the nation or act as a collection of individuals, each one making the most of the free market without transparency or regulation and concerned with his or her own well-being and self-interest.

Shifting aid to the fortunate (financial) sector from the unfortunate (manufacturing) sector, to the capitalist class from labor class, only exacerbates inequality in America and wrecks the families of working people. Both treasury Secretary Henry Paulson, under the Bush administration and now Tim Geithner with the Obama administration, bailed out Wall Street. Without question, they were personally close to the senior executives of the major banks, hedge funds and stock brokerage companies. Both resorted to using unprecedented amounts of taxpayer money, money from average Americans and many people who can barely pay their monthly bills, to save the nation's financiers from their own arrogance and mistakes. For example, by 2009 the U.S. Treasury Department reported 566 financial firms had received bailout money totaling in trillions. The difference in the way both worlds (Wall Street vs Main Street) were treated is striking.

Throughout history people who work with their hands have always been treated as inferior or second class compared to those who control the wealth and reap profits from information. Why should America be different? To be sure, big money has always been in bed with big government, not only in the U.S. but throughout the world. There has never really been much sympathy for workers; they are always treated as expendable items on the balance sheet. However, bankers have always been part of the political process and will always be protected by the system—the people in power—compared to workers who have done nothing irresponsible or fraudulent as their Wall Street counterparts. The same government officials who loaned the financial industry trillions in 2009 moaned and groaned over $50 billion in loans for the auto industry.

Mr. Paulson and Geithner were solely motivated to help big banking and Wall Street under the guise of getting credit flowing and solving the housing collapse. Excuses can always be conjured and delineated, but we are dealing with the same financial club that goes back to the Gilded Age—and hundreds of years beyond to the birth of the European banking system and European banking capitals of London, Paris, and Vienna. When pitted against each other, people who move money around and produce nothing are always the "winners," even when they make mistakes. The labor class who rely on their sweat and muscle are always the "losers," even when they play by the rules of society. This has always been the way of the world—since the beginning of civilization.

The chief executives of Citibank, Bank of America, Merrill Lynch, Goldman Sachs, and the Treasury Department Head (Mr. Geithner) are characters out of Dicken's novel *Little Dorrit*. The story is sadly familiar. A fund promises high returns, but you had to be well connected to get in on it. A prestigious banker, revered in financial circles, is running it. People are reassured. The fund is rock solid; it has "immense resources, high connections, [and] government influence." It's not the Madoff fund ($65 billion disappeared), nor the Stanford fund ($8 billion went up in smoke); it is a fund run by Mr. Merdle, the fraudent London banker who eventually brings wealthy investors to their ruin. But the story goes beyond financial bubbles; the subplots focus on greed, power, corruption and injustice. There is the description of debtors' prison—where people rot in jail for decades (the main character, William Dorrit, has been locked up for 23 years) and cannot even remember what bills went unpaid, while wealthy and well-connected financiers cheat and elude both creditors and the government prosecutors—too big to fail, too powerful and well-connected to go to jail.

Even Shakespeare captured the moment: How the fat cats enrich themselves at the expense of others. In "Henry IV," about Wall Street bonuses: "A little—more than a little is by much too much." Then about financial and banking executives, there is "Pericles" who states, "We would purge the land of these drones, that rob the bee of her honey." Now flash backwards, starting with the most recent economic meltdown in the U.S. and the collapse of Lehman Bros. Merrill Lynch, and Bear Sterns and the CEOs who plundered their companies and stockholders and made a host of mistakes and wrong choices in investments and yet paid themselves hundreds of millions of dollars. Then go back to the

2000 tech bubble and the same corporate disasters and mucho image of business leaders such as Dennis Kozlowski (Tyco), Ken Lay (Enron), and Bernard Ebbers (World Com). Now flip to the nineteenth century and the Gilded Age—how the American economy was in the gripes of the Goulds, Rockefellers, and Vanderbilts—an era when government regulation was nonexistent and truncated by greedy bankers and manufacturers at the expense of workers.

We can pooh-pooh these corporate realities as part of Social Darwinism and Ayn Rand's world that capitalism is where self-interest, greed, and competition meet—and are self regulating. We can also argue that government regulation is unnecessary and stifling, although anyone with an ounce of common sense understands that as a result of the recent financial crisis regulation has to happen, and the only question is how much. Now we can better appreciate and put in proper context the works of Dickens and insights of Shakespeare. Such ideas are perhaps best summed up in modern times by Joseph Othmer, an old-time business executive and author of the *Futurist*. He presents a view from the inside of corporate America, viewing capitalists as nothing more than "arrogant," reckless, and "unapologetic" criminals who think they "run the country" and are masters of the universe. They defy rules and ethics, charge dinners with fictional clients, throw lavish parties at the expense of stockholders, keep two sets of books and sell their stocks while telling shareholders "it's a bargain," even when they know the ship is going down. "They do it, all in the name of capitalism . . . and for America."

Regardless of which gray-haired expert you listen to when it comes to the state of the economy, from Pericles to the present, the money class has always kept the labor class in check. The rich emphasize shrewdness and strength to explain their own rise to the top while common people and working class remain in their station for life because of dullness and weakness. At the best, this is nothing more than Darwinism revisited, combined with the cult of the self-made man. On the other side of the ideological continuum, it tells us that money is power and the rich get richer by working the system to their advantage—and not necessarily by honorable methods.

THE CHANGING MARKET PLACE

Ordinary people, today, have to work two or more jobs and spouses need two incomes to keep up with a 1960s standard of living, an era portrayed by TV's popular show *Ozzie and Harriet* and *Father Knows Best*. Back then, it took a sociologist (like David Riesman) or psychologist (like Dr. Spock) to tell people what they were feeling. Now commentators like Lou Dobbs, Brian Williams and Diane Sawyer report to Americans how they feel, how they struggle to make ends meet, and, even worse, how our jobs are being exported abroad (85 percent of our retail purchases is now manufactured overseas), which in turn compounds the imbalance of trade (cheap overseas labor markets entering as goods on the U.S. market). Moreover, the outsourcing of jobs is now affecting middle-class and white-collar employment as such jobs increasingly include the engines of the knowledge, technological, and digital economy.

It started with a company named IBM in 2005, when it announced that it would shift 114,000 high-paying, high-tech jobs (paying $75,000 or more) to India at salaries about one-fifth of those in the United States and Western Europe. Hewlett-Packard stated the same year it would lay off nineteen thousand to twenty-five thousand employees earning between $50,000 and $125,000, representing a savings of $605 billion per year and build a new assembly plant in India. The next year Dell announced it would double the size of its software workforce in India to 20,000; it is also expected to shift tens of thousands of additional jobs once it set up a new manufacturing site in the country. Similar announcements were made by Cisco, Intel, and Microsoft, the engines of the technological future, which plan to double and triple their workforces in India. Cisco and Intel each plan to invest more than $1.1 billion in India, and Microsoft will invest $1.7 billion. Boeing, Ford, G.E., and Motorola are right behind these high-tech companies, opening up new factories outside the United States, in the Asian rim to save money. Even our old enemy Vietnam is on the radar screen for billion-dollar investments by high-tech firms such as Intel and Hewlett-Packard. Microsoft has also opened up a software center in Canada because of liberal immigration laws which make it easier to recruit qualified people from around the globe.

The outsourcing of jobs is bound to worsen if America's immigration policies are not softened. What we need to be doing is increasing student visas and paste green cards to science and engineering diplomas, so these qualified people become part of our economy, rather than losing them to another country and then having to compete with them. The ripple effect of these investments in terms of future science, research and technological jobs is estimated to create four times more the number of initial jobs. In other words, jobs create other jobs, and science and technology jobs have a fourfold impact in a growing economy—and the impact continues to multiply so long as there is a healthy growth pattern.

The fact is that nations are no longer able to isolate themselves and pursue policies that are incompatible with an increasing global market. The types of jobs and services that generate economic wealth for nations are more mobile than ever, based more on a broadband and Internet connection than geography, and policies that shackle international business hinder economic growth. With globalization, the average U.S. worker is exposed to much more competition and job insecurity. As the world becomes more globally interconnected, jobs became more mobile. Hence, the jobs at home that have become more plentiful are for less educated, displaced, or part-time workers—mostly low-paying jobs such as "hamburger helper" or Wal-Mart hostess (also called a "greeter"), which on the pay scale of one to ten (ten being the best) is ranked one or two. This is the future for our children and grandchildren unless we do something about it now.

To be sure, we are witnessing the emasculation and decline of ordinary Americans, the bottom 80 to 90 percent of the income scale. Having been systematically stripped of wages, jobs, health care, and financial security, they are unable to purchase new homes, automobiles, electronic devices and other consumer items. With corporate profits floating up the pyramid and cost savings at the expense of working—and middle-class Americans for the last 30 years, the average American is broke and consumed by plastic debt (more than $10,000 per household), banking penalty fees (amounting to $23 billion in 2009), devaluated homes and mortgages that cannot be paid.

On top of this body blow to Americans is the economic meltdown which began in 2008 and the millions of blue-collar workers who face long-term unemployment; their off-shore counterparts work for $2 or $5 per day. Then there are millions of technical workers with college degrees; their offshore counterparts work for 75 percent less. Obviously, these jobs are not coming back to the U.S., and a significant number of people in these groups will remain unemployed or underemployed at salaries much less than they once earned. The over-all outcome is, these people (about 33 to 50 percent of the workforce) will not only experience a significant drop in their standard of living, but also this trend is bound to influence the entire economy, including the professional class of accountants, lawyers, and physicians in terms of how much they earn or can charge their clients.

We are entering a new era: Where the function of government will be to find ways to take things from people to pay for services and programs. Not only will programs and services be trimmed, but also taxes will be imposed to help pay for mounting deficits which now average over $1 trillion a year. We are moving from the fat years (post World War II) to the lean years (post 2010), from the "Greatest" Generation to a "Forgotten" and "Downsized" Generation, from the most powerful nation to a nation in economic decline, and from the most egalitarian nation to an increasingly stratified nation.

According to Michael Mandel in *Rational Exuberance*, globalization and technology are coming together and creating the potential for future work and where we work. Off shoring jobs, for example, means that knowledge/information work can be broken into smaller tasks and redistributed around the world. Someone in Bangalore or San Paulo can do one aspect of the work, and someone in Hong Kong or Helsinki can perform another part of the job. Moreover, the Internet has enhanced all means of communication, creating "virtual worlds" and transforming the place of work and the speed of innovation.

For global corporations, the trend is to avoid bodies and offices in selected places like Silicon Valley or Shanghai. The idea is to get workers to collaborate instantly around the world. The typical hierarchical organization, with layers of management, has shifted to multiple sites, with an ever-shifting network of employees who work on a team for a single project and who communicate through e-mail and videocoms. Such corporations now hire people from around the world and then offer courses online to develop talent. People can obviously be hired in any part of the world to do the same work an American engineer or accountant can do—and for considerably less than the American salary. President Obama put it this way: "A child born in Dallas is now competing with a child born in New Delhi."

The "gathering storm" or slow demise of American innovation and knowledge is gaining momentum. American students are unable to compete on international tests in science and math, U.S science and engineering enrollments are down, the recruitment of top students from abroad has dramatically declined due to visa restrictions following September 11, and the world playing field has been flattened and made more competitive by the Internet. U.S. knowledge, information, and technology jobs, and other knowledge producers whose jobs are digitized, can now be replaced by a Google-ready or Windows-ready worker anywhere. Our children can only thank us for making it easier to communicate to the unemployment agency or finding some low-paying job via the Internet.

Skilled manufacturing jobs, once the backbone of the U.S. economy and the reason why workers once rose to middle class in America, have collapsed (once representing 1 out of 3 jobs; now representing 1 in 11 jobs). Now one of the last two remaining industries that America is still in a leadership role, that is knowledge and technology, is on the downward slide. Its decline is highlighted by the fact that American business values crumbled in the twenty-first century. Rather than investing in long-term products, services or technology, and related innovations that would benefit the nation and its people, short-term profits and risk-taking became the norm. The outcome was the dot.com bubble of 2000, followed by the worst financial crisis in 2008/2009 since the Great Depression.

Instead of venture capital coming after a product goes through research and development, the U.S. financial world threw money at Silicon Valley and the Golden Triangle. The money came first, instead of the product or item being made coming first. There was nothing being made, only fees being charged under the guise of packaging "financial products." This helped create the economic meltdown, costing some six million jobs, the shredding of pensions and 401Ks, as well as the evaporation of trillions of dollars of U.S. wealth. Even more disturbing, we have a growing number of college educated workers competing for fewer good-paying jobs in the U.S. When adjusted for inflation, the real salaries of U.S. workers with at least a bachelor's degree remained flat from 2000 to 2007, an unpleasant dose of reality in a society in which education is supposed to be the key to success.

Prior to 2000 expansion in technology and information-related jobs raised the income for those with sufficient skills and education to handle complex jobs. Those with minimal skills and lower levels of education did not benefit or receive income gains related to American productivity; the collapse of manufacturing and the union movement was a big part of it. But the resulting inequalities between the rich and rest of the nation was slightly masked by an increasing number of people receiving higher education degrees and moving up the wage ladder with good jobs. Now that outsourcing of high-tech and middle-class jobs are beginning to impact on the U.S. economy, we can expect increasing inequality in America unless the tax system is modified.

Beyond flattened salaries for people with college degrees and having our knowledge and technological jobs moved overseas, we are beginning to witness large movements of skilled workers crossing national borders in Asia and Europe, providing a hint of an increasing interconnected world and global economy. The question arises: Are we witnessing the beginning of a new world of empowered and mobile workers or a "brave new world" of virtual sweatshops—where multi-national corporations are able to depress employee wages? The emerging workplace is bound not to be a factory or assembly line, but don't expect it to be a place where the salaries of college educated or middle-class workers will keep up with inflation.

THE ROLE OF INNOVATION

Innovation is not invention, the latter which suggests a new paradigm or major shift in our thinking or production. Innovation is based on a spark or insight often derived in an office or research lab (or in the case of Steve Jobs in a garage), and represents a modification or improvement of an existing service or products which (1) creates value, (2) is brought to the market, and (3) boosts productivity. The overall effect is the creation of new jobs and even new industries. Innovation represents 20 percent of the economic output of the industrialized countries, supplying efficient products or services and economic growth. Innovation is part of the "knowledge" society and a nation's human capital; it is bottomless and limitless compared to economic capital which has a bottom line and limitations.

To be sure, innovation and entrepreneurialship are mainstream, embraced by all political stripes and popular and business heroes like Oprah Winfrey, Richard Branson, and Jack Welch. It wasn't always like that. Writers for the last sixty years have described the shift in culture in terms of the "organization man," "future shock," "the greening of America," etc. *The Organization Man*, described in William Whyte's best-selling book of corporate America, was a cousin or off-shoot to David Riesman's book. Published three years after the *Lonely Crowd*, both books described the "successful" corporate model, of people keeping their nose clean, following orders, and conforming to company rules and group norms.

Successful business people were not risk takers, innovators, or explorers. Knowledge workers sought a "good" job at IBM, AT&T, or G.E., and they relied on a combination of hard work, merit, and social skills. They dressed the part, with gray or blue suits and matching ties, and followed the expectations and preferences of their bosses; they had no interest in being too smart, "thinking out of the box" or creating a new idea or image. Innovative personnel were considered disruptive and not part of the team. Economists focused on traditional factors related to production—capital, labor, and equipment—and supply-demand curves. New ideas and copyrighted materials were not considered part of a company's financial statement or list of assets.

It took several decades for the informal atmosphere, combined with rewarding the creative talents of workers in Google, Nokia, and Wipro, to become an acceptable choice for other companies around the world. The current buzz involving innovation is based on a loose federation or network of corporate labs, government-sponsored labs and universities. Corporations often become the cord and implementer of new ideas from outside and inside corporate gates. They rely on the world-wide web for collaboration and communication, and they can integrate others' work around the world.

If it's not G.E., IBM or Google, then Apple is the apple of our eye, the eye of our innovative storm. When we think of Apple, we think of game-changing gadgets and the nurturing of new ideas. Apple represents a different innovative model, closely tied to the thinking and leadership of one person, Steve Jobs. There is a tight relationship between the personality of its leader and what it creates. The company's products eliminate complexity by purposely omitting things (originally designed by engineers) so as not to burden the user with too many choices. As one high-tech consultant puts it: "A defining quality of Apple has been design restraint."[57] But the key to Apple's success is the ability to hire people who think outside the box and beyond the curve, the so-called 10 percent or 20 percent smarter or more creative person who has a huge multiplier effect that distinguishes good products from excellent products.

The spirit of innovation and entrepreneurship, what the economist Joseph Schumpeter once called "creative destruction," has been embraced by U.S. business colleges, corporations, and governments. Schumpeter was one of the first theorists to recognize that the most important competitive factor was not lower land prices or labor costs but new ideas—what I refer to as part of human capital and what corporations and business pundits call part of innovation (and entrepreneurship). The story of the U.S. conversion from conformity to creativity in the workplace is evidenced by the number of endowed chairs of entrepreneurship in the U.S. business schools, from 237 in 1999 to approximately 500 in 2010.

For traditional knowledge workers, innovation is considered part of R&D spending and product development. In today's fast-changing society, innovation is considered the early stage of entrepreneurship and what may be called "innovation economics." And, it does not take a rocket scientist to figure out that more people around the globe are engaged in new ventures: From the slums of South Africa and Indonesia, to the bureaucrats in New Delhi and Shanghai, to big companies like Nokia and 3-M. Given today's global competitive spirit and quick access to information, many corporations now feel they must innovate faster just to stand still.

The U.S. still leads the world in innovation, having spent approximately 10 percent of the world's $480 billion on R&D in 2006, followed by the European Union which spent about 6 percent. Part of the reason for the U.S. lead has to do with its multiple sources of financial markets and venture-capital companies as well as the American spirit of risk-taking, the spirit of freedom, and spirit of individual achievement. Creative and innovative people need this open type of environment to stimulate, motivate and sustain their fresh thinking and human endeavor. So far America is ahead of the curve in terms of creating an atmosphere conducive to risk, freedom and achievement. What we have going is a culture that celebrates individual achievement and operates within a political and social atmosphere of freedom. Its universities are first rate and the nation as a whole has a long history of venture spirit capital and entrepreneurship that goes back to the Manifest Destiny and the "winning of the west."

European universities tend to be suspicious of private industry, relying more on government grants than private sector money. However, European venture-capital companies have adopted the American model and investment in new companies grew 23 percent between 2003 and 2006, compared to less than one percent in the U.S.—suggesting we have reached a "flat" period of innovation. Countries such as Denmark, Finland, Sweden and England, often criticized by American capitalists as too socialistic, have more venture-capital industries in relation to the size of their economies than America.

For all its economic problems however, the U.S. still leads the world in new start-up businesses and entrepreneurship—producing approximately 5 million new small businesses every year—some of them, rapidly growing into the world's largest corporations such as Wal-Mart, Microsoft, and Google. As many as 22 percent of the nation's Fortune 1,000 or biggest companies were created since 1980, illustrating the nation's continuous gospel of innovation and prowess of human capital. In a nutshell, given the last page of facts and figures, all these numbers suggest that American entrepreneurship is still very "venturesome," but it is beginning to flatten compared to other industrialized nations. The reason is not necessarily because the flow of money has declined rather because the U.S. companies are moving offices to other parts of the world.

Innovative businesses are also beginning to tap into emerging markets. China and India which spent less than 1 percent of the world's R&D in 2006 are now beginning to become innovative out of necessity.[58] Globalization and the spread of the Internet and technology have led to the spread of information and creation of new business models in Asia. Whereas originally noted as "copycats" of Western intellectual property rights (which cost Microsoft alone an estimated $50 million per year from 2000 to 2007), they are now moving into the innovative process in the (1) drug and pharmaceutical industries, (2) motorcycle and auto industries, and (3) electronic and communication industries—forming multinational companies and reaching markets in emerging countries in Latin America, Asia, and the Middle East.

While most of China's and India's innovators are not well known in the West, they will eventually challenge American human capital in the three aforementioned areas of productions. For example, India's Tata Motors is producing a "people's" car for $3,000, partially out of necessity, and China is boasting it will start manufacturing 500,000 electric cars by 2012—also out of necessity. According to Energy Secretary Steven Chu, if China's emissions keep growing at the rate of the last 30 years, the country will emit more greenhouse gases than the U.S. has for its entire history. If the emissions tide is not reversed, more people will be displaced by sea levels in China than any other country. The result: China is already producing clean-coal plants to cut down pollution in its cities. In the meantime, the U.S. is still debating whether it should drill for oil off shore. More troubling, there are over 500 computer chip companies in China, ready to challenge Motorola, Cisco, and AT&T.

If I had to bet on China or India, I would put my money on India. Comparing China and India, the human capital of India is young compared to China's population which is aging due to restrictions on family size and children. In 2009, India's 14-year old or younger population was 31 percent of its total, compared to China's 14-year old or younger population which represented 20 percent. [59] The outcome is that India with its 1.1 billion people and capitalistic spirit, represents the greater competition for America's human capital and potential for innovation than does China. The Chinese economy is based on manufacturing, a twentieth century model, not scientific or technical knowledge (India's prototype) which is a twenty-first century model. Actually, a few U.S. economists are concerned about the rise and potential of both countries—and future competition with the U.S. [60]

Now here is where I step in quick sand and voice a controversial position. I am inclined to wager my money long term on India, not on China, because the Indian education system is rooted in the Anglo perspective which puts a premium on creativity, inquiry and independent thought. The Chinese schools prize memorization and rote learning, an ideal that can be traced to a series of forty dynasties spanning more than 4,000 years, beginning with the Hsia dynasty in 2200 BC and ending with the Manchus in 1912 in which bright students studied diligently to pass a series of civil service exams in order to become scholar-officials and bureaucrats who governed China for the emperors.

The Chinese heritage has revealed persistent efforts to maintain unbroken traditions and cultural continuity, relying on respect for elders and old customs, and further promoted by the teachings of Mao up to Tiananmen Square just twenty years ago, whereby students were required to memorize and parrot the wisdom and thoughts of their leader. This type of thinking still characterizes the Chinese academic model in which conformity is crucial and questions by students are frowned upon in school because of fear of appearing stupid in front of classmates.

The teaching—learning process in China is not conducive for scientific, high-tech and innovative culture. The knowledge society we live in does not reward facts or trivia data that can be googled. What, when, and who questions and answers foster memorization and characterizes Chinese education; it is mistakenly assumes that people who know the answer are intelligent. Why, how, and what-if questions and answers lead to abstract thinking and discovery; it characterizes higher education in tier 1 colleges in the U.S. and other Anglo countries, as well as India whose schooling system is based on the British model. Chinese education authorities, with the approval of the central government, are just beginning to challenge traditional educational methods and study the U.S. and British education models, but they still have a long way to go in order to overcome 4,000 years of isolated history before they can laud the innovative mind.

But wizened old men realize the value for caution. The Western mind doesn't fully understand the Eastern mind, and no matter how naïve or immature we think the Asian perspective or philosophy, they know us better than we know them. Given a rapidly changing society that we live in, the future isn't what it used to be or expected to be. Therefore, everything I say about the Chinese and Indian mind and the spirit of innovation or discovery is nothing more than speculation that can be proven wrong by the winds of change (Chinese reform or Indian mismanagement)—and by a series of unspoken and unforeseen coalition of events.

Curtis Carlson, the co-author of *Innovation* captures the trend and puts it in blunt terms. "India and China are a tsunami about to overwhelm us." Millions of jobs are at stake and many are expected to be eliminated in the U.S. As Asia moves to a global center for innovation and new knowledge, most people in the U.S. are struggling to understand what is happening to the nation's economic luster and their own jobs. Are we on the way of the dinosaur—big, old and clumsy? As a nation are we on the downside of Darwin's theory of adaptability? We need to come to the realization that the emerging nations of the world will increasingly share economic power with the U.S. The hand writing is already on the wall. The ordinary person in America will have to adjust to a lower economic position on the totem pole of mobility, opportunity and status.

The "copycat" stereotype of Asia is vanishing. As purported by *Forbes* magazine, the number of engineers annually being produced by

China (600,000) and India (350,000) outnumber the U.S. (70,000) by more than thirteen times. According to the National Academy of Sciences, in its report, *Rising Above the Gathering Storm*, 4.5 percent of U.S. college students graduate with a degree in engineering compared to 20 percent of Asian students and 13 percent of European students. This difference is bound to accelerate the rate of innovation (and growth of middle-class jobs) in Asian countries and challenge Silicon Valley. Figuring a four to five year lag between the birth of an idea—from a computer model or experiment to research and development and then to production—in the next ten to twenty years the U.S. is going to wake up and find out that the low-paid, low-quality Asian worker has been relegated to the heap pile of history and replaced by a freewheeling, innovative workforce. The likes of G.E., Cisco, Hewlett Packard, etc. are going to experience major competition from China, India (and even Taiwan, South Korea, Japan, Singapore, etc.)[61] Americans will find the new Asian innovative models of growth and productivity possibly more threatening than the current demise of the U.S. manufacturing model—and the shredding of millions of more jobs to overseas competitors, with names we cannot pronounce and a culture and language we don't understand and never bothered to understand.

The only way to reverse this growing trend is to stop the erosion of U.S. innovation by (1) improving math and science education, K-12, including an additional course in engineering for talented students in grade 11 or 12, (2) offering scholarships or free college education to math and science teachers, engineers and scientists, (3) welcoming more talented immigrants and promoting their citizenship, (4) linking start-up companies with venture capitalists, (5) offering tax incentives to U.S. companies that invest in innovative products and services, and (6) discouraging or preventing the likes of Cisco, Intel and Microsoft from building new research facilities and offices in Asia or Eastern Europe. Dean Kamen, a college dropout, author and inventor who holds some 450 U.S. and foreign patents for innovation devices puts it this way. "We can print more money, but we cannot print more knowledge." That takes a generation to produce, some 12 to 16 years of schooling. More bailouts might help the economy in the short run, but only more Bill Gates and Steve Jobs can move us into prosperity over the long run.

In the U.S., the pressing need is to focus on talented students and math and science education and other innovative capacities (recommendations 3 to 6) in order to secure America's future prosperity and security. Here we are not talking about a new paradigm or transformative shift in society. What we need to do is to invest in incremental charges, more efficient-technology, and new industries—steady progress and development of ideas and human capital. In the final analysis, a nation is only as good as its next innovation. Transformative changes come in cycles and over several generations and cannot be easily predicted or counted on, unless you believe in a constant flow of "Sputniks." The last major paradigm shift had something to do with computers and the Internet. Unless someone has a crystal ball or a direct link to the Oracle, no one really has a clear idea when the next major shift or invention will take place.

As for developing countries, the situation for women is dim and there is need to broaden their basic rights, including access to education. However, the list of female-related problems include basic security issues—sex trafficking, child marriage, domestic abuse, gang rape as a military tactic, malnourishment, lack of medical care and maternal mortality. The key to fighting history is to stop ignoring the custom of devaluing women and to promote the education of women. If the third world is to prosper, the status of women must be improved for they represent 50 percent of a nation's human resources. Education can chip away at cultural practices in many parts of the world, and the outcomes are tied to economic growth in a knowledge and digital society.

As a capitalist society, the laws of economic individualism, competition, and achievement overshadow an economy based on safety nets and social programs, protection for workers or in which the free market is to be subordinated to the group. Although the natural law of competition is sometimes hard on the individual, the old-fashion capitalist might say: "If the strongest and swiftest win the race, and the rest falter and barely make ends meet, we may be consoled by recalling the sage advice of Shakespeare: 'The fault, dear Brutus, is not in our stars, But in ourselves, that we are the underlings.'"

The justification of U.S. inequality has been delineated since the birth of the nation. Going back to Alexander Hamilton, the first U.S. Treasurer, he felt the masses rise to the level that nature had intended and possess all the turbulent passions of an animal. The manufacturing and banking class were guardians of the public good, elevating society by providing people with opportunities to work in factories. The government had to support these economic elites and protect them from the influence of the labor class and "Jacobins" in the populous American towns.

More than two hundred years later Milton Friedman, another conservative pundit, argued that small government was the best government, since the big government jeopardizes individual liberties, especially property rights. Competition is the engine that drives the economy and inequality is the natural outcome when society allows individuals to compete and find their proper level and learn how to do that for which they are fitted by nature and nurture, as well as choice.

Under the Bush administration, the Hamilton-Friedman doctrines were followed and the government's role turned into one of promoting inequality by giving Wall Street and bankers free reign, cutting taxes for the rich, reducing social programs, and undermining unions and workers' benefits. The economic crisis that followed is too complicated to explain to most readers. Collateral debt obligations, credit default swaps, and Freddy Mac/Fannie Mae and Country-Wide toxic mortgages get in the way of a quick and easy read. Suffice to say that the Bush administration lifted government regulation of the financial sector, thus inviting the Wall Street and banking class in on a grand and greedy feast in which "financial products" were concocted and went hand-in-hand with fraud and corruption. When the bubble burst, the ordinary worker and taxpayer paid the price.

As capitalist doctrine has evolved, people are by nature unequal. Those who take risks, prove their ability and take responsibility, compete and excel, overcome obstacles and get ahead—are thus entitled to the rewards that may come from their efforts. Two classes of workers emerge within the capitalist system: *Performers* who entertain the public and generate *profits* or *revenues* for a business or corporation and *salaried employees* such as professionals (teachers, engineers, and accountants) and laborers (plumbers, hotel workers, and janitors) who are considered a *cost factor* or *expense item* in determining annual budgets. The goal of an organization is to keep costs down and maximize profits. For those who increase costs, the idea is to trim their salaries by considering supply-demand trends and eliminating jobs. Those who can bolster revenues or the profit column are paid handsomely for their efforts. For example hip hop's *Jay-Z* earned $34 million in 2007 and rapper *50 Cent* came in second with $32 million. Alex Rodriguez earned $27.5 million in 2008 and Derek Jeter earned $19 million. Tom Cruise and Sylvester Stallone each earned $15 to $25 million per movie.

[62] All of these people are brand names who perform for the public and realize profits for corporations.

In 2007 the average worker, a *cost factor*, earned $45,100, while the average teacher earned $51,000 and the average engineer was compensated with $75,500. Now compare these salaries with CEO's from the 200 largest companies who for the same year averaged $11.7 million, and those from the top 50 companies who averaged $20 million—or the four CEOs who earned $50 million or more: John Thain ($83 million) of Merrill Lynch, Lawrence Ellison ($61 million) of Oracle, Lloyd Blankfein ($54 million) of Goldman Sachs, and Kenneth Chenault ($50 million) of American Express.[63] Ironically, the run away salaries of top executives have little to do with performance, since many of the companies that paid the highest salaries often lost money that year (including three out of four of the companies listed above; the other company, Goldman Sachs, saw its stock tank the following year under Blankfein's helm).

The problem of the often overpaid, incompetent executive is especially upsetting when the rewards are subsidized by the U.S. taxpayer, including the single mother or typical laborer who works multiple jobs to make ends meet. It doesn't only occur when the feds bailout Wall Street. If executives, entertainers, and athletes are making millions of dollars, it has to come from someone's pocket; this is reflected in inflated prices for rock concerts and baseball tickets and depressed salaries for the average worker in the organization which pays high executives salaries, since there is a limit or percent of the firm's net revenue that goes to compensation and benefits for all employees. If we start adding up the ramifications of all these overpaid executives, there is more than a whisper of public frustration, not yet a shout, to put a lid on executive compensation and to improve the links between pay and performance.

What these kind of disparities create is a new group of "haves" and "have nots" within the nation, based on a flawed capitalist model that rewards those who make money for an organization and penalizes those who cost money for an organization. There is no sound reason to promote or defend this system of rewards other than some illogical reasoning based on greed and stupidity or some quaint notion that capitalists (now including brand name performers) receive their fair proportion from corporate profits while wage earners can enjoy a day at the beach on Sunday for free or a fishing vacation in some remote part of the country on the earnings of a week.

It's the Roman empire again—with highly paid gladiators who entertain the audience—coupled with the "robber baron" era again with all restraints vanished. The key question is whether Jay-Z is worth 63 times more than what a teacher earns or whether Alex Rodriguez is worth 37 times more than what an engineer earns, or whether the average large company CEO is worth 259 to 444 times more than the average worker. Let me state it in slightly different terms. Should Master Card's Robert Selander have received 287,341 shares of stock for free on the day the company went public, worth $13 million two weeks later, while each of the company's $4,400 employees received 100 shares, worth $4,700 for each employee. Is one person's value to a company worth 2,766 times more than the average worker in the same company? These monetary conditions lead to immense disparities and are symptomatic of the problem inherent in this capitalist system and the subsequent problem of inequality facing the nation.

We need to wrestle with these issues—and not pooh-pooh them away as part of the capitalist system. It is our teachers, scientists and engineers, and other knowledge and high-tech workers, that will save this country, not the hip hoppers or rappers, not our athletes or entertainers. In a fair society or good society, if inequality of income persists, it should be based on how much value a person's work is for the common good. The question then arises whether a teacher's or engineer's service is more valuable than someone who can sing songs or hit a baseball 400 feet.

What we need to do is find ways to reduce existing inequality. There is a lot we can do that is easy to implement regarding education, social security and health care. Canada, Australia, and many western European nations spend up to twice as much as we do on social programs and safety nets. Their unions are stronger than ours and their economies are growing on the same level or percentages, and in some cases better than ours. Why should entertainers earn $25 to $50 million? Should CEOs have golden parachutes comprising $100 to $200 million? Should hedge fund managers earn a half billion dollars or more? Why do the American people allow it? We don't need to be familiar with revisionary history to grasp that there is a point where financial rewards can become irrational.

Put these earnings in context with the average worker—whose salary when adjusted for inflation has remained relatively flat for the last 25 to 30 years—and then include the more than 10 million workers in 2009 earning the minimum wage ($7.25), another 15 to 20 million workers earning less than $10 an hour, another 7.5 million workers employed part-time who wanted to and could not find full-time employment, another 6.7 million workers employed fewer than 35 hours a week to avoid layoffs and still another 14.5 million workers out of work and unemployed. Then there are untold millions, merely best guesses, of people who have given up looking for a job—not part of these statistics—merely forgotten Americans, "unemployable" and poor people, nameless and faceless and unfit for any official job-related category. They are omitted from government employment statistics and ignored by the rest of us as long as they remain quiet.

CONCLUSION

What we have developing is a two-tier economy, one for "haves" and one for "have-nots"—and the majority trying to stay afloat and avoid the "have-not" sector. Proponents of the system rely on free-market theories to defend this dark side of the American dream. Myself and possibly other critics would interpret it as a rigged system which extends thousands of years back into history—a divide between 1 percent (the money people) and 99 percent (the working people). Bottom Line: We have large-scale suffering in the U.S., and it is likely to become part of the new economy and cast a shadow over the American dream for several generations to come. The official unemployment rate will eventually decrease, but the unofficial rate of part-time workers, under-employed workers (working for low pay and minimal benefits), and workers who have given up with few prospects will most likely become structured into the future economy. Sustained unemployment and underemployment will increase poverty rates, which in turn will effect education outcomes and the country's growth prospects.

In the end, our own values and reward system are going to topple the American civilization: First by choking the working and middle class—the populace or base that a democracy needs in order to function properly—and then by increasing the costs of goods and services which will make us less competitive with emerging nations. These countries are increasingly going to have a more competitive advantage because they stimulate their collective talent toward new ideas, new industries, and new markets.

In the meantime, there are a host of new books every year written by bright minds and toted by the *Wall Street Journal, Forbes* magazine, and *Business Week* on how to improve American corporations and how to become more competitive and win market share. These books are "feel good books," based on "puppy talk" and "wishful thinking"—designed to provide hope and perk up the nation's people. We need to change the message. Unless we rediscover and rebuild ourselves, unless we change our values and ethical standards, and unless we change our reward system, the U.S. downward slide will be more steep then we are prepared to imagine.

Thomas Friedman, the *New York Times* writer and author of *The World is Flat,* believes "the 21st century is still up for grabs." From my prospective, he is too optimistic. We need only to look in the mirror. Quick profits rule over long-term growth, Lehman Bros and Madoff are us! As the twenty first century evolves, the outlook of the economy is bound to change from one of optimism to one of pessimism. Put bluntly, if the corporate world doesn't change, the living standards of the average American must eventually decline.

Although I may be criticized as an idealog, I don't think I'm dreaming. A recent Roper poll concluded that 72 percent of the public believes there is a widespread wrongdoing in the business world. But the public feels helpless. In a Harris poll, 90 percent of respondents maintained that big business either highly influences or runs big government. The chief executive of Delphi, the auto parts company and former subsidary of GM, put it bluntly: "Society has come to believe that the term 'crocked CEO' is redundant."

Teddy Roosevelt was following public opinion when he broke up the monopolies at the turn of the twentieth century. One hundred years later, it's time to clamp down on business wrongdoing, better regulate big business, and require that shareholders approve executive pay and executive parachutes or tax exorbitant earnings at 90 percent as they do in some European countries. We also need to put sufficient pressure on external auditors and public attorneys, who we expect to guarantee public trust and ethical corporate behavior, to do their job. The only institution that can enforce these ideas is government, but it is deemed by the public as inefficient and incapable. I would add that government is unwilling to do it, because big business interests and lobbyists are in bed with politicians. What hurts the American workers most is not the dishonesty or crookedness of people in position of power, but the silence of the victims and bystanders who are capable of going to the ballot box and voting for reform, instead wink at betrayal or say "what can I do" or "losing is a way of life." Keep in mind there are few of them and many more of us—hundreds of millions in the U.S. and billions around the world.

NOTES

---

[1] See Allan Ornstein, *Class Counts: Education, Inequality and the Shrinking Middle Class* (Lanham, MD: Rowman & Littlefield, 2007).

[2] You can read more about the book by clicking: Classcounts.org.

[3] The median household income in 1977 was $13,572; adjusted for inflation (in 2009 dollars) it was $49,777. When conservative pundits celebrate the leap in America earnings, they often fail to point out that household incomes have remained stagnate for the last 30 years.

[4] Eric Konigsberg, "A New Class War: The Haves Vs the Have Mores," *New York Times*, November 19, 2006, Sect. 4, p.1.

[5] Charles Blow, "Empire at the End of Decadence." *New York Times*, February 19, 2011, p. A 23.1; Eduardo Porter, "Study Finds Wealth Inequality is Widening Worldwide," *New York Times*, December 6, 2006, p. C3.

[6] In fact, we have a host of financial wizards writing books on how to become a millionaire. Paul Farrel and Suze Orman, two financial gurus, mention the "lattee" effect and advise that you skip Starbucks. You can save, with compounding, $500,000 by retirement age. Orman also reminds us to manage money wisely and to avoid debt. David Bach, the author of *Automatic Millionaire* claims almost anyone in America can become a millionaire if they avoid extravagances and put away a chunk of change out of every paycheck and invest wisely. Robert Leeds, in *How To Make a Million Dollars* claims inspiration and perspiration is the engine of success. In *Rich Dad, Poor Dad*, Robert Kiyosaki talks about the concepts of leverage, risk and cash flow.

[7] "The Forbes 400," *Forbes,* October 19, 2009.

[8] Robert Kuttner, *The Squandering of America* (New York: Vintage Books, 2008); Allan C. Ornstein, *Class Counts: Education, Inequality and the Shrinking of the Middle Class* (Lanham, MD: Rowman & Littlefield, 2007).

[9] But, then Americans are not 100 percent innocent. We glorify the gladiator in movies like *Spartacus, Ben-Hur,* and the *Gladiator* with rugged and virile male actors; today, we recruit and train our gladiators from the lower classes and pay them huge sums of money to entertain us. We call them football and hockey players or boxers and wrestlers, and consider them heroes as we watch them crush their opponents in various forms of combat on playing fields in Roman-like coliseums, stadiums, and arenas across the country.

[10] Linda Bilmes, "The Trillion-Dollar War, *New York Times*, August 25, 2005; "Funny Money in Iraq," *Times Digest*, May 8, 2006; and Bob Herbert, "Add Up the Damage," *New York Times*, December 30, 2008, p. 25A.

[11] To be sure, there was a recent time (from 1930s to 1950s) when liberal and independent thought was mistrusted and considered anti-American, when language and the arts were tightly controlled by the U.S. government, and thousands of educators, journalists, artists and movie producers and stars lost their jobs. For those who are unfamiliar with the tactics of FBI Director J. Edgar Hoover or Senator Joe McCarthy, this may sound like mishmash or one huge polemical diatribe.

[12] Eduardo Porter, "Study Finds Wealth Inequality is Widening World rule." *New York Times*, December 6, 2006, p.c 3; Ornstein, *Class Counts: Education Inequality and the Shrinking Middle Class.*

[13] Gretchen Morgenson, "Wall Street's Tax on Main Street," *New York Times,* August 7, 2011, pp. Bu 1, 6.

[14] Julian Von Reppert-Bismark, "How Trade Barriers Keep Africans Adrift, *Wall Street Journal*, December 27, 2006.

[15] Sewen Can, "Poorer Nations Get Longer Rate in World Bank" *New York Times*, April 26,2010, p.B3.

[16] Allan C. Ornstein, *Class Counts: Education, Inequality and the Shrinking Middle Class* (Lanham, MD: Rowman & Littlefield, 2007).

[17] Herbert J. Gans, *More Equality* (New York: Vintage 1973).

[18] *Eduardo Porter, "Study Finds Wealth Inequality is Widening Worldwide," New York Times, December 6, 2006) p. C3.*

[19] Joe Klein, "The Rock Builder," *Time*, May 4, 2009, p. 32.

[20] The distinguishing characteristics of a WASP, according to Tad Friend in *Cheerful Money*, is the family history (how many generations can you trace your family tree, hopefully to colonial America, and claim branches of

the tree to include governors, senators, judges, corporate leaders, ministers, etc.—and where you and your ancestors were educated and what church you attend. Of course, going back to medieval England, Scotland or the Netherlands, and tracing your ancestors to the dukes and earls and privileged nobility, is irresistible and stylish and wins oohs and ahs from peers and outsiders alike.

[21] Allan C. Ornstein, *Class Counts: Education, Inequality and the Shrinking Middle Class* (Lanham, MD: Rowman & Littlefield, 2007).

[22] "Bank Chief Resigns" *New York Times*, October 3, 2009, Section 4, p. 2; "Of Layoffs, Bankruptcy and Bonuses" *New York Times*, October 5, 2009, pp. Bu 1,9.

[23] Devin Leonard, "Bargains in the Boardroom?," *New York Times*, April 4, 2010, pp. B1, B8.

[24] In 2005, Goldman paid more than 50 employees more than $20 million each. See Graham Bowley, "3.4 Billion Profit at Goldman . . ." *New York Times*, July 15, 2009, pp. A1,A13. Also see Graham Bowley and Jenney Anderson, "For Goldman, A Swift Return To Lofty Profits." *New York Times*, July 13, 2009, pp. A1, A3; Aaron Lucchetti, "Big Pay Packages Return to Wall Street," *Wall Street Journal*, July 2, 2009, pp. C1, C3.
In 2007 Lloyd Blankstein, Goldman's Chief Executive, was paid $68 million in bonuses, the year before the sky caved in. He did not receive a bonus in 2008, to reduce public backlash, and his bonus check for 2009 was a mere $9 million. See Graham Bowley, "Record Profit at Goldman," *New York Times*, January 22, 2010, pp. B1, B4.

[25] Graham Bowley, "Goldman Bonus Pool . . . ," *New York Times*, October 16, 2009, p. B1, B7; Bowley, "Morgan Stanley's Quarter Is Weak, Unlike Its Pay Pool," *New York Times*, January 21, 2010, p. B1, B8; Zachery Kouwe, "Wall Street on Track for Record in Profits," *New York Times*, November 18, 2009, p. 24A.

[26] David Segal, "Trader's $100 Million Payday Poses Quandary for Regulator," *New York Times*, August 2, 2009, pp1, 19, Louise Story and Eric Dash, "Bankers Reaped Lavish Bonuses During Bailouts," *New York Times*, July 31, 2009, ppA1, A3.

[27] "What About The Raters?", *New York Times*, May 2,2010. P. A22.

[28] Bill Vlasic, "A G.M. Vow to Get Leaner," *New York Times*, July 11, 2009, pp B1, B3; Bill Vlasic and Nick Bunkley, "Automakers Seek $14 Billion More, Vowing Deep Cuts," *New York Times*, February 18, 2009, pp A1, A18.

[29] John Bogle, cited in Sewell Can and Eric Dash, "A Skeptical Reception," *New York Times*, January 22, 2010, p. B4.

[30] One hundred years later Ayn Rand would write her 1957 novel *Atlas Shrugged*—similar to Harris' philosophy—about the virtues of self-interest, competition, unfettered capitalism, and limited government. As social and progressive measures are introduced the economy collapses—sought of today's reality-based economy, as perceived by the followers of Ayn Rand and the preview and early warnings of Harris. Some readers might argue that in the interpretation of social/economic laws it's a stretch to jump from Harris to Rand, but in their minds and hearts both authors saw the world fixed by laws of nature, any extension of state activity in the economic order as a betrayal of individualism nurtured by capitalism, and the worst political leaders could do was by ignorance or by undue influence of labor mar the operation of the social/economic laws.

[31] Allan C. Ornstein, *Teaching and Schooling in America: Pre-and Post-September 11.* (Boston: Allyn and Bacon, 2003) p. 249. Original data from *Digest of Education Statistics,* 1982, 1985,1989,2000,2007.

[32] Ibid.

[33] Susan Dominus, "$400 Hourly To Get Them Off The Sofa," *New York Times*. March 6, 2010, p. A16.

[34] Charles Murray, "Intelligence in the Classroom," *Wall Street Journal*, January 16, 2007.

[35] Robert Frank, "Not Being Smart Makes You Rich?" *Wall Street Journal*, May 5, 2007, p. B4.

[36] Allan C. Ornstein, *Class Counts: Education, Inequality and the Shrinking middle class* (Lanham, MD Rowman and Littlefield, 2007).

[37] Ibid.

[38] Nelson D. Schwartz and Louise Story, "Hedge Fund Pay Roars Back," *New York Times*. April 1, 2010, pp. B1, B10.

[39] The buying and selling of derivatives is the most outrageous part of the financial system, a $42 trillion industry. Speculators bet for and against a company—creating a web in which a default in one company can threaten to produce a chain reaction and possibly economic collapse of the global financial market. This is exactly what occurred in 2008/2009. Reforming this aspect of the market is essential if ordinary people are to be protected in the future. See Gretchen Morgenson, "Don't Let Exceptions Kill the Rule," *New York Times*, October 18, 2008, pp. Bu1, Bu7.

[40] "A Brief History of Credit Cards," *Time*, May 4, 2009, p.16.

[41] In 1943, manufacturing jobs accounted for 38.75% of U.S. jobs. By 1950 it represented 30%. In 1970, manufacturing jobs accounted for 26.5% of U.S. jobs. Forty years later, in 2009, it accounted for 9%. Bureau of Labor Statistics; http:images.google.com

[42] "Help Not Wanted," *Economist,* April 12, 2008, p.38.

[43] Actually English is a more precise language than Mandarin. That said, Mandarin will be increasing spoken at Asian business meetings, but business contracts will most likely remain in English.

[44] "Not the Ace in the Pack," *Economist,* October 27 2007,p.60

[45] Thomas L. Friedman, "America's Real Dram Team," *New York Times,* March 21, 2010, Sect. 4, p. 10.

[46] "Immigrants Big in Tech Start Ups," *Seattle Times,* January 4, 2007.

[47] "Help Not Wanted," *Economist,* April 12, 2008, p.38

[48] Torsten Husen, *International Study of Achievement in Mathematics: A Comparison of Twelve Countries*, Vols. 1 and 2. (New York: Wiley, 1967).

[49] L.C. Comber and J.P. Keeves, *Science Education in Nineteen Countries.* (New York: Wiley, 1973).

[50] Sam Dillon, "Top Test Scores for Shanghai Stun Educatiors," *New York Times*, December 7, 2010,pp. 1-A, 27A.

[51] Chester E. Finn, "A Sputnik Moment for U.S. Education," *Wall Street Journal,* December 8, 2010.

[52] Fred C. Lunenburg and Alan C. Ornstein, *Educational Administration: Concepts and Practices*, 6th ed. (Belmont, CA: Cengage, 2011).

[53] Bureau of Labor Statistics, 2009; *World Almanac* 2010, p.154. 1980 is a turning point in labor; a year later President Reagan fired the striking air-traffic controllers nationwide, fostering a steady deterioration in the union life cycle and where the rank-and-file experienced a decline in wages and working conditions. Also see "Prime Number," *New York Times*, November 15, 2009, sect. 4, p. 4.

[54] Hiroko Tabuchi, "China's Day Arriving Sooner than Japan Expected," *New York Times*, October 1, 2009, pp. Bu 1-2.

[55] David Barboza. "China's Sprint for the Gold," *New York Times*, November 15, 2009, Sect 4, p.4.

[56] In 1971, when President Nixon visited China and started trade relations, the exchange reserves of China were less than $200 million. Between 2000 and 2009, the U.S. trade deficit with China spiked from $84 billion to $266 billion. China's exchange reserves have now topped $2 trillion, with 75 percent invested in dollar assets (sought of a dollar trap for China).

[57] Steve Lohr, "The Apple in His Eye," *New York Times*, January 31, 2010, Sect 4, p. 6.

[58] Japan and S. Korea are expected to produce 1.5 million hybrid or all-electric cars by then—compared to North America making 265,000: See Keith Bradsher, "China Vies to Be World's Leader in Electric Cars," *New York Times*, April 2, 2009, pp.A1, A20.

[59] See *World Fact Book* (Washington D.C.: U.S. Government Printing Office, 2010).

[60] But there is a flipside or softbelly to India's future growth and that flies in the face of its prospective superpower image. The country is beset by an entrenched smug elite, tied to a caste system and perpetuated by centuries of racism and injustices. Notwithstanding the enormous economic gains made by India, far beyond even what optimists would have predicted a few decades ago, the country is flawed by the dust heap of custom and tradition. It's history (and current policies) is plagued by the brutal methods of the police, unethical practices of business people, payoffs and favors expected by an army of government bureaucrats and regulators, and a slow-moving, class-biased judiciary system—all which currently vye to slow down India's economic miracle.

[61] All of these countries consistently out score American students on international tests in science and mathematics.

[62] Endorsement and investment income of these people are not included. For example, *Jay-Z's* total income was $82 million and rapper *50 Cent* was $150 million in 2007, according to *Forbes* magazine.

[63] Claudia H. Deutsch, Executive Pay: A Special Report, *New York Times*, April 6, 2008, p.Bu1, 7-11; Eduardo Porter, "More Than Ever, It Pays to Be the Top Executive," *New York Times*, May 25, 2007, p.A1, C7.